TOP TEN WEDDING SURVIVAL TIPS

tear here

1. Allow plenty of time to plan. If you can allow at least one year to plan your wedding, you'll be able to take care of all the details and still keep your sanity.

2. Develop a system to help you get organized. Use a three-ring binder, a shoe box, or a folder with pockets; find some way to keep all your wedding information together and organized.

3. Set a realistic budget. Get everyone together who has a part in paying for this event and discuss how formal you want the wedding to be and what you want to include in the wedding. The "What's Important to Us" and "Cost Comparison" worksheets in Chapter 3 can help you through this process.

4. Work within your budget. Do your homework and become an intelligent wedding consumer. Shop around, ask questions, and try to get the best value for your dollar.

5. Learn to compromise. Some compromise will be necessary to keep costs under control, so be prepared to identify the things that are important to the two of you and let go of the little things.

6. If you get into an argument, take a deep breath and start over. This is good advice anytime, but the wedding planning process can be especially stressful. Try to relax and find the humor in every situation.

7. Only take your mother and one friend with you to shop for your gown. The more opinions you consider, the more difficult it will be for you to make a final decision.

8. Make time for recreational activities that you enjoy. Exercise and recreation can help reduce your stress level and help you stay relaxed, yet focused.

9. Eat right and get enough sleep. You need all the energy and level-headedness you can muster. You won't get far if you don't keep your body well-nourished and rested.

10. Enjoy this time. Sure, there is lots to do, but take the time to relax and enjoy this special time of your life. It should be fun!

alpha books

GETTING READY FOR THE BIG EVENT: IMPORTANT CALENDAR ITEMS

Six to twelve months before the wedding:

Find a system to keep you organized.

Talk with a bridal consultant.

Decide on how formal you want the wedding to be.

Use the Cost Comparison Worksheet in Chapter 3 to determine your wedding budget.

Decide who will pay for what and then set a realistic budget.

Set your wedding date.

Reserve your ceremony site and talk to the officiant.

Reserve your reception site.

Reserve your caterer.

Investigate photographers and hire one.

Check out videographers and hire one.

Select a florist.

Book your musicians.

Ask friends to be in your wedding party.

Shop for your gown.

Five months before the wedding:

Order your wedding apparel.

Four months before the wedding:

Order your invitations, other wedding stationery, and paper supplies.

Three months before the wedding:

Make reservations for your honeymoon.

Two months before the wedding:

Order the wedding cake and groom's cake.

Six weeks before the wedding:

Plan the rehearsal dinner with the caterer.

One month before the wedding:

Arrange for special transportation.

Send invitations.

The COMPLETE IDIOT'S GUIDE TO
the Perfect Wedding

by Teddy Lenderman

alpha books

A Division of Macmillan Computer Publishing
A Prentice Hall Macmillan Company
201 West 103rd Street, Indianapolis, Indiana 46290 USA

For Floyd, my dear husband, and our two sons, Andy and Ben—the men in my life. I'll love you forever!

©1995 by Alpha Books

International Standard Book Number: 1-56761-532-5

Library of Congress Catalog Card Number: 94-072726

98 97 96 95   8 7 6 5 4 3 2 1

Interpretation of the printing code: the rightmost double-digit number is the year of the book's first printing; the rightmost single-digit number is the number of the book's printing. For example, a printing code of 95-1 shows that this copy of the book was printed during the first printing of the book in 1995.

Photos in this book are reproduced with the kind permission of Wyant Photography, Inc.

Printed in the United States of America

Publisher
Marie Butler-Knight

Managing Editor
Liz Keaffaber

Product Manager
Tom Godfrey

Senior Development Editor
Seta Frantz

Development Editor
Jodi Jensen

Production Editor
Kelly Oliver

Manuscript Editor
San Dee Phillips

Designer
Barbara Kordesh

Cover Designer
Karen Ruggles

Illustrator
Judd Winick

Indexer
Jeanne Clark

Production Team
*Gary Adair, Stephen Adams, Dan Caparo, Steve Carlin, Brad Chinn,
Kim Cofer, Lisa Daughtery, Dave Eason, Jennifer Eberhardt, Rich Evers,
David Garratt, Karen Gregor, Erika Millen, Beth Rago, Bobbi Satterfield,
Karen Walsh, Robert Wolf*

*Special thanks to Gerard J. Monaghan for ensuring
the accuracy of this book.*

Contents at a Glance

Contents

Foreword

Marriage is one of the major rites of passage in life, a change of status with all the emotional baggage that comes with such changes. It also ranks as one of the more serious stress-producing events in our lives.

The other rites of passage and stressful events are beyond our control: birth, death, death of a spouse, corporate downsizing, and so on. Marriage is one of the few rites of passage that we choose to undertake. (Let the psychologists and sociologists explain *why* we choose to do it.)

Once you have decided to get married, your next step is planning your wedding. This really is simple. All you have to do is coordinate the activities of about 20 participants in your ceremony, color-coordinate and select clothes for them, find and deal with as many as 40 vendors, throw a simple family party for about 200 people, and plan a vacation—all at the same time—while you still work for a living and maintain other relationships.

That is why it pays to deal with reputable wedding professionals and hire a bridal consultant—a person who does this for a business, knows how to plan your wedding on or under budget, and can help ease much of the stress normally associated with a wedding.

Another invaluable tool in planning your wedding is a wedding planner. There are scores of them on the market: written planners, video planners, and audio planners. Many offer good, solid advice; some have more fluff than all the tulle you'd ever hope to use at your wedding.

This wedding planner book is very special, for many reasons. It has something too many wedding planners lack: a light-hearted touch. Your wedding is supposed to be fun, right? Then why are so many wedding planners so serious?

More than a sense of humor, this planner has tons of great advice from someone who knows. Teddy Lenderman, who operates Bearable Weddings by Teddy, in Terre Haute, Indiana, is a consummate professional who has coordinated more weddings than a bridesmaid would think of attending in a lifetime.

She has been a member of the Association of Bridal Consultants (the international trade association representing the wedding industry, with

1,400 members in 16 countries) since February, 1986. I first met Teddy at an informal Association dinner meeting in Indianapolis in July, 1986, and saw her potential for becoming a great credit to the wedding business.

She has been an active participant in Association annual conferences from Hawaii to Boston and has served as Indiana state coordinator since January, 1992. As state coordinator, she is the Association's representative in Indiana, working with members on a local, personal level.

Teddy also holds a very special designation from the Association. She has earned the title of Master Bridal Consultant, based on her work through the Association's Professional Development Program, continuing education, recommendations of peers and brides, and her continuing service to the wedding business. It is a designation not easily obtained. There are only four Master Bridal Consultants in the world.

So, when Teddy speaks, listen. Chuckle at the humor. Share the horror stories with your family. Then listen again. The information in this book is priceless—and thoroughly professional.

Gerard J. Monaghan
President, Association of Bridal Consultants
New Milford, Connecticut
December 8, 1994

Introduction

It sometimes seems that you have to be a genius to pull off a successful wedding. Thousands of complex questions are just lurking out there, waiting to be answered. It's hard to know where to go or whom to turn to for help. You start thinking, "I must be an idiot. I don't have the faintest idea where to begin."

Well, you're not an idiot—not even close. You are, however, about to become a wedding consumer. You will have lots of questions, and you will need many, many answers.

You deserve honest answers to your questions and some guidance from someone who knows this industry inside and out. You also deserve to be treated with respect by vendors. This book tries to answer your questions and provide you with the information you need to gain the respect of vendors. It also attempts to guide you through the months of planning that lie ahead.

This book is the result of the experience and satisfaction I have gained in helping more than 200 couples enjoy the wedding of their dreams. In 1985, I began my wedding consulting business, Bearable Weddings by Teddy. In the ensuing 10 years, I have shared ideas with and learned from dozens of other wedding professionals through countless seminars and conferences. I have learned the hard way how to choose competent and professional vendors and how to avoid potential nightmares. I have also broadened my horizons through the give and take of teaching a noncredit course called "How to Plan and Enjoy Your Wedding" for Indiana State University, Terre Haute, Indiana.

I've always been a believer in continuing education, and in 1993 I obtained the highest level of recognition that the Association of Bridal Consultants awards: Master Bridal Consultant. It took me seven years to achieve that, but my learning never stops. I learn so much from the brides and grooms I've had the pleasure of working with—that alone could fill a book.

I've been where you are right now about 200 times. I know the frustration you are feeling, the intimidation, and the feelings of being overwhelmed at the same time that you're so happy you could just burst.

Well, slow down. Take a deep breath and get ready for some major work on understanding the wedding industry. That knowledge will help you gain an insight into a field you probably know nothing about. Once you have some understanding and knowledge of what is out there as far as the wedding industry goes, you will be better equipped to be an intelligent wedding consumer.

You wouldn't rush right out and buy a new car without first studying the car industry and trying to figure out what is best for your particular needs and value. No, you'd pick up brochures, talk to friends and family, go into the car dealer and look around, ask questions, get a feel. Right? So what's so different about shopping in the wedding industry? Nothing—absolutely nothing.

That's what this book is all about. You—the bride and groom—will learn what can help make your life and the lives of your family and friends so much easier. It's really not difficult, but it will require some time and energy on your part. The sole purpose of this book is to take the overwhelmingly complicated task of planning a wedding and make it E A S Y.

How to Use This Book

Before you spend that first dime, I suggest that you read this book from cover to cover. Try not to get so carried away with the romance and the newness of being engaged that you lose your sense of perspective.

Use a highlighter to mark the points you need to understand more fully. Take notes on possible vendors you want to contact. Use this book! The book's unique design will give you all the help you need. The more you use it, the easier your planning will be. Do not rush right out and reserve a catering hall before you read this book. Let me help you determine what to look for in a facility that's going to be a big part of your wedding day and your wedding dollars.

Pick up this book and read it (that always helps), and go forward with your wedding plans. Become an intelligent wedding consumer and spend your dollars wisely. Understand your responsibilities and figure out the best way to approach them. Most of all, enjoy this time in your life. It should be one of the most pleasant, fun-filled, exciting times in a couple's life. This book can help with that. It won't make it perfect, but it can help take the bumps out of the road to a very bearable wedding.

Included in this book are worksheets associated with a particular chapter. For example, the chapter on photography contains a worksheet to help you select your photographer. Record your discussions with the photographer on the worksheet and make notes on anything else you feel is important. Within each chapter, you will be given questions to ask the professionals. Read those sections very carefully so you can ask intelligent questions.

In the front of this book is a tear-out card containing the Key Survival Tips for planning your wedding. While this card can't possibly sum up what the book covers, it does offer some key points for you to consider. Tear out this card and carry it with you over the months of planning.

To help you get the most out of this book, you will see the following special information boxes scattered throughout this book:

Bet You Didn't Know... Wedding trivia provided just for comic relief.

Tips or timesavers that can help you be more efficient.

Warnings and solutions to common problems you may encounter.

Information about some of the minitopics not specifically discussed in the text.

Acknowledgments

Having never even dreamt about writing a book, much less writing a 400 page book in less than four months, there are several individuals I would like to acknowledge for their endeavors. To Tom Godfrey, Product Manager (who thought I was the author to do this work and believed all along that I could write 325 pages); Kelly Oliver, Production Editor; San Dee Phillips, Copy Editor; and Seta Frantz, Development Editor, a great big thank you for all your patience and guidance with me, the new kid on the block. And to Jodi Jensen, my development editor, words alone cannot express the sincere appreciation I have for everything you did to help make this book a reality. Your encouragement, patience (!!), and dedication will forever be etched in my soul. Thank you from the bottom of my heart.

Thank you also to Wyant Photography, Inc., for kind permission to use their beautiful photographs in this book.

Wyant Photography, Inc.
Indianapolis, IN   (317) 788-7300
Zionsville, IN   (317) 873-2282

Part I
Don't Spend a Dime Yet!

You're engaged to a wonderful person. You have been floating on cloud nine since the proposal. You have announced the good news to your family and friends, and now you can't wait to get started on the wedding plans.

Catch your breath, let your feet touch down for a moment, and turn to Part I. This Part introduces you to some of the things you should know before you write that first check. You'll find advice on how to start your planning, which questions to ask, and where to go for help. You learn how to determine the type of wedding you want to have and how that decision affects your wedding budget.

Planning a wedding is a big deal and the wedding business is BIG business. The more you know about the industry and how to use it to your advantage, the better your planning will be and the more relaxed you will be when you finally walk down that aisle.

Chapter 1

Getting Started

In This Chapter

➤ Getting organized

➤ Investigating bridal shows

➤ Examining other helpful resources

Examining the Wedding Industry

The first thing you need to know about weddings in this country is that the wedding industry is big business. In 1993, the wedding industry grossed $32 billion in retail sales, second only to Christmas retail sales. That, my dear readers, is a lot of wedding cake. That is also something that many first-time wedding couples fail to understand. Just knowing how big the industry is may help give you some perspective of why you don't want to rush right out and reserve the first reception site you see. This wedding process will cost you some money. You don't have to mortgage the house to have the wedding of your dreams, but you do have to plan wisely.

Finding a System to Keep Yourself Organized

The number one suggestion I make to the brides I work with is to find and use some kind of organizational system. It doesn't matter what it is, whether it's a three-ring binder, a folder with pockets, or a shoe box. (Obviously, this book will be a big part of your system, and it should be.) The type of system you choose to use really doesn't matter. What matters is that you *use* it. Keep everything that relates to your wedding in this system: receipts, contracts, material swatches, a calendar with appointments marked, phone numbers of all your vendors, and re- minder lists. Make sure you have this "system" with you whenever you visit a vendor. Even if you are not an organized person, force yourself to become more so. Let me explain why this is so important.

 Be patient with yourself! Taking some time now to read and understand what you need to do will pay off later on.

Keep *every* receipt, and keep them together in one place! You never know when you may have to produce one quickly.

Usually, I pick up my client's bridal gown the day of the wedding and take it to the ceremony site for her. On one routine run to a bridal shop to get the gown for a bride, I told the shop owner who I was and what I was there for, whereupon she informed me that the bride still owed $350 on the gown. Now, during the years, when the situation warranted it, I have purchased small, last-minute items for brides and we have settled later. However, $350 was a bit beyond a small item. I called the bride and explained the problem. The lovely bride not only told me the shop was in error but also produced the receipt for the gown marked "Paid in Full." So, I drove to her home, picked up the receipt, and drove back to the shop. The owner grudgingly admitted that the mistake was hers, and I left the shop with the gown. Moral of the story: Had the bride not been organized and able to produce the receipt (a mere three hours before the wedding), she would have handed over another $350 to get the gown out of hock. Keep yourself organized, even if it's not some- thing that comes naturally to you. It will pay off in the end.

Investigating Bridal Shows

So you've figured out a system you're comfortable with and one that you will use. Now what? Depending on how much time you have, you may want to attend a bridal show in your area.

What to Expect

Bridal shows are great ways to meet the vendors from your area whose services you will be using. These shows are usually promoted by area merchants to let the community know what wedding services are available in that area. Merchants rent booth space to display the products or services they can offer the customer. Interested customers enter the facility and visit with these merchants at their booths. The usual format for such events may include time to talk with individual vendors at their booths, a fashion show by area bridal shops, and sometimes drawings for door prizes the vendors provide. One bride I know attended a show two years ago and won the grand prize: two round-trip tickets to Hawaii! Not a bad deal for giving up a Sunday afternoon.

The whole idea behind bridal shows is twofold: you get to see what's available in your area, and the vendor gets your name and address for possible contact. You, the bride and groom, or parents of a bride or groom, may browse the different vendors and get a feel for what they have to offer. Sometimes, by just looking at the booth setup, you will be able to tell whether they can provide what you need. If crepe paper streamers and balloons decorate the booth and you are thinking more in terms of satin ribbon and crystal, then you should look at other displays.

Bet You Didn't Know... One reason the diamond is a popular stone for engagement rings is because the ancients believed that its sparkle arose from the flames of love. Ancient people also believed that the bride should wear a diamond on the third finger of the left hand because that finger is said to have the only vein that runs directly to the heart.

How to Get the Most from a Bridal Show

Okay, so you're walking around the floor of the local civic center trying to take in all this wedding stuff, with your arms getting longer by the moment as your little tote bags get weighted down with brochures, pamphlets, and other promotional items. To get the most from your visit, you need to talk to the folks behind the booths, although the better vendors will *never* be *behind* their booths. They will be out in the aisle, meeting and greeting prospective clients. Hear what they have to say. Is it hard-sell? Does the product look like something you would want to have at your wedding? Are the vendors personable? Do they seem to know what customer service means? Pick up any handouts or brochures they offer and make notes on items you particularly like. When you get home, you can spread out your notes and brochures and see what's available. This can give you a good starting point.

 Watch for professional behavior from vendors: appearance, mannerisms (gum chewing—yuk), good grammar, eye contact, and so on. How do they present themselves? Do they act bored or interested?

The real reason the vendors at a bridal show agree to give up an entire Sunday is that they receive a list of all attendees at the show. You will probably receive some flyers or direct-mail pieces from some of the vendors following the show. Many times, you will receive additional coupons or discounts from these vendors after the shows.

Now, remember: Not all wedding vendors use the medium of the bridal show to advertise. Many bridal shows are very expensive for participants. You may find that several of the more established vendors choose not to participate in shows. Every wedding professional has a preferred method of advertising, and bridal shows are only one of those methods. Bridal shows can give you a feel for the services offered in your area.

Using the Library

The library is another dependable source when getting started with your wedding plans. Libraries contain many resources, the most obvious being magazines that you can browse through and dream on. Libraries also may have a resource guide to either wedding vendors in your area or a resource guide of other wedding-related materials. For example, a local library may list possible wedding sites and the contacts for those facilities in one of its resource guides. It never hurts to check out your local library.

Asking Friends for Suggestions

Friends, both well-meaning and otherwise, are another source of information during the early stages of wedding planning. Friends who have married recently can be especially helpful. Find out who they used for the various service providers and what they thought of the vendors. Find out where they held the reception, whether they were pleased with the facility, and what it offered. Ask which caterer they used and which florist. Find out if they were pleased with the wedding photography, and how and when photographs were taken. What would they do differently now?

Find out how the wedding day went and what they could have done to make it better. Ask about any problems they had and what they could have done to prevent them. Pick their brains; most newly married brides and grooms are pretty talkative about their wedding day. Try to pin them down. If Mary Ann tells you that her wedding day was one of the most embarrassing days of her life, find out why. Did the wrong flowers arrive at the church? Did the cake really fall over into the punch bowl?

Bet You Didn't Know... You think you have problems? How would you like to select a new wedding ring every year? That's what the early primitive brides had to do. Their rings were circles of hemp or rushes woven together into the shape of a circle. Because the fibers disintegrated over a period of time, women had to replace their rings every year.

If the couple had to do it over again, what would they change or what would they do the same? Get specifics! Generalities in this area don't offer you much insight. "The flowers were pretty" may be a nice sentiment, but it's more helpful to know whether the florist followed the color scheme, had a professional business manner, and delivered the flowers on time. In other words, was this florist a vendor that you should consider contracting? Get all the details you can.

Taking a Class to Learn More

Many colleges offer adult education classes. Many of those classes are offered solely for enjoyment and cover a wide range of class topics. If there is a college or university in your area, you should check out the resources there.

Since 1988, I've taught a noncredit course for Indiana State University called "Enjoy Your Wedding." It runs for five weeks every spring and sometimes also in the fall. I've had good comments from the students, and I have learned so much from them, too. I know they are learning the information they will need in order to wade through the countless hours, days, and weeks of wedding planning.

So if you are trying to figure out where to begin with this monumental task, or if you need some direction in finding and dealing with vendors, see if you can take a class in your area that can provide you with some guidance and some answers.

The Least You Need to Know

Well, you're off to a good start! Remember these tips as you begin your planning:

➤ Take your time. Spend the time now to become informed. Read this book thoroughly and take notes, and browse wedding magazines. Determine what you want your wedding to be.

➤ Use a system of organization—such as a shoe box, notebook, or folder—to hold your receipts, brochures, fabric swatches, appointment calendar, and so on.

➤ Ask recently married couples for advice. Get all the specifics you can. Find out what they would do differently and what they were happy with. Find out the *details* of why they liked or disliked particular vendors.

➤ Look for adult education classes that can help you get started and that can provide some guidance as to how to deal with vendors.

Chapter 2

Wake Me When It's Over: Hiring a Bridal Consultant

In This Chapter

➤ What is a bridal consultant?

➤ How to determine if you need one

➤ How to choose and use a bridal consultant

➤ What a bridal consultant can do to help you

So Who Are These People, Anyway?

First of all, let's define some terms. A *bridal consultant* is someone who consults with brides and grooms (and often with members of their families) about planning, coordinating, or arranging for a wedding. An *independent bridal consultant* is a consultant who does not work with another vendor, such as a florist or caterer, but instead has a self-contained bridal consulting business. A *wedding coordinator* is someone who helps coordinate or conduct the wedding activities. A *wedding day coordinator* works on-site for the rehearsal and for the day of the wedding to ensure that the wedding flows smoothly.

A *wedding director* is similar to a wedding day coordinator. The term is relatively common in the South. A *church wedding coordinator* is someone on the staff of a church or in a church's women's group. Usually, she is not a true wedding consultant or coordinator, but rather someone who makes sure the church's rules are followed. There is also the *wedding professional*, which describes anyone in the wedding business but doesn't specifically mean the person is a consultant or coordinator.

Sounds pretty confusing, doesn't it? The independent bridal consultant and wedding coordinator are the focus of this chapter. For simplicity's sake, the term "bridal consultant" is used to cover both consultants and coordinators unless specifically stated otherwise. Although they sometimes have different responsibilities, many of their functions overlap. Some bridal consultants, for example, do not coordinate the activities on the actual wedding day, but most do.

The Evolution of the Bridal Consultant

One of the rapidly changing areas of the wedding industry today is the increase in the number of bridal consultants being hired by couples. These professionals, out of simple necessity, are becoming an integral part of the wedding industry. Today, in our society, the boy next door seldom marries the girl next door. Families often live in various parts of the country, and there is a need for someone local to be available as a "home base."

The development of bridal consulting parallels—and in some ways has helped create—the development of the wedding "industry." Before 1980, there usually was little coordination among vendors. In some cases, for example, the photographer might not even know what the gown looked like before the wedding day. The consultant helps ensure that all the vendors communicate with one another and that the wedding "industry" pulls together to make each wedding a coordinated affair—as close to perfection as possible.

I often help out-of-town brides who want someone to coordinate the details with the folks at home. For example, the local newspaper called a couple of years ago to interview me for an article on the "business of weddings." They wanted to follow one bride through the last month of her wedding planning stages. They wanted to go to all the final consultations, have a photographer capture the moment on film, and see just how that last month of planning ticked off. Of the five weddings I had scheduled for that June, only *one* had a local bride. All the others were out-of-town brides who hired me to make sure someone on the home turf knew what was happening and to take care of the details. This is one of the prime reasons you may want to include a bridal consultant on your vendor list.

Another major reason the bridal consultant has become so popular is the fact that so many women are working full time—often in time-consuming, fast-track careers—and simply don't have the time or energy to take on the monumental task of planning a wedding. Gone are the days when Mom was at home and had time for such large projects as planning her daughter's wedding. Most of the mothers I work with also are career women. Time is a valuable commodity and career women understand that.

The bridal consultant also serves other purposes. Even if the couple and both sets of parents are local, unless they plan weddings for a living they will have little experience dealing with wedding vendors. That's why Chapter 1 emphasized just how big the industry is. When you choose a bridal consultant who has planned many weddings in your area, she knows which vendors to steer you to for the budget you have in mind. She also knows which vendors to avoid and why. She is a combination counselor, financial advisor, etiquette expert, organizer, referee, and, at times, a good friend. She can make your life so much easier. It's still *your* wedding; it is not the consultant's wedding, your mother's wedding, or your fiancé's mother's wedding. It is the wedding that you and your fiancé want it to be. The bridal consultant's only purposes are to make your plans come true, to make your day run smoothly, and to help make both of you look your best.

As an example of how a bridal consultant can help you, let me tell you a story. For the second wedding that I coordinated back in 1985, I was brought in to make the long-awaited day a reality. The mother of the bride and the bride had done most of the legwork and brought me in during the last month to pull things together.

On the big day, the bride and bridesmaids were busy getting dressed when the mother came up to me outside the dressing room. She had that panicked look on her face that I have now come to know and understand. She said, "Okay, now what?" I explained that everything was running on time and smoothly (so I thought at the time), and she should go back into the dressing room and savor this time with her daughter. With a huge sigh of relief, she returned to the dressing room, thrilled that she didn't have to perform any other task at that moment.

Meanwhile, back in the church lobby, I discovered the florist had forgotten all three grandmothers' corsages, so I called the florist to have them delivered. Then the trumpet player called the church and informed me that he'd had too much to drink at the rehearsal dinner and couldn't play for the wedding. I immediately inquired whether he needed help dressing and driving to the church or if he could manage that himself. He was so taken aback that I didn't excuse him that he muttered something about not needing any help. He showed up a little green but played a fine trumpet, and that's all I cared about. And the flower girl (ah, children in weddings, now that's an entire chapter in itself—Chapter 8, to be exact) caught the flounce of her dress on a nail and ripped off the entire thing, except for four inches. I thought, "Geez, what else," and then found out how handy a stapler could be. I was able to staple the dress and flounce together and no one was the wiser. Neither the mother, nor the bride, nor anyone in the family knew a thing about all this turmoil taking place just an hour before the wedding.

It just so happened that this particular mother of the bride was a writer for the local paper. Two weeks after the wedding, the mother's column, entitled "The Wedding Day," appeared in the paper. It was about being in that dressing room helping her daughter prepare for her wedding and remembering bringing her home from the hospital, the tomboy stages, going off on her first date, the proms—all those wonderful things that mothers and fathers store away in their memory banks. Hiring a bridal consultant to attend to all the last-minute crises and details gave that mother and daughter time together at a very special moment in their lives. Had the mother been out arguing with the florist and the trumpeter or trying to coax a four-year-old into holding still long enough to have her dress stapled, she would have missed that time with her daughter.

Obviously, there is another benefit the professional bridal consultant offers: quality time. Keep that in mind when you look for a bridal consultant. You want someone who is going to give you peace of mind and quality time on your wedding day.

What You See Is Not Always What You Get

Along the path leading up to your wedding, you are likely to run into wedding professionals who refer to themselves as bridal consultants. The florist who works with the bride is consulting the bride about the flower needs for her special day. The salesper-son in the bridal shop may also refer to herself as a bridal consultant because she works directly with brides concerning gowns and accessories. The photographer, the catering manager, and the reception site coordinator all may refer to themselves as bridal consultants. Most of the time, how-ever, their expertise is in a particular area of the wedding business, such as a *floral bridal consultant*. Don't confuse these specialized consultants with a bridal consultant who deals with the entire wedding process. Use your Yellow Pages wisely. Just because the DJ is listed under *Wedding Consultants* does not mean that he knows the first thing about plan-ning a wedding.

Read the Yellow Pages carefully! Don't be fooled by the heading under which you find a vendor's name. Make sure that vendor's expertise and experience match the qualifi-cations you are looking for.

What Is the Consultant's Role?

Working one-on-one with the bride and her family from the engage-ment to the honeymoon, the bridal consultant can ensure that all aspects of your wonderful day happen as you had planned. Some couples hire consultants as soon as they announce their engagement. I've actually had mothers call me for advice and counsel before their daughters even have a ring, much less have a date chosen. Other couples choose to hire a consultant near the end of the process   six weeks or so from the actual day—to pull together those loose ends and to oversee the rehearsal and wedding day activities. The bottom line here is that you should decide just how much you want to involve the bridal consultant. You are the boss; the final choice should always be yours.

You may decide you just want to bend a consultant's ear for a couple of hours to help you get started. I've had several brides being married away from my area who made an appointment to get some advice about how to begin. That's fine. If that's all the help you think you will need, then definitely take that route.

Some Words on Wedding Etiquette

Traditional wedding etiquette is something most consultants know very well. American rules of etiquette haven't changed much since the beginning of this century when Emily Post and Amy Vanderbilt wrote their now famous treatises. While some practices probably will always be frowned upon, other customs have relaxed over the years. At the turn of the century, for example, proper wedding etiquette dictated that the receiver of a wedding invitation must respond formally, in writing, to the sender. There were no response cards enclosed back then. While that idea is literally still "proper etiquette," that practice is all but forgotten and the enclosure response card is a standard part of wedding invitations today.

There are no "wedding police" out there. If you truly want to do something at your wedding or during the planning stages that others say is not proper etiquette, get some impartial advice. Try to determine whether the custom truly is not in good taste or whether it simply wasn't a custom practiced at the turn of the century. It may be one at which no one would bat an eye in 1995.

How to Find the Right Consultant for Your Wedding

As mentioned earlier, you can check out the Yellow Pages as a first step in locating a competent bridal consultant, but you have to review the listings carefully. The best method, however, is to ask friends and family for names of consultants they have used. Many vendors also will recommend bridal consultants in their area that they have worked with and with whom they feel comfortable. In addition, your clergyman may have worked with a bridal consultant he felt especially good about having at the wedding. You can also get the names of consultants in your area by contacting certain trade associations, such as the Association of Bridal Consultants. The Association is located in Connecticut (203-355-0464; FAX 203-354-1404) and will be happy to give you names of members in your area.

Asking the Right Questions

Start by making an appointment with the bridal consultant. Telephone interviews leave a lot to the imagination. You'll understand who you're dealing with if you sit down face to face. Sometimes there is a charge for this meeting, so ask about charges when you call for the appointment. Ask for references of other brides with whom she has worked. Ask how she charges. Is it by the hour, a flat fee, or a percentage? Make sure you completely understand the money part here. Ask about what she can do for you

Any time you ask for a reference and the vendor won't provide it, look elsewhere.

and, at the same time, ask if there are things she will not take care of for you. Does she use a contract? A letter of agreement? A contract should protect both you and the consultant from problems caused by misunderstandings. Make sure it spells out, in reasonable detail, who—including you and Aunt Tillie—will do what, when, and for how much. Does the bridal consultant require a deposit or retainer? Get a feel for who this person is. She should put you first. You should feel as though you are her only client and that she will bend over backward to make your wedding special and as stress-free as possible.

As I said earlier, this is your wedding, not the bridal consultant's, and you need to know and understand just what role the bridal consultant will play in your wedding. Ask if she takes commissions from vendors. Although it is perfectly acceptable for her to do so, you still should decide which vendors you will use.

On occasion, I have had prospective clients ask if they can observe me at a wedding before they make the decision to hire me. I have absolutely no problem with that as long as they dress appropriately, let me do my work, and I have my client's approval. They can see me in action, doing what I'm good at and what I love. And so far, they have always decided to hire me.

Be aware that, just as with other service providers, there are bad apples in the bridal consultant barrel as well. Analyze the conversation in your first meeting with the consultant. If she uses the word *I* lots in the conversation with you, hear what she is really saying. "*I* want to have candy for your favors." "*I* want the flowers to be in shades of pink." "*I* see your wedding as a very formal affair." "*I* hope you'll use engraved invitations." "*I'm* sure you'll want a seated dinner instead of just hors d'oeuvres." Hey, whose wedding is this anyway? Listen carefully to what she says and how much pressure she asserts.

Many people call themselves bridal consultants simply because they have assisted with a family or friend's wedding. These individuals most likely do not have the experience and resources you will find with a professional bridal consultant who has been in the business for a while and whose very livelihood depends on maintaining a good reputation.

Deciding Whether a Consultant Can Help You

Okay, you've met with a bridal consultant. You've found out what she charges, and you like what you are hearing. She has lots of experience and her credentials are great. Her references check out, but you're just not quite convinced.

Let's get practical here. The bridal consultant can save you time, money, and energy. Because of her "repeat buying power," she can sometimes negotiate prices for you with vendors that the individual cannot. Many times, the bridal consultant will receive a discounted price for suggesting a particular vendor and pass that savings on to you, the client. Say you want to contract a certain reception facility and it rents for $400. You may be able to contract it for less, maybe as much as half, through your experienced bridal consultant. The vendor knows that if his work is good, the consultant will return with other clients. That's what I mean by "repeat buying power."

I refer to bridal consultants as female because the majority of them are. There are very good, competent male bridal consultants out in the trenches, too. According to the Association of Bridal Consultants, about 2% of all consultants are male.

Aside from the "repeat buying power" issue, you may find that there are vendors who may not do business with individual couples. There is a facility I occasionally use that will not rent for wedding receptions unless the couple is my client. This facility knows that I will do all that is possible to make sure the facility is not harmed.

One bride was on a tight budget but felt she needed the extra guidance and help of getting the most for her dollars. We met with the florist and worked out a flower plan. The bride wanted huge bouquets of spring mixed flowers, including iris, roses, orchids, lilies, snapdragons, and tulips. When the estimate came back, it was three times what was in the budget. The bride called, very upset, and asked what to do. Because of the good working relationship I had with the florist, he wanted to work with us and make the bride happy. For less money, we were able to create the same look with less expensive flowers. (The first thing we did was replace the orchids—at $15 apiece that seemed like a good place to start.)

The consultant's fee should be included in the overall budget, not an add-on. For example, let's say you have $10,000 to spend on the wedding. If the consultant's fee is $1,000, then she should be able to give you a $10,000 wedding for $9,000. Most times, if you engage a bridal consultant, you will stay at or under budget and get more for your money.

Look for a bridal consultant who is a member of an organization of wedding professionals. This generally indicates that the consultant is continually learning, growing, and keeping aware of changes and trends in the wedding industry.

Your best friend who offers to coordinate your wedding does not have that "repeat buying power," nor the resources or experience to make your day bearable. You need someone impartial. If your best friend is afraid to tell you that your idea stinks because she doesn't want to hurt your feelings, how does that help you? While the bridal consultant doesn't want to hurt your feelings either, she also does not want you to be embarrassed. She will find a tactful way to tell you the truth, and you will thank her for that honesty.

A bridal consultant or wedding coordinator isn't for every bride. However, you should at least be aware that they are one option you can choose in your wedding planning. And they're not just for the big budget weddings, either. A good consultant can be a valuable asset in putting together the wedding of your dreams.

The Least You Need to Know

➤ Bridal consultants and wedding coordinators can help you with the smallest details of your wedding from the engage ment to the honeymoon or just for the wedding day itself.

➤ Interview the potential bridal consultant and ask many questions. Find out about her fee structure and whether she requires a contract. Ask what she is willing to do and what she will not do.

➤ Listen carefully to her presentation in your initial meeting. Is she focused on making this the wedding you want? Check her references.

BRIDAL CONSULTANT/WEDDING COORDINATOR WORKSHEET

Name: _____

Address: _____

_____

Telephone: _____

Referred by: _____

Other references: _____

_____

_____

_____

Fee: _____

How to be paid: (installments? retainer?)

Contract required? Yes_____ No_____

Questions to ask:

　　How long in business?

　　How many weddings has she coordinated?

　　Professional associations?

　　How does she view her role?

　　Professional education?

　　Describe a typical wedding day.

　　What can she do and what will she do?

Other questions you may want to ask:

　　What are the consultant's background and credentials?

　　How does she keep up with changes in the industry?

Simple or Extravagant: Setting Your Budget

Determining How Formal Your Wedding Will Be

Determining how formal you want your wedding to be will help you establish the basis for your overall wedding strategy. The level of formality you choose determines, to a great extent, the overall cost of your wedding. It's a good idea for all players to sit down together—the bride, the groom, the in-laws, and anyone else with a financial interest in this wedding—and figure out just how fancy you want this affair to be. Essentially, you can choose from the following four levels of formality:

➤ Ultraformal

➤ Formal

➤ Semiformal

➤ Informal

Ultraformal: Glamorous and Glitzy

The fanciest type of wedding you can have is *ultraformal*. This is the kind of wedding a movie star, Princess Diana, or the President's daughter would have. An ultraformal wedding is always very large, both in the number in the wedding party and in the number of guests invited. For an ultraformal wedding, you can expect to have 6 to 12 bridesmaids and more than 350 guests.

Decorations at the ceremony site are extensive, complete with large floral arrangements, many candles, garlands of greens, and tulle and ribbons everywhere. The attire for the wedding party is formal. The bridal gown is elaborate and includes beading, pearls, and sequins. The gown usually has a cathedral-length train and also may have a floor-length veil. The bride's attendants dress similarly, with either tea-length or full-length dresses to complement the bride's gown. The men dress in tails, complete with white tie.

Ultraformal weddings are always conducted after 6 p.m. The reception almost always includes a sit-down dinner and dancing, and the band or orchestra usually performs a variety of music for the guests' dancing pleasure. The determining factor that marks a wedding as ultraformal is that most of the guests also dress in formal attire. The men usually dress in tuxedos and the women in formal dresses—either cocktail or full-length. Favors are often a big part of the ultraformal wedding, and guests may leave the reception with elaborate gifts, such as silver picture frames; individual, monogrammed boxes of candy; or a set of crystal candlesticks.

Making a List, Checking It Twice

A large factor in determining how formal your wedding will be is deciding how many guests you want to invite. Start with a number you can comfortably entertain at the reception and divide that number by four. This process can vary depending on your personal family situation, but normally the bride's parents, the groom's parents, the bride, and the groom all submit guest lists. There may be duplicates on the lists, so check for that. If that number is too high, begin eliminating names by whatever means you can determine. Many families invite only those friends who know the bride or groom well, leaving out the business associates. Many couples want those in attendance to be only people who are special to them.

Formal: Elegant and Graceful

The *formal* wedding currently is a typical type of wedding in the United States. A formal wedding normally includes three to eight bridesmaids and from 150 to 350 guests. The bridal gown may still be elaborate, but may include a chapel-length, rather than cathedral-length, train. The attendants' dresses complement the bride's gown, and the men are dressed in formal wear, but usually not white tie.

A formal wedding generally is conducted in the late afternoon or early evening and usually offers a buffet, a sit-down dinner, or very elaborate hors d'oeuvres. As with the ultraformal wedding, dancing usually is part of the reception, with band music or a DJ. Decorations both at the ceremony site and the reception may be extensive and usually include flowers and candles. While not quite as grand as those found at an ultraformal reception, table decorations still may include elaborate centerpieces. The guests most likely will receive mementos, although not as elaborate as the favors at an ultraformal reception.

Weddings tend to grow in size and complexity. Think carefully now about your options and what you want to include. As you start adding to your "must have" list, the complexity and costs can begin snowballing.

Semiformal: Tasteful and Dignified

The *semiformal* wedding generally includes one to four attendants and 100 to 150 guests. Decorations are less extensive, both at the ceremony site and the reception. The bride's gown may be full length or tea length and she may or may not wear a veil. She may opt for fresh flowers in her hair. Likewise, her attendants are dressed more simply.

Semiformal weddings are often conducted in the late morning or the early afternoon, and the food at the reception is much less elaborate. You may choose to serve finger sandwiches, cake, and punch or champagne. Frequently, both the ceremony and the reception are in the same facility for a semiformal wedding. There may be dancing—usually to the tunes of a DJ—or you may opt for background music.

Informal: Casual and Comfortable

An *informal* wedding usually is conducted either in a judge's chambers or in a home setting. Generally, an informal wedding includes fewer than 50 guests, and the bride and groom each have one attendant. The bride may choose to wear a suit or fancy street-length dress, and the groom may wear a suit. The honor attendants dress appropriately.

The reception for an informal wedding may consist of cake and punch, and perhaps champagne for the toast. Decorations may simply be flowers for the wedding party and a cake top. Dancing is not appropriate at an informal reception, but you can have a reception at a later time to which you invite more guests and include dancing in the festivities. Technically, this would not be a reception, but rather a "party in honor of the couple."

How the Level of Formality Affects Your Budget

The type of wedding you decide to have—ultraformal, formal, semiformal, or informal—plays a huge part in determining the overall cost of your wedding. The standards that determine the level of formality, however, are not carved in stone, and there are no hard and fast rules. Your wedding may cross over into a couple of formality levels, but you do need a starting point. Choose the level of formality with which you are most comfortable and which seems to fit best within your budget.

If dancing is very important to both of you and the budget will allow it, then by all means, include that aspect into your reception plans. If you want a small intimate wedding, attended by only a few friends and family members, then you may want to go with an informal wedding. If you want a full-blown affair complete with dancing, lots of flowers and candles, a cathedral-length train on a dress full of pearls and beading, then just be sure you understand that you will pay much more than you would for an informal wedding in the judge's chambers. Use the What's Important to Us Worksheet at the end of this chapter to determine the elements you believe are important to include in your special day.

Setting a Realistic Budget

The Budget! This probably is the biggest area of turmoil for most couples. No one, I repeat, no one wants to talk about the cost of the wedding. But ultimately, you *do* have to talk about it; the earlier you begin talking about it, the better.

Now comes the real issue. Just how much is this whole affair going to cost? Well, it's not going to be cheap, but I firmly believe that you don't have to mortgage the farm for your wedding. Let's define what we mean by a *wedding budget*. A wedding budget is what you can *realistically* expect to spend on the wedding and reception, and it includes an estimate of all your other wedding expenses.

Cost Comparison

Turn to the end of this chapter and glance at the Cost Comparison Worksheet. This worksheet lists all possible wedding expenses. The purpose of the worksheet is to find the norm for your market area and determine what sets each estimate apart. It won't help you one bit if I quote you the cost of hiring a photographer in Indiana if you live in Boston. You have some homework to do here, but it will pay off in the end (literally).

Now is the time to begin reviewing those names of possible vendors you have gathered from bridal shows, your family, your friends, and maybe from your bridal consultant. Call at least three vendors under each entry to determine where their prices fall.

To give you an idea of how to use this worksheet, let's take the photography section as an example. Suppose photographer A charges $1,000 for 36 8x10 photos and three hours of his time; photographer B charges $1,500 for 30 8x10 photos and four hours of her time; and photographer C charges $500 for 30 5x7 photos and four hours of his time. Now determine what is important to you and your fiancé and what appears to be the best deal. Are 8x10 photos really important to you? What about the amount of time spent at the wedding by the photographer? What is photographer A's overtime fee? If it's $150 an hour (which it can be) and you go over by two hours (which can happen), then you're right in the ballpark with photographer B. It takes time to do a cost comparison, but it can be a valuable tool.

Putting Your Budget on Paper

When you've finished the Cost Comparison Worksheet, you can turn to the Wedding Budget Worksheet at the end of the chapter. Using your completed Cost Comparison Worksheet (hint: use a pencil), run down the list of service providers. If you decided back on the Cost Comparison Worksheet that either photographer A or B would be okay price-wise, write down their fee estimates on the sheet. This is only a starting point, but it will get you moving in the right direction. Continue to do the same with each entry on the budget sheet, then add everything up and see what ballpark you're in. You may be way, way out of the park, or you could be right on target. So many times, couples don't have any idea what a wedding will or should cost in their area. Even the president and vice president of the Association of Bridal Consultants—who know what weddings cost—said they were in "sticker shock" when their elder daughter married in January, 1994!

 The more open you are to compromising with the budget, the less stress over money matters you are likely to have later on. You are also less likely to be disappointed because your budget cannot accommodate your dreams.

Even they were shocked to find out what some of the expenses are. By using the Cost Comparison Worksheet and then putting those figures down on paper, you know what kind of money you're going to be spending.

The next step is *compromise*. If you want a dinner reception for 650 of your closest friends but you just can't figure out how you can afford it, see where else you can cut costs to make up the difference. Maybe you can serve less elaborate food for the reception, have fewer flowers, or cut your guest list a little. You have to be willing to give and take. Unless you have unlimited resources or Uncle Ralph died and left you a huge inheritance, you have to be cost conscious in your thinking. If you want that number-one-rated photographer in your area who costs $2,000 just to book him, then think about ways to decrease your flower bill or go with a DJ rather than a band. Give and take—that's the name of the game.

Let's say you have $12,000 to spend on this wedding. Your parents are contributing $4,000; the groom's parents are adding another $4,000. That leaves $4,000 for you and the groom to come up with. And remember, you have to cover everything with that amount— EVERYTHING.

Included in that "everything" are the rings, the honeymoon, the reception, the photographer, the bride's gown, the veil, the accessories, and so on. That's why it is so important to determine early what kind of dollars you are willing to spend on this wedding. I've seen too many couples and parents so stressed out over the cost of the wedding that they lose sight of the joy and excitement of the time. Don't let the almighty dollar sign ruin your day. Set a budget and follow it closely.

Whom to Involve

When determining your wedding budget, be sure to include all members of the wedding finance committee. That may include the bride and groom, all parents, grandparents, and others. Sit down in a relaxed atmosphere and talk about the expenses of this wedding. Most of all, think positive and be willing to give and take.

The groom does have responsibility for some parts of the wedding costs. Traditionally, the groom and his family cover the bride's bouquet, the flowers for the groomsmen, the rehearsal dinner, and the flowers for the mothers. Sometimes, the groom's parents also may offer to pay for part of the cost of the reception, the photography, or the floral bill. Etiquette dictates that the bride or bride's parents cannot ask the groom's parents to help with the expenses. If they offer, however, the bride's parents may choose to take them up on the offer. After all, it is their son's wedding, too, and they may want to feel as though they are contributing a part.

Never leave key players out of the budget discussion. If you don't have the financial resources to spring for this wedding on your own, you need backing from family. Play it smart.

Who Pays for What?

Weddings are considered traditional ceremonies of a life passage. As customs and traditions have changed during the years, so have the rules for "Who Pays for What." Traditionally, the bride's family has paid for the majority of the wedding costs. However, that is changing, and more and more couples are coming up with creative ways to meet their financial obligations. Today, it is not uncommon for the couple to help pay expenses and for both sets of parents, grandparents, and even close friends to pitch in.

The Who Pays for What Worksheet at the end of this chapter gives you an idea of the traditional items in a wedding budget. But this worksheet is only a guide. These are the '90s, and there are many ways to divide wedding expenses. Find the way that works best for you.

The Least You Need to Know

➤ Determining your formality early on lets you decide what is important. It also enables you to establish a realistic budget.

➤ There are no hard and fast rules concerning the levels of formality. Find a starting point—even if the wedding you want seems to cross a couple of formality levels.

➤ Use cost comparison to determine prices in your area. You can't begin putting together a budget if you don't have an idea of the going rate for services in your area.

➤ Sit down in a relaxed atmosphere with everyone who needs to be involved with the wedding finances. Be realistic in what you want and what you can afford. When you have established your budget, do your best to work within it.

➤ Think positive and be willing to give and take!

WHAT'S IMPORTANT TO US WORKSHEET

Number of guests:_____

Number of attendants: _____

Time of day:_____

Time of year:_____

Other: Limousine, photography, videography, special items (hot air balloon, vintage cars), decorations (balloons, flowers), flowers (silk vs. fresh), and attire.

_____

_____

_____

Reception:

- ❑ Cake and punch
- ❑ Hors d'oeuvres
- ❑ Buffet
- ❑ Sit-down dinner
- ❑ Open bar
- ❑ Limited bar
- ❑ Cash bar
- ❑ Champagne toast
- ❑ Music
- ❑ Dancing
- ❑ Favors

Other ideas:_____

COST COMPARISON WORKSHEET

Item	Vendor Name & Contact	Cost Estimate

Jewelry store
   Engagement and
   wedding ring
	_____	_____

Bridal consultant	_____	_____
Ceremony site rental	_____	_____
Reception site	_____	_____
Caterer	_____	_____

Bridal shop
   Gown, veil,
   attendants' dresses
	_____	_____

Wedding stationery
Invitations
   Announcements,
   enclosures,
   other paper
	_____	_____

Photographer	_____	_____
Videographer	_____	_____
Florist	_____	_____

Musicians—
    Ceremony

Musicians—
    Reception

Wedding cake

Groom's cake

Attendants' gifts

Men's formal wear

Party rental equipment

Limousine

Favors

Programs

Honeymoon
    Hotel, travel, tours,
    wardrobe, gifts

WEDDING BUDGET WORKSHEET

Item	Estimate	Actual
Rings		
Engagement ring	$_____	$_____
Bride's wedding ring	$_____	$_____
Groom's wedding ring	$_____	$_____
Other	$_____	$_____
Bridal consultant	$_____	$_____
Other	$_____	$_____
Ceremony		
Site rental fee	$_____	$_____
Officiant's fee	$_____	$_____
Ceremony assistants' fee	$_____	$_____
Other	$_____	$_____
Reception		
Site rental fee	$_____	$_____
Food	$_____	$_____
Beverages	$_____	$_____
Service personnel	$_____	$_____
Party rentals (chairs, tables, linens, etc.)	$_____	$_____
Other	$_____	$_____
Wedding cake		
Charge for cake	$_____	$_____
Delivery fee	$_____	$_____

Groom's cake	$_____	$_____
Other	$_____	$_____

Reception

Napkins	$_____	$_____
Personalized matches	$_____	$_____
Favors	$_____	$_____
Toasting goblets	$_____	$_____
Cake knife	$_____	$_____
Scrolls	$_____	$_____
Other	$_____	$_____

Bride's clothing

Gown	$_____	$_____
Headpiece and veil	$_____	$_____
Alterations	$_____	$_____
Shoes	$_____	$_____
Gloves	$_____	$_____
Hose	$_____	$_____
Jewelry	$_____	$_____
Garter	$_____	$_____
Lingerie	$_____	$_____
Other	$_____	$_____

Photography

Engagement announcement photo	$_____	$_____
Wedding portrait	$_____	$_____
Wedding photographs	$_____	$_____
Wedding albums	$_____	$_____
Other	$_____	$_____

continues

Videography

One camera	$_____	$_____
Two cameras	$_____	$_____
Three or more cameras	$_____	$_____
Fee for extra tape	$_____	$_____
Editing charge	$_____	$_____
Other	$_____	$_____

Flowers

Ceremony flowers	$_____	$_____
Reception flowers	$_____	$_____
Personal flowers	$_____	$_____
Other	$_____	$_____

Wedding stationery

Invitations	$_____	$_____
Announcements	$_____	$_____
Reception cards	$_____	$_____
Response cards	$_____	$_____
Thank-you notes	$_____	$_____
Informals	$_____	$_____
Maps	$_____	$_____
Newsletters	$_____	$_____
Other	$_____	$_____

Music

Ceremony

Soloist	$_____	$_____
Organist/pianist	$_____	$_____
Reception	$_____	$_____
Other	$_____	$_____

Groom's clothing

    Tuxedo or suit $_____ $_____

    Shirt $_____ $_____

    Tie $_____ $_____

    Vest or cummerbund $_____ $_____

    Shoes $_____ $_____

    Accessories $_____ $_____

    Other $_____ $_____

Gifts

    Attendants $_____ $_____

    Gifts to each other $_____ $_____

    Parents' thank-you gift $_____ $_____

    Other $_____ $_____

Transportation

    Limousine $_____ $_____

    Parking $_____ $_____

    Other $_____ $_____

Rehearsal dinner (Included, even though traditionally
paid for by bridegroom's family)

    Food $_____ $_____

    Beverages $_____ $_____

    Service personnel $_____ $_____

    Room rental charge $_____ $_____

    Flowers/decorations $_____ $_____

    Other $_____ $_____

Honeymoon

    Hotel accommodations $_____ $_____

    Transportation $_____ $_____

continues

Tours	$_____	$_____
Meals	$_____	$_____
Passport	$_____	$_____
Traveler's checks	$_____	$_____
Other	$_____	$_____
Additional expenses		
Marriage license	$_____	$_____
Postage for invitations	$_____	$_____
Gratuities	$_____	$_____
Blood tests/physicals	$_____	$_____
Hair stylist	$_____	$_____
Makeup artists	$_____	$_____
Birdseed or petals	$_____	$_____

WHO PAYS FOR WHAT WORKSHEET
The Bride and Her Family:

➤ Wedding dress, headpiece, and accessories

➤ Ceremony site rental

➤ Bridal consultant

➤ Reception site rental

➤ Reception food and drink

➤ Flowers for the ceremony

➤ Flowers for the reception

➤ Groom's wedding ring

➤ Invitations, announcements, enclosures

➤ Gift for the groom

➤ Gift for the bridesmaids

➤ Photographer

➤ Videographer

➤ Musicians (both ceremony and reception)

➤ Wedding cake

➤ Transportation from ceremony to reception

➤ Bride's physical and blood test

➤ Accommodations for out-of-town attendants (optional)

➤ Personal stationery

The Groom and His Family:

➤ Bride's engagement and wedding rings

➤ Gift for the bride

➤ Rental of formal wear

➤ Marriage license

- ➤ Officiant's fee
- ➤ Boutonnieres for the men in the wedding party
- ➤ Bride's bouquet
- ➤ Corsages for mothers and grandmothers
- ➤ Rehearsal dinner
- ➤ Groom's physical and blood test
- ➤ Accommodations for out-of-town attendants (optional)
- ➤ Honeymoon expenses

The Wedding Party:

- ➤ Their wedding attire
- ➤ Accessories to go with the attire (shoes, headpieces)
- ➤ Gift for the bride and groom
- ➤ Transportation to the city (if out-of-town)

Part II
First Things First

This Part of the book talks about what you need to reserve first and how far before the big day you need to make the reservations. Although it may not seem like it now, there is a method to all this madness. The chapters that follow take you step by step through what you need to do next and explain the order in which you need to do things. You don't, for example, want to rush right out and order your invitations. You have several major items to pin down first. Read through all of Part II before you even begin to think about going out to meet those vendors. The information here should give you a fundamental understanding of what you need to do and when you need to do it before you put down that first deposit or order that first corsage.

A Check-Off List is provided at the end of Part II to help you keep things organized and to prevent you from forgetting any important details. This list shows you exactly what you need to be doing from six months before the wedding right up to the big day. Keep this Check-Off List with you during these planning months, and you'll feel more relaxed and confident as you plan.

Get Me a Church on Time!

Probably some of the most obvious items to cover in the beginning of your wedding planning are setting a date, finding a place, and making the arrangements for someone to perform the service. These tasks are not as time-consuming as meeting with the caterer or visiting the reception facility, and they need to be done first. After all, if you don't have a date, how can you plan anything else? Read on!

Setting the Date

Before you can reserve one of the "biggies," you need to determine a date for the occasion. When choosing a date for your wedding, keep in mind family commitments (birthdays and other anniversaries), holidays, how far guests will have to travel, special events and tourist activities taking place in the area, and weather conditions.

Plan Around Big Events

Planning a May wedding in Indianapolis around the time of the Indianapolis 500 race probably is not a wise move. In fact, it would likely be a very expensive proposition. Hotels and motels double their room prices, crowds swell the city beyond imagination, and many of the ideal reception spots are booked years in advance for 500 activities. If you can wait until June or move the date up to April you'll be in much better shape to deal with the rest of the stress that comes with planning a wedding.

Be sure to refer to the Planning Check-Off List at the end of Part II to help you remember what to do in the months before your wedding day.

Likewise, a wedding in New Orleans during the Mardi Gras is not a wise idea. Again, you have tons of tourists and inflated prices, plus the difficulty of booking a reception site. Save yourself a lot of planning nightmares by checking out the tourist trends in your area. Try your best to avoid scheduling your wedding at the same time as a popular special event.

Other dates during the year that you should try to avoid—mainly because of the floral difficulties during that time of year—are Mother's Day weekend and Valentine's Day weekend. Both of these times are very, very busy times for florists. They will be much more accommodating at other times during the year and can give you the service and products you deserve. There are florists who will not accept a Mother's Day weekend wedding. It just takes too much manpower to handle the pressures of a wedding and the Mother's Day floral orders.

You also can check with the Convention & Visitors Bureau to make sure there are no really big conventions in town that will take up many hotel rooms and reception sites.

Holidays: Pressure Cookers or Money Savers?

Holiday weddings, especially during the Christmas season, can be stressful—given the very hectic nature of the season—but they can also be money savers. Most facilities are already decorated for the holidays and you can save big bucks. The cost savings don't come without a price, however. We all know the kind of stress that can accompany the holidays in everyday life; add the task of planning a wedding, and you compound that stress many times over. However, if you love Christmas and can handle the added pressure, you can save substantially on your decorating costs.

One of the prettiest Christmas weddings I can remember included 500 white poinsettias, candles on every aisle, red ribbons and fresh greenery at the entrance, and a large Christmas tree in the lobby area. The church congregation had already decorated for the season and it was breathtaking. The best part was that the couple didn't spend a dime on any of it.

Waltzing with the Weather

Be sure to take the area's weather into consideration for the time of year you are planning your wedding. For my own January wedding back in 1971, I never even considered the weather as a factor. Now, since I'm from Indiana, not California, I should have known better. It snowed eight inches on the day of the wedding. Lucky for us, the snow came straight down, it didn't really drift much, and everyone was able to drive to the church.

When I coordinated a January wedding a few years ago, I drove 35 miles on solid ice to get to the church the morning of the wedding. Everyone, including the groom, was late. You can't control the weather (although at times, I sure wish I could), so if you live in an area where bad weather conditions may be a problem, try to take the weather into consideration when you set the date.

Don't Forget the License!

One simple thing that can easily sneak up on you is remembering to apply for the marriage license. Each state has different requirements and policies, including the length of the waiting period, the ages of both parties, whether you need a blood test (or other medical examination), identification requirements, and how much the license costs.

Within each state, each county may have its own set of rules. Your first step should be to call the office of the Marriage Clerk or County Clerk in your county seat and ask how to proceed. You should investigate the requirements several months before your wedding date. Many counties now make allowances for long distance couples, but you should find out all the requirements well in advance of your wedding day.

Consider Other Commitments

Family commitments also make a difference in setting a date. Make a list of those commitments before you look for a date. You can say to Aunt Martha, "We're thinking about sometime next May for our wedding. Can you think of any dates that you and Uncle Fred may not be able to attend?" You don't have to do this with all your relatives, and unless you have a very small family, you can't, but try to consider the schedules of those people whose presence is especially important to you.

If you and your groom have school commitments or careers that are affected by the time of year, take those commitments into account. The main reason I was married in January was because my husband is a farmer and January is his off season. If you're an accountant, then a wedding date before April 15 is probably not wise planning.

Be sure to check with family members and others whose presence at your wedding is especially important to see what scheduling conflicts they may have.

If you take some time now to plan around other family commitments, your local traditions (festivals, large sporting events, and so on), the holiday schedule, your own work or school schedules, and your local weather conditions, you can please more of your guests in the long run and make life a little easier.

Selecting the Ceremony Site

Okay, you have a date in mind. Now, you need a place to get hitched. After you determine when and how formal you want this wedding to be, you need a place for the ceremony.

The place where you choose to have your wedding ceremony can be as unique as you, the couple. The obvious choices are those with a religious tone. You may have the ceremony in a church, cathedral, chapel, or temple. You can also choose a hall, private club, hotel, restaurant, garden or other outdoor setting, your home, or a judge's chambers. You may also choose a truly unique setting. Couples have married in hot air balloons, at the top of roller coasters, on horseback, on the beach, and even underwater.

Choose a ceremony site with some special significance for the two of you. For example, if you met each other at church or maybe in a park, then those sites may be appropriate for your wedding because they have significance for you. Most couples who choose a religious setting are married in their home church or temple. If you are not a member of a church, or if your home church isn't large enough to accommodate your guests, you may consider renting church space. Several denominations rent to nonmembers, but tracking down these organizations can sometimes be difficult.

Examine the Facility Firsthand

Whether it's your home church or you are renting space, look at the physical side of the facility. How many guests can it comfortably hold? I coordinated a wedding several years ago at a church with a capacity of 300. The couple, however, expected 450 guests. We had to bring in 150 folding chairs to have on hand in case we needed them. We did. It was not an ideal situation, but at that point, we had no choice.

Check the musical equipment that comes with the facility. Do they have an organ or piano? What are the restrictions? Can any organist play the available equipment? Also check the sound system and availability of microphones for soloists, if appropriate.

Check parking availability. Is it ample to meet the needs of your guests? Will the guests have to walk far? What about lighting and safety considerations outside if the service is at night? I once coordinated a wedding in which the couple hired four off-duty policemen to guard the guests' cars during a service in a part of town that was considered "risky."

If you plan to get dressed at the ceremony site, ask to see where the bride traditionally dresses. In the Midwest, most brides dress at the ceremony facility. So check out the dressing rooms for mirrors, rest rooms, and electrical outlets. A dressing that doesn't have an outlet for hair dryers or curling irons is a pretty frightening possibility if it has to accomodate eight woman. What about the lighting in the dressing room? Is it adequate? Do you need to bring a lighted makeup mirror?

Ask to see the sanctuary or the room in which the ceremony will be held. If you have 40 attendants, make sure that the facility can handle that number. I once coordinated a very large wedding party in a church with an altar area that was so tiny we literally had to stack the attendants in sideways just to get them situated. At the end of the ceremony, the bridesmaid on the end turned too quickly, and her bouquet stabbed the next bridesmaid in the nose. Not exactly the finale of your dreams!

Understand the Fees and Policies

Be sure to ask about fees. Yes, a church is a business, and many of them charge for the use of the facility. Some of these fees can be quite steep. Ask what the fee includes. Churches that charge a single fee that includes all the necessary services (musicians, janitor, officiant, and rent) probably offer the best deal. You're going to have to pay for those services anyway, so if you can line them all up with one stop, that's not a bad option.

 Make sure that you read and fully understand the church wedding policies before your wedding day. If you can't work with the policies, look elsewhere. If there are restrictions on certain parts of the church rental, be sure to let the appropriate person know about those rules.

Ask if there are any wedding policies for the facility. Many churches and other sites where weddings occur regularly provide a wedding policy booklet that explains the rules—what you can and cannot do in the facility. Get a copy of this booklet for yourself and a copy for your bridal consultant if you have hired one, and review the policies with her. Be sure to abide by these rules. They were written for a reason. If there are any restrictions on decorations, music, or photography, be sure to let your vendors know. You don't want surprises on your wedding day when the florist is told he can't use the lovely pew bows because the church has a rule against it, or when you find out that the videographer cannot work in the sanctuary during the service.

Use the Ceremony Site Worksheet at the end of this chapter to ensure that you have asked all the right questions and have thoroughly investigated a facility before you actually write the check to reserve it.

Working with the Officiant

Someone has to perform your service. That's a given. Whether that person is a justice of the peace, a judge, a priest, a rabbi, or a minister, someone with the legal authority allowed by the state must preside at your marriage. My best advice when working with this person is to make him your friend, not your enemy. After all, he is going to perform a very important ceremony in your life and you want fond memories of this event.

Susan, a bridal consultant in a western metropolitan city, shared one experience with me that emphasizes the importance of working with your officiant. Some years ago, Susan coordinated a wedding in which the mother-of-the-bride got into a power struggle with the clergyman. This mother called the clergyman all hours of the night to ask silly questions that could have been answered during normal working hours. If the clergyman suggested something, the mother always had a reason not to do it his way. She wouldn't budge. Susan said you could tell, as the wedding plans progressed, how stressed the mother was making the clergyman, almost as if this task had become her advocation. So, the day of the wedding arrived and all systems were "go." Susan had everyone lined up ready to make their grand entrance when all of a sudden, the clergyman appeared in front of the church and launched into a stand-up comedy routine. Whether he had always wanted to be on "The Tonight Show" and had never been asked, no one will ever know. What we do know is that he proved to the mother who was really in charge. It was payback time.

Within the first 35 minutes of the wedding, he rearranged the entire wedding plan. First of all, he asked the bride's guests to get up and trade places with the groom's guests. He said he wanted everyone to get to know each other. Then he started telling jokes, "Did you hear the one about the priest…." After 35 minutes of joke telling and musical chairs, he proceeded with the ceremony.

The mother was beside herself. Her daughter's wedding was turned into something far different from what she had imagined. The clergyman not only had the best lines, he also had the last laugh. Some of the guests found the situation humorous; some left the church for a smoke; others wandered down to the corner bar. On top of everything, the bride was crying. Susan, who normally is completely composed and in charge, was also rapidly losing her grip on reality. (This is why bridal consultants usually have gray hair.) All this chaos occurred because, instead of working with the clergyman, Mom created an adversarial relationship.

The officiant is your link to the legal aspects of your wedding. Without his consent and cooperation, the wedding may take place, but if the officiant doesn't complete the legal paperwork to validate the marriage in the state, the union won't be legal. So although you may have different ideas about what you want to include in your service, a wise bride-to-be or mother approaches the officiant cautiously. Meet with him. Ask for opinions and advice. Get the officiant on your side first and then talk about the particulars of your service. It helps to have an amiable relationship with your officiant.

I have actually coordinated a wedding in which the officiant refused to marry the couple just two weeks before the wedding. It wasn't that the officiant was concerned about the marriage itself, he just didn't like the way in which the couple answered a question he posed to them. He called the mother two weeks before (invitations had been out for weeks at that time, the reception was arranged, and all systems were go) and told her to find another officiant. It was not an easy task given the particulars of that wedding. And it is certainly something that you would not want to go through two weeks before your big day.

It's always a good idea to befriend your officiant. Besides helping the ceremony to proceed smoothly, the officiant must properly complete all legal paperwork in order for your marriage to be valid.

These stories aren't meant to frighten you, although they certainly may have that effect. However, please understand that they are true. Certainly most officiants are pleasant and friendly and want to help make your wedding day memorable. The reason I mentioned these tales of uncooperative officiants is that you need to understand that a little common respect and courtesy can go a long way toward making the officiant a friend. When I was married, we met with the officiant and what he said was the rule; you didn't ask questions. We don't have that type of society anymore. People ask questions. They want things done their way and no other way, and everyone, from the officiant to the couple, can be disrespectful of each other's feelings. The bottom line here is that you most assuredly need the officiant to be your friend. Do your best to work *with* him, and he will do his best to make your wedding ceremony a very pleasant experience.

The Least You Need to Know

➤ Consider weather conditions, family commitments, and local special events and celebrations when you select your wedding date.

➤ Select a ceremony site that best suits your needs, such as the size for the number of guests, location, size of altar area, and parking.

➤ Treat the officiant with respect. Try your best to work with your officiant to ensure a smooth road both to the church and down the aisle.

CEREMONY SITE WORKSHEET

Name of facility: _____

Address: _____

Telephone: _____

Contact: _____

Fee: _____

(Includes:)

    Organist _____   Officiant _____   Janitor_____

    Kneeler _____   Aisle cloths _____   Candelabra _____

Meeting with contact: _____

Number of guests facility can accommodate: _____

Musical equipment provided: _____

Dressing room facilities: _____

Parking areas: _____

Wedding policy booklets: _____

Facility restrictions:_____

_____

_____

Added fees rental items (such as candelabra, kneeler,
aisle cloth): _____

Special accommodations for the handicapped (parking, access,
restrooms, and so on)_____

Notes: _____

_____

_____

_____

_____

Scheduling Your Soirée

Reserving the Reception Site

After you choose the site for your ceremony and find someone to perform the ceremony, the next most important item to reserve is the reception site. Many reception sites—whether a private club, a hall, the church's social hall, a restaurant, or civic center—will accept early reservations. You can reserve many of the prime reception sites at least a year in advance; you can book some sites in the larger cities as much as 18 to 24 months in advance. Hopefully, you will have some choices in your locale. If possible, visit potential sites while weddings are being set up. It will give you a better feeling than looking at an empty room.

Be sure to refer to the Planning Check-Off List at the end of Part II to help you remember what to do in the months before your wedding day.

Ask friends, family members, and certainly recently married couples where they had their reception. That's a good starting point. Also, check in the Yellow Pages (under headings such as "Banquet Facilities," Hall and Auditoriums," and "Party Centers") for sites you may not have thought about. Many times, private clubs will rent facilities out. I know of a beautiful old Victorian house that has been turned into a women's club that can be rented for wedding receptions. Look at the local university or college. Possibly there are sites on those campuses. Of course, many hotels have banquet facilities you can use for receptions.

If you don't have many choices for a reception site and the weather in your area will permit, consider having an outdoor reception, either at your home or in a park or garden. (See the "Outdoor/ Garden Weddings" section in Chapter 17, "What's in a Theme?" for more information about planning an outdoor reception.)

Is It Big Enough?

The biggest factor in booking a reception site is determining whether the facility is large enough to handle the number of guests you anticipate. How is the traffic flow inside the facility? Your reception manager should be able to make suggestions, based on past experience, for the best traffic pattern for a wedding reception at that facility. Also check floor plans. Many times, reception sites will list that number of guests

Make sure the reception site is large enough to accommodate your guests. Don't guess on size; get the facts. How many guests can they seat comfortably along with the activities you want to include?

that can be accommodated based on total square footage of the room, not taking into consideration the size of the head table, cake table, dance floor, and other minor disruptions, such as support columns (although they may come in handy, if you want to seat behind them that obnoxious aunt you really didn't want to invite in the first place).

I coordinated a lovely wedding a few years ago followed by an equally lovely reception—except for one small detail. The reception hall was on three different floors. There was an elevator, but most guests had to walk up and down three flights of stairs. Most of the food was set up on the first floor, and dancing and some finger foods were located on the third floor. The rest rooms were located on the second floor. I remember trying to move a guest in a wheelchair through the crowd and wondering what I should do if anyone yelled "Fire!" That reception would have been so much nicer and easier for the guests had the bride made the reservation earlier and reserved a larger one-floor facility.

What about Services and Restrictions?

Check with the manager about the restrictions the facility has for food and beverages. Can you bring in a caterer of your choice or do you have to use the facility's *in-house caterer*? An in-house caterer is the caterer responsible for that facility's food service. An *outside caterer* is a person or organization not associated with the facility who comes to the facility to prepare the food.

Are there ample rest rooms? Can they accommodate the handicapped (most public facilities today must meet those requirements)? Are microphone hook-ups available? Will the DJ or band have any trouble setting up their equipment?

What does the facility provide? Make sure you have that part in writing. Linens? Table skirting? Security guards? Get estimates on the price and what the price includes.

Check about parking facilities. Is it adequate for the number of guest cars you expect? How far will guests have to walk? How far is the site from the ceremony location? Are there good, well-traveled roads between the two? Handicapped parking?

Look at the Choosing the Reception Site Worksheet at the end of this chapter. Also, check out Chapter 10 for more details.

Who's in Charge Here?

Try to gauge whether you will be able to work with the reception manager. You don't want to hear "That can't be done." "Let me see what we can do" is the response you want. You're going to be spending a lot of time with these people and you want it to be a pleasant experience. It is *not* the reception manager's wedding reception. You are the client and her only job for that day is to make you look good. If you look good and are happy, the reception manager (and the facility) looks good.

Choosing a Caterer

After you select a reception site, the next step is to find a caterer. If the reception facility you reserved provides an in-house catering service, you have no choice. Most of the larger facilities, such as hotels, country clubs, colleges, or universities provide in-house catering.

If you decide to hold your reception in a hall, art museum, home, church social hall, or outdoor setting, you must arrange for a caterer to provide the food. If the choice of caterer is up to you, then shop around and find someone who can give you the food choices you want at a price you can afford.

Friends, family, and recent couples are your best bet when discussing possible caterers. Ask the reception facility manager, too. Sometimes, facilities limit which caterers may come into their facility. They may give you their "preferred caterer list" and ask you to chose a caterer from that list. This usually means that those caterers are competent, provide quality work, and take care of the facility so the reception manager doesn't have to worry about damage from the caterers.

Look at the Choosing the Caterer Worksheet at the end of this chapter. There is also detailed information about caterers in Chapter 10.

Bet You Didn't Know... The largest wedding dish ever prepared was a roasted camel. The camel was prepared in the following manner:

Eggs were stuffed into fish
Fish were stuffed into chickens
Chickens were stuffed into a roasted lamb
The lamb was stuffed inside the whole camel.

The entire camel was then roasted and served to the wedding guests.

Guinness Book of World Records

May I Serve You?

Your menu choices can be as basic as cake and punch. Traditional etiquette says that the only thing you must offer your guests at the wedding reception is something to eat and something to drink. Cake and punch or bread and water will do the trick. Anything else is icing on the cake (pardon the pun). The simplest type of wedding reception is a cake and punch reception, with some mints and nuts thrown in for good measure, if you so desire.

off
off

You may want to move up one step and serve hors d'oeuvres and a limited bar. A limited bar means that you limit what is served to your guests. You may opt for only wine and soft drinks or beer. One step up from this would be an open bar and hors d'oeuvres.

Then there is the simple buffet for guests. A simple buffet includes one entrée plus other side dishes. You can expand this into a more elaborate buffet by simply adding more entrées and other side dish choices.

The most elaborate reception meal you can offer would be a five- or six-course dinner served to guests, including wine with the meal. If you choose this option, consider hiring extra wait staff. If the facility's price normally includes one waiter for every two tables (20 guests), consider adding enough to have two waiters for every three tables (30 guests). It will speed the service and make the guests feel more special.

So, What Will It Cost?

After you decide on the kind of meal you want to serve, start getting price estimates. Most caterers figure their prices per person except for hors d'oeuvres, which sometimes are figured per dozen. For example, you may order 15 dozen water chestnuts at $8.20 per dozen. Other items may be priced per item, such as large fruit trays or blocks of cheese and crackers at $25 per tray.

A nice touch to add to your reception is to have the wait staff wear white gloves. Classy look!

Unless you have your heart set on particular food items, it often works well to give the caterer a price per head and let them be creative. They can choose the food, subject to your approval, based on seasonal availability. Also, be wary of caterers who refuse to deviate from their standard menu. Good caterers will be willing to take your favorite recipes and price them out for your reception. This is great if you have some foods you particularly like or that are family traditions (like Aunt Eileen's traditional Irish Soda Bread). We'll talk more about actual menu selection in Chapter 10.

Ask about the caterer's policy on guaranteed numbers. This is an important concept for you to understand before you begin contacting caterers. If you plan to serve major food items, you must have an accurate guest count for the caterer. The caterer obviously isn't providing this food just for the pure pleasure of it. It comes with a price tag, and here's how it works. Most caterers give you a 5 or 10 percent window above or below your guaranteed number. If you guarantee them 100 guests and only 95 people show up, they only bill you for 95 guests. The same rule applies if you are substantially under your guaranteed number. If you guarantee them 100 guests and only 50 people show up, they still bill you for 95.

The caterer usually only prepares food for 5 or 10 percent above your guaranteed number. So if you guarantee them 100 guests and 120 show up, you will only have enough food for 110 (that's at 10 percent, which is on the high side). That means 10 guests are going to go without food. That probably doesn't leave a very good taste in your mouth (another pun). This is the biggest reason to make sure you have an accurate count for the caterer.

Catering to the Masses

Build in some extra time for checking out caterers and reception sites. This is one area of wedding planning that can carry a heavy price tag, and you want to find a facility and a caterer that offers you the best value for your wedding dollars.

Also, get the catering details in writing. This can save you a great deal of grief later as you try to remember exactly what was quoted, including the 5 or 10 percent window above and below the guaranteed number.

Liquor: To Drink or Not to Drink

The decision of whether or not to serve alcohol to your guests is solely a personal one. If you are going to offer alcohol with your reception, you need to engage a caterer with a liquor license or a liquor licensed dealer. It is a wise move considering the liability issues presently in focus in the country.

Many states now make the host liable for accidents involving guests at a party. (Direct any concerns about local laws regarding alcohol to the liquor licensed dealer.) While all caterers are supposed to ensure that their bartenders comply with local laws, it may be wise to brief them (or have the wedding consultant do it) on specific guests they should watch for and to ensure they know when and how to cut people off tactfully. We'll talk specifically about designated drivers in Chapter 24. If you are planning to serve champagne, also provide non-alcoholic "sparkling grape wine" so those who wish not to drink can have something "bubbly" for toasts.

Most religious facilities do not approve of liquor on the grounds. Again, that's why you need to read and understand the wedding policy booklets they may provide. If you want champagne at your reception and the reception is scheduled for a church social hall that will not allow liquor, then having champagne is no longer a choice. As I said above, whether or not you offer liquor at your wedding reception is a personal choice. Just because everyone else does it, doesn't mean you have to.

If you are considering offering liquor at your reception, get the terminology down now so you can ask intelligent questions.

Limited bar means you limit what is served to the guests. This is your choice. If you only want to offer wine and something non-alcoholic, that's fine. Often with a limited bar in the Midwest, it will offer both wine and beer plus soft drinks or maybe punch.

Open bar means a bar containing hard liquor for mixed drinks, plus beer and wine and maybe even after-dinner drinks. Here again, you want to make sure you provide nonalcoholic beverages also.

Cash bar brings both smiles and frowns to people. If you offer a cash bar at your reception, your guests will pay for their drinks. You may offer wine and soft drinks, and then if guests want something else in the way of liquor, they can buy it from the bartender. Many people feel that a cash bar is insulting to their guests. You wouldn't make your guests pay for a drink in your home, so why make them pay for one at your reception? The other side of that philosophy is that if guests are paying for their own drinks, they may not be as free with the liquor and watch consumption. It's your call.

Pricing for liquor at receptions can vary. You want to know what system the caterer uses to arrive at the figure that appears on your bill. There are several methods; you just need to know what system they use.

One method is for the caterer to charge a per drink tab at the bar. Most bartenders aren't crazy about this system because it is time-consuming. When they have 200 guests to serve liquor to, it can become cumbersome to count drinks.

Another method is for the caterer to charge a price by the bottle. You choose the type or brand of liquor you want to serve. At the end of the reception, the caterer charges you for all the opened and empty bottles. You can have your choice of the liquor served. The cheapest brands are "house brands," the next step up are "call brands," and the most expensive are the "premium brands." The bottle price should include the fee for the bartender, mixes, and glassware.

The one other charging system I've run across is a per-person charge. The client who used this system was very satisfied with the price and didn't have to worry about counting bottles at the end of the reception. With this system, you are charged so much for each guest. It doesn't matter whether every guest drinks alcohol or not. You still pay a set price for each person. This system is supposed to strike a balance between those who drink and those who don't.

Keep in mind that if your caterer uses the open and empty bottle system, someone has to go to the bar at the end of the evening and count the used and open bottles. I've done this over the years for clients and have had no problems until about a year ago. I told the bartender that I would count bottles at the end of the reception. When the reception ended, the bartender I had spoken with had the bottles all lined up in nice, neat rows. We counted together and came up with a total of 35 bottles that we had consumed. A second bartender then came along (I didn't find out until later that he was the owner) and started mixing up the lines of nice, neat bottles so that they were no longer even. Then he counted again.

I watched him very closely, because a big red flag went off in my head when he undid the even rows we had established. As he counted along, I watched him count one row twice. Okay, I was onto him, but I learned a long time ago that it is sometimes better to play dumb—at least for the moment. I coyly suggested that the other bartender and I had only counted 35 bottles, not 42 like he had, and that maybe we should count again. He started to count again, but I stopped him, and in my most motherly, demure voice said, "Oh, now look, we've got these bottles all out of line. Let's line them up nice and neat and count them again. Your friend and I only counted 35." To say he was angry is an understatement. But guess what? I didn't care. He was trying to overcharge my client by seven bottles and at $65 per bottle; it doesn't take a brain surgeon to figure out how much money he was going to make.

Moral of the story: Have the bottles counted by a neutral person and watch carefully. At the next wedding reception I had with this liquor outfit, the owner saw me coming at the end of the evening and without saying a word had the bottles all lined up in nice, neat rows.

Bet You Didn't Know... The word *bridal* comes from the old English term *bride-ale* which refers to the mead drink (a fermented beverage made of water, honey, malt, and yeast) they consumed for thirty days following the marriage.

The Least You Need to Know

➤ Ask lots of questions about the physical layout for the reception. Make sure the facility can accommodate the number of guests you are inviting. Also check whether parking is adequate.

➤ Make sure the reception facility has a good traffic flow pattern. Too little room to comfortably allow for the number of guests you expect can be frustrating for everyone involved.

➤ Make a list of questions for the caterer before you meet with him. Get the details of what the caterer will provide in writing.

➤ Understand your legal responsibilities if you decide to serve alcohol at the reception.

CHOOSING THE RECEPTION SITE WORKSHEET

Facility: _____

Rental Price: _____

Includes:

❏ Linens

❏ Skirting

❏ Tables

❏ Chairs

❏ Security

❏ Plants, decorative items

Ample parking? _____

Distance from ceremony: _____

Catering requirements: _____

In-house : _____

Outside : _____

Number of restrooms? _____

Handicapped accessible? _____

Date available: _____

CHOOSING THE CATERER WORKSHEET

Names: _____

_____

_____

Referred by:

_____

_____

_____

Available on: _____

_____

_____

Pricing system: _____

Per person: _____

Per item: _____

Labor charges: _____

Linen charges: _____

Delivery charges: _____

Plate charge: _____

Menu format (Buffet, hors d'oeuvres, seated dinner): _____

_____

Will incorporate family recipes? _____

Chapter 6

Photos, Flowers, Gowns, Music, and All That Jazz

In This Chapter

➤ Asking the photographer and videographer the right questions

➤ Finding a good florist

➤ Choosing your bridal gown

➤ Choosing your musicians

Choosing a Photographer

The next element you want to consider in your wedding planning is the photographer. Photography is an expensive undertaking for most couples. You want good pictures that capture your special day, but that means you're going to have to spend some time investigating your choices now and allow for enough money in your budget to accomplish that goal.

So Many Questions, So Little Time

When you meet with the photographer, there are several items you need to consider. The first thing you should look at is the quality of the photographer's work. Does the photographer's work capture the moment? Look through the display albums. Do the pictures express the romance of the day? What catches your eye? Are they straight shots?

Be sure to refer to the Planning Check-Off List at the end of Part II to help you remember what to do in the months before your wedding day.

Do the pictures tell a story? Find out whether the photographer will take candid shots; many photographers will not. Is the photographer available on your wedding date? What is the fee? What kinds of packages does he offer?

Be sure to find out what kind of contract the photographer uses. Does the contract include a time limit? You want to avoid having to pay overtime to your photographer. Overtime can add up to big money very quickly.

Make Sure That What You See Is What You Get

Ask what percentage of the photographer's work is in wedding photography. Is his business mostly weddings or is he primarily a studio photographer? It takes a certain personality to take wedding pictures, so you want to be sure you hire an experienced *wedding photographer*.

As you are looking over the work displayed in the studio, be sure to ask whose work you are viewing. If Mr. Smith took the pictures they are showing you, but Ms. Jones will be the photographer shooting your wedding, ask to see Ms. Jones' work.

If it is a large studio, make sure you know who will be photographing your wedding. One couple I worked with a few years ago was very excited because they had booked one of the biggest studios in town for their wedding. I knew that the studio contracted out some of its photography work to other photographers, but the couple didn't know this. When I asked who was going to take pictures at the wedding, they responded that Mr. Smith, the owner, was going to shoot the wedding. I asked if they were sure about that, and they were very surprised that I asked this question. When they checked with the studio, they were shocked and disappointed to find out that Mr. Smith was not going to photograph the wedding pictures, but instead their wedding had been contracted out to someone they had not met. Had they read their contract more carefully, they would have discovered that fact sooner.

Do You Have That Warm, Fuzzy Feeling?

One of the most important questions you have to ask is whether you both feel comfortable with this photographer. Be honest with yourselves. You will spend a lot of time on your wedding day with this person. If you don't like the person, for whatever reason, it will show in your pictures. Over the years, I have watched brides who were so obviously annoyed by the photographer that the only things that came across in the finished product were clenched teeth and forced smiles. Not good! It's important to have a good rapport with your photographer.

Make sure you examine the work of the photographer who will be taking your wedding photographs. Looking at the work of another photographer from that studio won't help you decide if the photographer you are considering is right for the job.

Hiring a Videographer

After you have hired a competent photographer to shoot the still pictures for your wedding, you may also want to consider booking a videographer. Video taping by an experienced videographer can add so much life to your wedding memories that it is fast becoming a very popular wedding component. Some couples are even opting for a professional video in lieu of professional photography. With developing technology, it is possible to pull still frames from a video.

When you check out a video company, always ask to see a demo tape. This should give you an idea of the quality of work they provide. When you view this tape, look for clarity both in film quality and in the coverage of events. Does the tape flow smoothly from one portion of the wedding to the next? Make sure you understand whether the tape will be edited or unedited. Edited is what you would most likely prefer.

One couple didn't check and ended up with 12 hours of unedited tape. Can you imagine inviting friends over to see your 12-hour wedding video? Ask to see a recent tape (not just the demo that will be the best one ever shot).

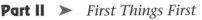
The biggest complaint I hear from brides who asked Uncle Henry to tape their wedding is "I thought it would be just like TV." Well, it's not. For a videotape to have some of the major components of a TV show, you will need at least two cameras, and three would be better. Ask the video company whether they can provide the groom with a wireless microphone to pick up the vows segment of the ceremony.

Is there music that will be added to your edited video? Will you have a choice in the selection of music? Can you order extra tapes? Approximately how long after the wedding will you receive the tape? Does he use a contract? (Most do.) Is there a time limit on his contract? Does he charge for overtime? What do the videographers wear for the wedding?

Choosing Your Gown

You should order your gown at least six months before the wedding. It doesn't take six months for your gown to arrive at the shop, but with delays in shipping, manufacturing problems, and alterations, it's best to allow six months. If you don't have six months lead time, make sure you mention that to the shop. There are several bridal gown companies that specialize in short order times.

Bet You Didn't Know... The traditional color of a bridal gown was not white until very recently. In ancient times, red was a favorite color, along with other brightly colored materials.

In the mid-nineteenth century, Empress Eugenie, wife of Napoleon III, broke the medieval tradition of wearing a brightly colored wedding gown and chose white.

In the Victorian period in this country, brides who were from affluent families began wearing white gowns to show that they could afford to have a special dress they would wear only one time. Most women simply wore the best dress they had at the time. A white gown did not come to represent purity until the 20th century.

When shopping for your wedding gown, look at many different styles of dresses. You may be really surprised to find that a gown style you thought would not complement you really does. Shop with an open mind. Take one or two people with you when you shop. One or two trusted friends or your mom can offer plenty of advice. Do not go armed with your entire wedding party when you do your bridal gown shopping. Too many people giving you advice will only cause you more stress. Too many opinions also make it harder for you to choose the dress that is right for you.

If possible, make an appointment with the bridal shop. That way, you are guaranteed the time you need to try on the various gowns. Ask about alterations; they can add a hefty amount to the price of the gown. Ask if they will deliver the gown to the ceremony site. Some shops provide that service. All gowns should be pressed and bagged for delivery. Ask if they will stuff the sleeves with tissue and if they use a bodice form. These things help keep your gown looking fresh even after it leaves the shop.

Talking About Tuxedos

Many brides think that when they order their gowns, they should also take care of ordering the formal wear for the men. That process can wait until later on in the calendar schedule. Most men rent formal wear and alterations are usually kept to a minimum, so it isn't necessary to worry about the men's formal wear at this stage. We'll cover that in Chapter 12, "Puttin' on the Ritz."

Deciding on a Florist

I mention the florist here as an early booking duty, but under normal circumstances, you don't really have to decide on flowers until two or three months before the wedding. The reason I mention the florist here is that if you are being married in a prime wedding season (June, May or August), or if you are being married around a holiday (Christmas, Valentine's Day, or Mother's Day weekend), it is wise to go ahead and reserve your florist for your wedding day. Some florists will only service one or two weddings a weekend because weddings are such labor-intensive productions.

Bet You Didn't Know...

The very first types of bridal bouquets included not only flowers, but also herbs and spices. Especially popular were strong scented ones, such as garlic, to ward off evil spirits.

Various kinds of flowers have different meanings. Ivy represents fidelity; lily-of-the-valley represents purity; red roses mean love; violets represent modesty; forget-me-nots mean true love; orange blossoms represent fertility and happiness; and myrtle is the symbol of virginity.

My personal pet peeve is a florist who says to the bride-to-be—who has no idea which flowers she wants or even knows the available options—"Oh, honey, we'll do anything you want." NO NO NO. You are paying that florist for his ideas; you are paying for his expertise. This attitude is fine when and if you know what you want, but if you're like most brides, you do not know what you want or what your options are. Try to stay with seasonal flowers if at all possible. Tulips in December will be expensive and won't be the quality of tulips in April, when they're in season.

My favorite florist story goes back many years, before I was officially in this business. I was planning my out-of-town sister's wedding and was meeting with the florist to finalize the wedding flowers. I went to the appointment armed with a picture of my sister, a picture of her gown and a swatch of the fabric from the bridesmaids' dresses. I sat facing the florist who was seated at his desk. While I talked and described the wedding, the reception site, the number of bridesmaids, and the formality of this wedding, Mr. Becker was drawing on a pad. When I finished describing the details, he handed me the piece of paper he had been working on. There in black and white was a sketch of my sister, in her wedding gown, with the appropriate bouquet that would not only complement the gown, but would also complement her. He then drew pictures of the bridesmaid's dresses and their bouquets and what he saw to be the total picture. It was perfect, and it all blended and fit together wonderfully.

Now, obviously, most florists don't have the ability to sketch out the bride with her bouquet, but I think you get the point. A good florist will assist you in determining what you can and cannot do with your flowers for your wedding. They will offer suggestions and ideas, and they will help you work within your budget. Before you meet with them, ask if they are familiar with the ceremony and reception site. If they are not, ask if they can visit the sites before your appointment. At minimum, provide the florist with photos of the sites. That will help you be more practical when you discuss the options you have for decorations.

Some general questions you can ask the florist would also include whether he uses a contract. How is pricing done? Usually, you will pay per item. If you are having six bridesmaids and each of their bouquets will cost $20, then 6 × $20 = $120 in bridesmaids' bouquets. The only other charge that may come into play—and that depends on each individual florist—is a labor charge for extensive setup. Often, the labor charge is built into the flower pricing. As with any vendor, check references.

Choosing the Musicians

You must reserve wedding music early, both for the ceremony and the reception. Music completes your wedding atmosphere. Because it stays in the background, music is also one aspect of wedding planning that is easy to overlook.

Music for the Ceremony

For the ceremony music, you have many more options than just an organ or piano. I've coordinated weddings with music as formal as a string quartet to a full choir, to bells and chimes added at the conclusion of the service. A harp is a wonderful instrument for a wedding. Its soft and harmonious tunes can make you feel as though you're listening to angels playing. Trumpeters are a great addition to the processionals. There are several pieces written solely for trumpet and organ that are simply majestic. I worked with one bride on a tight budget who hired high school orchestra students to play for the ceremony rather than use the string quartet from the local union. The kids were thrilled to get some experience, were very inexpensive, and were quite good.

You must be certain that you can bring in musicians of your choice to the ceremony setting. Many facilities authorize only certain musicians to play their particular instruments. For instance, pipe organs are very, very expensive to buy and even more so to maintain. One wrong move by a musician who doesn't understand the pipe organ (it is different from an electronic keyboard or piano) and he could ruin the organ. So, many times, especially in religious settings, you will be given a list of "acceptable" musicians. You may also have no choice at all. "Ellen Jones is our organist. Period!"

Some popular choices for ceremony music are as follows:

Processionals: "Bridal Chorus" by Lonengrin ("Here Comes the Bride"); the "Wedding March" from Mendelssohn's *A Midsummer Night's Dream*; "Rondo," the Masterpiece Theatre theme, by Mouret; "Prince of Denmark's March" by Clarke; "Fanfare" from *The Triumphant*, Couperin; "Sarabande" from *Suite No. 11*, Handel; theme from "Love Story," Sigman, Lai; "Trumpet Tune," Purcell; "Trumpet Voluntary," Clarke; and "Water Music," Handel.

Ceremony Music: "Jesu, Joy of Man's Desiring," Bach; "Cannon in D Minor," Pachebel; "A Wedding Prayer," Williams; "Wedding Song," Stookey; "One Hand, One Heart," from *West Side Story*, Bernstein, Sondheim; "Somewhere," from *West Side Story*, Bernstein, Sondheim; Theme from *Romeo and Juliet*, Roto, Kusik; "Sunrise, Sunset," from *Fiddler on the Roof*, Harnick, Bock; "Evergreen," Barbara Streisand; "The Hawaiian Wedding Song," Williams; theme from *Ice Castles*, Melissa Manchester; "On the Wings of Love," Jeffry Osborne; "The Hands of Time" ("Brian's Song"), Michel LaGrand; and "The Lord's Prayer," Malotte.

Music for the Reception

The type of reception you plan will influence your music selection for the reception. You can choose from background music for a cake and punch reception to the sound of the Big Band era. Some of the best bands I've seen at wedding receptions have had Big Band sounds.

Set up an interview with the band leader and listen to some of the band's tapes. Ask about a contract and ask who exactly you are hiring. Ask if they have liability insurance. Many facilities require this, but a lot of bands and DJs do not carry it. It's probably a wise move to make sure the band has liability insurance. One thing you want to make perfectly clear is that you want all their equipment set up and ready to go long before the guests arrive. At one wedding reception, a wave of panic hit me when I entered the reception hall and noticed that something was missing: THE BAND! The area where they were to be set up and ready to go was empty. They were driving in from out of town, and the mother had paid some heavy change for this group. We tried calling their office and only got a recording. Luckily, guests were having cocktails in another room and didn't notice the band moving in its equipment in cut-offs and tee shirts.

Ask if the band offers a song list from which you can make selections. Ask also if they will help with introductions and the bouquet and garter toss. Ask about how cooperative they will be with the volume. Too many times, the music is so loud that the guests cannot carry on a conversation. The musicians should be in tune (another pun, sorry) with the volume level during the reception. Please take your guest's hearing into consideration. Some guests prefer to sit at their tables and chat with family and friends. If they cannot hear themselves over the music, it's too loud. You want the volume loud enough for those on the dance floor to appreciate, but not so loud as to make other guests shout to each other at their tables.

If you are able to see the band live in a performance setting, notice their poise and interaction with the audience. What is their appearance like? Do they wear formal clothes? Are they in costume? What about their timing? Timing is crucial with a wedding reception. Your band or DJ must be able to read the crowd and decide what is working and what isn't working. You want your dance floor active most of the evening. A good band will make that happen.

A DJ (short for disc jockey), is another avenue for your reception music. I've seen good disc jockeys and I've seen bad ones. Any form of music makers at your reception can make or break the reception. Make sure you've seen their performance and understand what they will do and what they won't do. Read their contract carefully. Note how long they will play and how many breaks they will take. Check out whether they will need any extra electricity at the reception. Make sure they will be dressed appropriately.

Several years ago, I had a client who searched long and hard for a really good band for her daughter's wedding. She went all over the state listening to bands and finally found one she liked. She had all but signed the contract when she asked if they needed anything extra from the reception facility. It seems this band had to have a certain type of electrical wiring, and the reception facility didn't have that type. It would have cost an extra $1,500 just to get the right wiring for this band. Needless to say, she shopped elsewhere.

The Least You Need to Know

Understanding what to look for in the photographer, videographer, musicians, and florist and finding the right gown are all important aspects of your wedding planning. Every part of a wedding needs to blend, fit together, and flow smoothly. And every part is important, no matter how large or how small.

➤ Examine samples of the photographer's work. Make sure you are viewing the work of the photographer who will actually be shooting your wedding.

➤ Make sure you use an experienced wedding photographer, not simply an established studio photographer. The bride and groom should feel comfortable with the photographer.

➤ Be sure to view video demos shot by the videographer you are considering. Ask whether the tape will be edited or unedited, and whether music will be added.

➤ Try on many different styles of gowns to find the one most becoming to you. Check whether your gown price includes alterations.

➤ Make sure the florist you choose can offer suggestions and ideas. Remember, you are paying for the florist's expertise.

➤ Be sure to interview any band you are thinking of hiring. Try to gauge its stage presence, and ask if you can make selections from a song list. If possible, see the group perform before you sign a contract.

O.K. GANG LET'S TAKE IT FROM THE TOP!!

Chapter 7

Cast Party: Arranging the Rehearsal Dinner

In This Chapter

➤ What's behind the tradition?

➤ Whom to invite

➤ Incorporate your own personal style

Examining the Tradition

After you've reserved the church, reception site, and some of the fundamental elements of the wedding day (photographer, flowers, and music), you should begin thinking about a place to hold the rehearsal dinner. Usually, the rehearsal dinner immediately follows the wedding rehearsal, although it can be held just before the rehearsal or even on an entirely different day.

Despite what some folks may think, the idea behind the rehearsal dinner is not just to make sure that the groom or his family has to pay for some part of the wedding. The rehearsal dinner is a time to get friends and family members together to relax, to get to know one another, and to celebrate this wonderful occasion. In some cases, a family member or close friend may even offer to host the rehearsal dinner.

Regardless of who is going to act as "host" and invite the guests to the rehearsal dinner, some coordination among all the players is important. The hosts, whether the groom, his family, or other relatives, need to work with the couple—both the bride and the groom—to determine their likes and dislikes. Even though the hosts can do what they want, they really need to work with the couple.

Make sure to check with all the players involved with the rehearsal dinner to ensure that no one is accidentally left off the guest list. Usually, the bride's family submits a guest list to the groom's family.

Getting to Know You

Because we are such a scattered society, the rehearsal dinner has become a very important part of the wedding activities. Many times, this is the first opportunity for the bride and groom's families to meet each other. It isn't unusual for the two sets of parents to live on opposite sides of the country, and getting them together before the actual wedding isn't always feasible. The rehearsal dinner is a time when you can bring everyone together to meet and get to know each other in a relaxed setting—before the formality and pressures of the wedding day.

As a couple getting ready to blend family and friends, you can use the rehearsal dinner to begin forging a united front. You want your parents, your grandparents, aunts, uncles, and friends—people who are special to each of you—to get off to a congenial start. Take this time to make people feel welcome and at ease with each other. Try your best to make these special people feel special.

Even though the groom or his family traditionally hosts the rehearsal dinner, some thoughtful planning, and perhaps compromise, is in order. Because it is so important for all guests to feel comfortable, the setting for this dinner is an important factor—especially when your families come from different backgrounds.

In my situation, for example, my father was a businessman—part of the suit and tie crowd. My husband-to-be's parents were involved in agriculture; blue jeans and work shirts were their appropriate attire. When Floyd (my husband) asked advice on the type of facility we should look into for the rehearsal dinner, we chose a restaurant in which both families could feel comfortable. If one family is accustomed to the country club and the other family is more comfortable with beer and pizza at the local pub, make a compromise for the rehearsal dinner. You want both families to feel at ease.

Whom to Invite

Your guest list for the rehearsal dinner should include all the key players who normally would attend the rehearsal. That may include the wedding party and their spouses or dates, the parents, the grandparents, the officiant and spouse, and sometimes some of the other key players of the wedding "team," such as the organist and soloist if you know them well. Otherwise, while certainly a nice gesture, inviting the entire choir or string ensemble isn't necessary. You may also want to invite those out-of-town family members or close friends who arrive the night before the wedding, or close friends who live nearby but whose presence would make you feel more comfortable.

Many couples chose to send invitations for their rehearsal dinner. As long as the invitation is not more formal than the wedding invitation, you can do what you please. Maybe a phone call inviting guests is enough for you, or maybe you've seen some wonderful informal invitations that go with the wedding theme. There are also companies that offer some great rehearsal dinner invitations. Being a mother of two sons, (I'll never be mother of the bride—interesting...) I have envisioned different kinds of invitations to our son's rehearsal dinners. We'll just have to wait and see what the future Mrs. Lenderman thinks.

Young children who are part of the wedding party probably should not be included in the dinner unless they are old enough to enjoy it. However, even if they don't attend, do include their parents on your guest list. Basically, your guest list depends on what your budget will allow and the size of the facility you choose for this function. There are large guest lists for rehearsal dinners and there are small intimate guest lists. The choice of how large or small the guest list can be is ultimately the hosts' choice.

Giving It Style

The rehearsal dinner does not have to be a formal, sit-down affair. Some of the more successful rehearsal dinners that I've heard about have been very relaxed and informal. Brides and grooms sometimes

73

choose to have picnics, pizza parties, cook-outs, or even carry-in suppers instead of a formal dinner. Remember, the primary purpose of the rehearsal dinner is to get newly merging family members together in a relaxed, informal setting.

Have It Your Way

Some couples go with a theme for the rehearsal dinner. One couple opted for an old-fashioned, midwestern picnic supper on their lake property and finished the evening with a dramatic display of fireworks. To dress up this rehearsal dinner, they used red and white gingham-checked tablecloths and napkins, real china, and real silverware. They still served hamburgers and hot dogs, but it was more elaborate than using paper plates.

Other ideas you can use may include a beach party rehearsal dinner. Those near the water may find a picnic on the beach with volleyball and hot dogs a fun way to get folks together. Or, how about a river cruise for the rehearsal dinner? If you're near a river and have access to a riverboat, it could be fun to take it sailing off into the moonlight following the rehearsal.

Combine the ethnic food touches from both families to have a heritage rehearsal dinner. Offer foods special to both the families along with a list of the ingredients and an explanation of why the foods are so special; the list could look something like a playbill.

You can move the rehearsal dinner outside. Whether you're in the backyard or a formal garden, with candle light and soft music, can't you just see the fireflies buzzing by? Of course, if you want an elegant formal dinner for your rehearsal dinner, then do it. Add place cards for each guest, some candles and floral centerpieces, and you can have a lovely affair.

Whatever you decide to do, just make it enjoyable for your guests. Make your guests feel relaxed, welcomed, and special. They are all nervous about meeting the "other side," so try to put them at ease. You may want to assign a host or hostess to each table at the rehearsal dinner to help keep the conversation moving and to make sure guests are cared for. Another way to help avoid some extra stress for your guests is to assign them a seat for the meal. That way you can put who you want to next to crazy Cousin Cindy (every family has one, you know), and not worry about your future mother-in-law sitting next to her.

Another benefit of seat assignments is that it makes people get to know those they don't know. Often, guests like to be directed to a table assignment. The well-experienced and kind hostess will never place total strangers at the same table without at least two people who know each other.

What's on the Agenda?

Take the opportunity at either the beginning or during the meal to introduce your families to the others. The bride can take her side and the groom his side. Add a little personal comment about some of the guests to the introductions to make them more personable. ("This is my Aunt Helen, who helped Mom make all the centerpieces for the tables tonight.")

You may want to add some fun activities to the evening. I know of several instances in which brides and grooms have shown home videos, set to their favorite music, during the rehearsal dinner. These videos showed the couple growing up—from babies up to the present. Although these can sometimes be tear-jerkers, they also can be tension relievers. I have found that if the mothers cry at the rehearsal or the rehearsal dinner, chances are they will be tearless during the ceremony.

Another rather fun activity you can add to the evening is for the couple to "roast" each other. Make sure that you have someone you both trust to act as MC for this portion of the evening. Handled in the right spirit and all in good fun, a roast can help make your rehearsal dinner both relaxing and unique.

One couple took one of the informal engagement pictures and had it matted with an extra wide matting. It was displayed on a table at the rehearsal dinner. As guests were having cocktails, they were asked to write their names or a message on the matting. The couple later had it framed, and even today, it hangs on their living room wall, a reminder of a great time.

A Time to Say Thank You

The rehearsal dinner is a good opportunity for both of you to give your attendants their gifts and to say your thank-yous to your family members for all their support.

The groom's father (if he is the host), should offer the first toast of the evening, and he should offer that toast to the bride. His next toast

The rehearsal dinner should never be more formal or more elaborate than the wedding reception.

should be to the bride and the groom, as a couple. He most likely will also welcome guests and thank them for coming. The floor is open for additional toasts after those first two. This would be an appropriate time for the father of the bride to welcome the groom to the family. At this time, the bride and groom could also offer a toast to their parents, thanking them for all their love and support.

The Least You Need to Know

The rehearsal dinner is an event that can bring both your families together in a calm, relaxed, fun atmosphere. It needs careful planning and attention to meet those needs. It is the springboard to a wonderful time in your life. (Be sure to use the Rehearsal Dinner Worksheet at the end of this chapter to help you make this a relaxing, memorable evening.)

➤ The rehearsal dinner should be a time when family and friends—the special people in your lives—come together in a comfortable setting to meet each other and to help you launch your new life together.

➤ Include all members of the wedding party and their spouses or dates. It's not mandatory to invite very young children from the wedding party, but do include their parents.

➤ Rehearsal dinners do not have to be formal. Make it whatever you want—sit-down dinner, picnic, carry-in supper—just make it a setting in which both families will feel comfortable.

➤ Use the rehearsal dinner as a chance to say thank you and to hand out your gifts to the wedding party.

REHEARSAL DINNER WORKSHEET

Place: _____

Address: _____

Telephone: _____

Contact: _____

Time to begin: _____
Time to end: _____

Menu ideas: _____

_____

_____

Meal price: _____

Bar charge: _____

Agenda ideas ("Roast the couple," slide show, etc.):

_____

Equipment needed:

_____

_____

Invitations ordered: _____

Responses received:

Guest's Name	Address	# Attending
_____	_____	_____
_____	_____	_____
_____	_____	_____
_____	_____	_____
_____	_____	_____
_____	_____	_____

Guest's Name	Address	# Attending
_____	_____	_____
_____	_____	_____
_____	_____	_____
_____	_____	_____
_____	_____	_____
_____	_____	_____
_____	_____	_____
_____	_____	_____
_____	_____	_____
_____	_____	_____
_____	_____	_____
_____	_____	_____
_____	_____	_____
_____	_____	_____
_____	_____	_____

Chapter 8

The Wedding Party: A Circle of Friends

In This Chapter

➤ Determining the size of your wedding party

➤ Deciding whom to include

➤ Finding other jobs for friends

One of the better parts of planning your wedding is telling your friends the good news and asking them to share this wonderful time with you. Most people consider it an honor to be asked to be part of a dear friend's or family member's wedding. Because you are asking someone to stand with you on one of the most significant days of your life, be sure to put careful thought into choosing your wedding party.

Determining the Wedding Party Size

A complaint I hear frequently is, "My groom wants to ask 14 guys to be groomsmen. I have only 8 friends for bridesmaids. Where can I get some more maids?" Well, it's probably not a good idea to "rent-a-bridesmaid," although sometimes it may seem like the only option you have left. The number of men and women in the bridal party does not have to match. Figure out exactly how many people the two of you want to stand up with you and then figure out which other jobs you can delegate to friends.

Talk with parents or older relatives about their wedding party. How many of the friends they "just had to have" are still friends? Do they even know where some of them are today? How close are some of those "best friends?" Twenty years from now, will you look at the wedding pictures and wonder who those people are?

If the ceremony site has a large enough altar area, and you have 40 of your best friends lined up to be in the wedding party, then go for it. However, if the area will only accommodate a total of 12 people (that's the two of you, plus five bridesmaids and five groomsmen), you're going to have to prioritize who you want to do the honors. You need to try to coordinate the size of your ceremony area with the size of your wedding party. I've been "church shopping" several times to find a church large enough to accommodate a large wedding party. Armed with a tape measure and a couple of assistants, we go into the sanctuary area and figure out how much room we have and whether a large wedding party will fit.

Size probably doesn't matter as much as your feelings for the family and friends you're about to ask to be part of one of the most wonderful days of your life. These should be people you feel especially close to and really want to participate in this occasion.

Finalizing the List

Your wedding party will consist of several groups of people. The first people you will ask to be a part of this day will be the maid or matron of honor and the best man. You may refer to these people as the *honor attendants*; however, in current use, an honor attendant refers to a male "maid of honor" or a female "best man." The special honor of being your maid or matron of honor may go to a sister, a cousin, or a very close friend. You can even choose to have both a maid and matron of honor. Just be sure to decide before the ceremony which duties each will perform. Maybe the maid of honor will hold the groom's ring, while the matron of honor will help you arrange your train. Both can help you with some of the preliminary duties, such as running errands, being a good listener when you need it, and organizing some parties for you. Of course, this all depends on whether your honor attendants live in your area.

Likewise, the groom chooses a best man. He can decide to have two best men, although this is not as common as having both a maid and matron of honor. The groom might ask his father to be his best man. (What an honor for any father!) The best man helps the groom prepare for the wedding, making sure he arrives at the ceremony site on time. He holds the bride's ring during the service and offers the first toast to the new couple during the reception.

You will also ask friends to be brides-maids at your wedding. Traditionally, these are young women who are close to the bride. These may include sisters, cousins, the groom's sisters, and good friends.

The groom then chooses men to serve as his groomsmen. These can be from a group of brothers, the bride's brothers, cousins, or good friends. Groomsmen have no official function in the wedding party. They generally are not ushers, but simply are friends chosen to dress up and be part of the wedding party.

Bet You Didn't Know... Choosing a best man keeps with the ancient custom of finding a good friend, most likely a tribal warrior, to help shield the bride from abductors known to prowl around the ceremony site.

The remaining members of the main wedding party include the ushers, usually one usher for every 50 guests. Sometimes, the grooms-men double as ushers. There usually isn't a problem with this system, although it helps to have at least one usher in the back of the church to help with late arrivals or unexpected happenings.

If one of your attendants drops out of the wedding plans because of illness or other circumstances, you have a couple of choices. You can ask someone else to step in if they are agreeable, and if (for the women) the outfit will fit the new attendant. Or you can just go as is and not worry about having even pairs. You don't have to have matching numbers of attendants.

Other attendants making up the wedding party may include the flower girl and ring bearer, candle lighters, train bearers, Bible bearers, junior groomsmen, junior bridesmaids, and pages. You may give these assignments to children or young adults.

Using Children as Attendants

Children, as members of the wedding, can add joy to the day. They represent innocence and remind us of the circle of life we all share. They can also detract more than you think from the wedding ceremony. You need to remember that children in wedding parties are still kids. They are not little adults in children's suits. They think like children, they behave like children, and they will be unpredictable like children.

Kids Do the Darndest Things

Do not expect four-year-old Karen to walk down the aisle in front of 650 guests and not act timid. Unless she has maturity beyond her years, she will be shy. She may say, "No way, I'm not going down there. You can't make me!" (It happens frequently with flower girls.) Or you could have the darling little ring bearer, dressed to the limit, who stops short of making it down the aisle, throws down the pillow, and stomps out because he's not used to so many people (and so many strangers), not to mention that funny-looking guy in the bathrobe—the clergyman—at the end of the aisle.

I coordinated one wedding in which the flower girl decided that the basket she was carrying was just too heavy for her to hold and asked the minister if he could hold it for her. He politely declined saying he was busy at the moment. You must treat children as children. Do not expect children to be more than they are capable of being. Then you will not be disappointed when they don't perform as you had hoped.

Find the Right Jobs for Kids

When you consider having children as part of your wedding party, do think about their age and maturity. A child of four—maybe even a very mature three-year-old—is probably old enough for the responsibility you are asking him or her to perform. Children much younger than three are a risk.

If you really want a particular young child to participate in the festivities, why not list her name in the program as "Honorary Flower Girl." That way the child is being honored (which is what you are doing in the first place), but it doesn't end up being traumatic for the child and a nerve-racking experience for you. Don't put Junior in a situation he is not ready for and one in which he doesn't understand what you expect.

Here are some jobs you may consider assigning to special people you want to honor:

Children younger than four are probably too young to handle the pressures of "performing" at your wedding.

Ring Bearer (age: 3–6)

Flower Girl (age: 3–6)

Train Bearer (age: 4–8)

Guest Book Attendant (age: 12+)

Program Attendant (age: 12+)

Coat Checker (age: 10+)

Gift Attendant (age: 13+)

Candle Lighter (age: 10+)

Altar Boy or Girl (Catholic service) (age: 10–15)

Gift Bearers (Catholic service) (age: 13+)

Petition Reader (Catholic service—older child) (age: 16+)

Scripture Reader (age: 16+)

Page (age: 6+)

Junior Bridesmaid (age: 10–16)

Junior Groomsmen (age: 10–16)

Greeters (age: 14+)

Musician

Soloist

Assigning Other Fun Tasks

Okay, you have your wedding party all lined up, but you have some more friends you want to include in the festivities. Well, there are other jobs that need attention and are an honor to be asked to perform.

Some of the more obvious jobs are:

Guest Book Attendants   This person, male or female, greets guests as they enter the ceremony site or reception site (depending on where you want the guest book placed) and asks guests to sign the guest book.

Bird Seed or Petal Attendant   These are the folks who will distribute bird seed or petals to guests at the appropriate time (your exit) so that you can be "showered" with it.

Program Attendant   This person usually stands by the guest book and distributes the wedding programs; this person also acts as a greeter.

Readers (both Scripture and poetry)   During the service, you may have several readings. This is a responsible job for the right person.

Gift Bearers   During the Catholic service, the Gift Bearer brings the bread and wine to the priest.

Personal Attendant   This is a close friend of the bride who is there to help, run errands, and be a support.

Gift Attendant   At the reception, this person is in charge of taking gifts from the guests and placing them in the appropriate spot (either a gift table or locked room).

Reception Assistants   These folks, usually ladies, are asked to help with the reception foods, mostly cutting and serving of the wedding cake.

These jobs can be assigned to folks who you want to include as honorees. Make all your wedding party people feel special. Whether someone is taking care of gifts at the reception or acting as your maid of honor, they all need to know that you are excited they have agreed to serve and that you really want and need their help.

Consider asking friends to mingle at the reception. Tell those you know are socially outgoing that you're counting on them to roam the reception seeking out those who seem to be alone to engage them in conversation, ask them to dance, or introduce them to others. It makes these friends feel special and helps all the guests feel more like family.

If you are not hiring a wedding coordinator, consider asking a very special friend with organizational skills to help oversee the reception, keeping an eye out for potential problems. It's a big responsibility, but one you (and your mother) won't have time for on the wedding day.

Getting a Little Help from Your Friends

Over the years, I've heard statements like these from time to time: "Aunt Shirley is going to cater my wedding." "My friend Ellen is doing the flowers." "Jennifer, my sorority sister, is going to coordinate my wedding." "Uncle Harvey likes to tinker with a camera and will be taking the pictures."

All of these examples have two common elements: The bride thinks she is saving money, and she expects a professional job. She most likely will be disappointed on both counts.

There is nothing wrong with asking your friend Ellen to take care of your floral needs. She's a good friend and you know she'll do her best. The problem comes when she doesn't or can't deliver what you expect. When those flowers arrive, you find that Ellen wasn't really right for this task. The colors are all wrong, the arrangement doesn't look anything like the picture you showed her, and she forgot the main centerpiece for the head table at the reception.

One rather bleak example of using friends for tasks that they may not be prepared for involved a bride who was on a very tight budget. A good friend volunteered to prepare some food for the reception as her wedding gift to the couple. The bride couldn't afford a caterer and was grateful to her friend for offering. The friend volunteered to bring in enough meatballs, fruit trays, and cheese and crackers for 175 guests. Two days before the wedding, the bride called this friend to inquire whether the friend needed help with any of the arrangements. The good friend shrugged off the question with, "I changed my mind. I found you another gift instead." Needless to say, the

Don't assume that just because someone is your friend she has the expertise to handle a particular task. Even with her best efforts, these jobs may be too much for her to handle. Unless your friend or family member is a florist, photographer, or caterer by trade, it's probably a good idea to leave these tasks to the professionals.

bride was devastated. Here she was without much of the food for her reception, and to make matters worse, the good friend didn't even seem to feel any regret or concern about not following through with her promise. That close to the wedding, it was too late to hire a caterer to come in and save the day. The stressed bride got lucky. The groom's aunt heard about the plight and volunteered to provide the necessary food. This situation could have been a disaster!

The moral of this story, and the point I want to make, is that you should be very careful when you ask friends or accept offers from friends to take on major responsibilities for your wedding. If that task is normally handled by a professional, then it's almost always better to let the professional handle it. If Aunt Charlotte is a florist and wants to make you a good deal on the flowers, go for it. Saving some pennies here and there is great. But if Aunt Charlotte just likes to play with flowers, you might want to use caution when you are discussing your wedding needs around her.

The Least You Need to Know

➤ Make sure the church or other ceremony site can comfortably fit the size wedding party you are planning.

➤ Wedding party members should be those individuals you feel close to and want to include as a special part of your day.

➤ Use good judgment and common sense when you choose to include children in your wedding party. Remember, children will almost always act like children. That can make for some unpredictable moments.

➤ Think carefully before you ask a friend, or accept an offer from a friend, to take on a major responsibility of your wedding that is normally handled by a professional. Usually it's best to let the professionals handle the big items.

Romance and Roses: Planning Your Honeymoon

In This Chapter

> ➤ What type of honeymoon do you want?

> ➤ Where are the popular honeymoon spots?

> ➤ Where is the best place for you?

Although it may be an easy one to overlook in the hustle and bustle of planning for the wedding itself, your honeymoon reservations are one more thing you need to consider early in the planning stages. Depending on where you plan to take your honeymoon, you need to arrange reservations and details as early as possible.

Finally, Some Time Alone...

Ah, the honeymoon. Finally, you will be able to get away and be alone. The wedding and reception will be behind you and your wedding day will be only fond memories and warm fuzzies to remember. With all the pre-wedding parties, check lists, and appointments, the two of you won't have much time together. You're definitely going to be ready for some quality time with each other.

Communication Is the Key

So, now you're planning for this wonderful time away, alone together for the first time as husband and wife. Where do you start? First, talk to each other and decide what your options are, how much time and money you have, and what your likes include. It's very important to discuss openly and honestly with each other what you want to do on the honeymoon.

 You will be tired. You will be physically exhausted from the wedding activities. Don't let anyone else convince you otherwise. Make sure your honeymoon plans include plenty of time to rest and regenerate after all the hectic months you've both just survived.

When I was married, my soon-to-be husband wanted our honeymoon to be a trip to Mammoth Cave in Kentucky. Now, I usually don't get real excited about cold, damp, dark places where bats fly around freely and things slither on their bellies. I just didn't find this cave idea very romantic. So we did some soul searching and some more talking and found out we both really liked and enjoyed winter sports. We were married in January, so instead of heading south to a warmer climate, we ventured north to a wonderful mountain lodge complete with fireplaces, snowmobiles, cross-country skiing, and a huge toboggan run. We had a great time because we talked first and looked at our options, including what we could afford and what was within our reach. By the way, just so you don't think I was totally insensitive to my husband's feelings, on our first anniversary we headed south to Mammoth Cave. It was actually a very nice place.

Whatever you choose for your honeymoon, whether it's a two-week cruise down the California coast, a luxury resort in the Hawaiian Islands, or a weekend in the big city, make it special. Make it your time to be alone together, to reflect on the wedding, to get to know each other, to start out this marriage on the right foot. It doesn't have to cost you a bundle either. Talk early on about the amount you realistically have to spend on this honeymoon.

Honey, Why Are You Crying?

A couple of things to watch out for as you head out on your honeymoon: you may feel much more tense than usual and you may even cry more easily. Relax and accept that these feelings are all part of normal wedding stress.

After our wedding and reception, as we were heading to our wedding night destination, I started to cry. I couldn't explain to my new husband why I was crying and I couldn't stop. The more he asked what was wrong, the more I cried. In looking back on our wedding, I now know that it was nothing more than all the wedding stress coming out. The tension of keeping it together for those long months of planning finally had taken its toll.

We talk more about wedding stress in Chapter 16, "I Think I'm Losing My Mind." For now, the bottom line on your honeymoon is to make it special for both of you. Plan early and find a good travel agent who knows what your budget is and will help you stick to it. Be sure to ask about special packages, especially those made just for honeymooners. Likewise, if you don't want to be identified as honeymooners, don't pick a honeymoon package or go to one of the traditional "honeymoon locations." Get all details ironed out before you leave.

Bet You Didn't Know... The word *honeymoon* comes from the days of marriage by capture. A man would see a woman he liked, capture her (many times against her will) and hide out for a moon (30 days—one full moon to another full moon) or a month. During that time they would drink a concoction sweetened with honey. Thus, *honeymoon*.

Get Thee to Paradise

As with any trip or vacation, deciding where to go on your honeymoon is a very personal decision for the two of you to make. You've probably heard about some of the "traditional" honeymoon spots, however, and you may want to give them some consideration. The following list describes a few of the current "hot spots."

Hawaiian Islands. All the islands offer the right weather with the right atmosphere for some very romantic times. These islands are about as close to Eden as you can get. The islanders have that "hang-loose," "don't worry," "it's going to be okay" attitude that makes you feel so welcomed and relaxed. Friends of ours traveled there earlier this year. They were headed for the Big Island. They took the wrong island hop plane and landed on the opposite side of the island—more than three hours away. They called the hotel where their reservations were and told the manager, "We've got a problem. We landed at the wrong airport." The manager replied, "There are no problems on Hawaii, only solutions." Makes you feel good, doesn't it?

Having just returned from a "Second Honeymoon" to Hawaii, I can attest to the wonderful, laid-back attitude and beautiful scenery. When we finally arrived at our resort, we were behind our "schedule." After we had checked into the hotel, the bellman had our luggage and I said to Floyd, "Come on, we have to hurry." The bellman stopped me and said, "Mrs. Lenderman, you are in Hawaii now. We have a much different philosophy from you on the mainland. It takes us an hour and a half to watch "60 Minutes." And he was right. We slowed down and savored every moment of our trip.

Watch for specials during the fall and early January. This is an affordable vacation spot for lots of couples. If you watch for a price war on air fares, you can get some pretty good rates.

The Poconos. The "honeymoon capital of the world" includes four counties located in Northeastern Pennsylvania and consists of 2,400 square miles of majestic mountains, wonderful views, rivers and streams, and beautiful forests. There are many resorts to choose from in this region. Any of the four seasons are perfect for a stay in these resorts. These resorts are made to fit all types of activities: winter sports, water skiing in the summer, and walking along mountain paths in the fall foliage. They offer both earthy pleasures and fantastic accommodations. If you dream of a heart-shaped bathtub in your private cabin, then one of the resorts in the Poconos might be just right for you. If you've always wanted to spend the night in a 1900 farmhouse, a charming country inn, or a French chateau, then a resort in the Poconos may be just the ticket.

There's also lots of shopping here. Over 100 factory outlet stores within driving distance of the center of the mountains. Don't forget your credit cards!

The Poconos area offers a "Honeymoon Planning Kit." Simply call 1-800-POCONOS to receive the information.

Caribbean Islands. Located on the eastern side of the United States and running from south of Miami to South America, there are many islands to choose from. Watch for specials during the low season (April to October). It rains more at this time of year so prices run about 30% lower than the high season, which is November to April. Cruise several islands or fly off to a remote island.

They call this paradise and there is a reason for that. With their gorgeous beaches, clear waters, and fun nightlife, many of the islands bid for the honeymooner business.

Just as the Association of Bridal Consultants can provide names of consultants in your area, they also can provide names of destination and honeymoon travel specialists who are also members. Call 203-355-0464.

Jamaica, with Montego Bay, is a popular honeymoon choice with a variety of accommodations and activities.

There are six main resort areas in Jamaica, and they each have a different style. Montego Bay is Jamaica's primary port. Other cities famous for honeymooners are Ocho Rios, Negril, Port Antonio, and Kingston. Tucked away in the center of the island is Mandeville. While much will depend on what you want to do with your honeymoon time, each of these areas offers different points of interest to the honeymooner.

Other islands in the Caribbean area that can delight the honeymooner are the Virgin Islands, Puerto Rico, Bermuda, and the Bahamas. All have wonderful beaches, terrific night life, and tremendous accommodations.

Mexican Riviera. South of the Western United States, the Mexican Riviera boasts 2,000 miles of white sand beaches. Some favorite honeymoon spots here include Acapulco, Cancun, and Puerto Vallarta. Again, they offer great night life and fantastic resorts.

Hilton Head, South Carolina. This romantic city by the sea is fast becoming a popular honeymoon site. With a variety of condos and hotel prices to choose from, almost any couple can spend some time here walking along the beach or sipping a cool drink on the hotel balcony.

Las Vegas, Nevada. Las Vegas not only represents a wedding ceremony site for many couples, but offers some excitement for the honeymooners, too. Las Vegas means "The Meadows" in Spanish. It's nestled in the heart of the Mojave Desert in western Nevada. You can find some of the most famous hotels in the world on "The Strip." Their off-season is November to January.

Some sites around the area include Death Valley, Grand Canyon West, Hoover Dam and Lake Mead. For information, you can call The Chamber of Commerce at 702-735-1616 or the Nevada Commission on Tourism at 1-800-NEVADA-8.

San Diego, California. The city was once a remote Spanish mission. It lies just north of the Mexican border. Famous "must see" sites are Balboa Park and the San Diego Zoo. San Diego is full of history and has a near perfect year-round climate. Many people want to retire here, but don't let that stop you from considering it for a honeymoon spot. It has action, too. Contact the Visitor's Bureau at 619-232-3101 or the Chamber of Commerce at 619-232-0124.

San Antonio, Texas. Located in south central Texas, its name means "Saint Anthony's City" in Spanish. One famous point in San Antonio is the Alamo, where Davy Crockett and Jim Bowie fought the huge Mexican Army. The Alamo lies in the center of town along "The River Walk." The downtown area is delightfully filled with cafes, boutiques, and hotels with tropical gardens. You can call the San Antonio Visitor's Bureau at 1-800-447-3372.

Breckenridge, Colorado. If it's snowy weather and skiing you dream of for your honeymoon, then you should venture to Breckenridge. The city actually got its start in 1859 with a gold rush discovery. Since then, the town has enjoyed activities for all the seasons. There are many historical buildings in Breckenridge, and its Victorian charm lures honeymooners from all over. For more information, call 1-800-800-BREC.

Cruise ships. Many couples feel an ocean cruise is the ultimate honeymoon idea. One price gets you almost everything (except for alcohol, which usually is not included in the price). You can be entertained, if you want, or left alone for a romantic walk about the deck in the moonlight. There are hundreds of activities to fill up your day, including the sights and sounds of the neighboring islands (when in dock), along with swimming, sunning, exercise classes, aerobics, gambling, disco, and cabaret shows. Other activities include board games, basketball, skeet shooting, Ping-Pong, sauna, country and western nights, piano bar, library, beauty shops, arts and craft classes, massages, laundry services, on-board doctors (sea-sick medicine), midnight buffets, room service, duty-free shopping, movies, and endless eating.

Here are some points to consider if you are thinking about a honeymoon cruise. The age of passengers varies, not only on ship but by area of the world. For example, travelers on cruises in the Caribbean usually are younger travelers than those traveling in the Alaskan waters or the Baltic seas. The size of the vessel will help determine what kind of cruise you want. Those carrying over

When packing for a cruise, shorts or slacks with elastic waist bands are a needed item because of the availability of all the food.

1,200 passengers will offer more activities than the smaller ships. Price is very important. Check with travel agents who specialize in cruise ships. Departure days don't vary much; most cruise lines depart on Saturday. There are a few that sail on Sunday to accommodate the honeymooners who have married on Saturday. Be sure to check with your travel agent about the cabin accommodations. If you want a king or queen size bed in your cabin, understand that not all cruise ships offer that option. Check about shore excursions before you sail. In many places, these can be an unnecessary purchase. (Strolling through the local village market can be fun on your own; you may not want to go on-shore in a group.) In some cases, though, the excursion may catch your eye (hiking through a rain forest, riding horses on the beach, or snorkeling in clear blue waters). Ask your cruise travel agent for a list of ports where it would be better to go solo for sights and those ports where you will need a group tour.

Disney World. If it's action you want, then head south to Orlando for a time of fun and excitement amid the king of entertainment, Mickey Mouse. The various hotels in the area are geared to offer all the extras for the honeymooners and you shouldn't be bored for lack of something to do.

Hints for Honeymooners

Here are some tips to help you take some of the worry out of your honeymoon travels:

➤ Take most of your money in traveler's checks. Be sure to get some in smaller denominations ($20) because some areas will not honor larger denominations ($50 and above).

➤ Rental car companies require a major credit card.

➤ Keep a list of your traveler's checks' numbers, credit card numbers, and checking account numbers separate from where you keep the checks and cards themselves. Also take the phone numbers for these companies with you. In case any of these items are lost or stolen, you can get help much faster if you have phone numbers and account information.

➤ Label luggage both inside and outside with your name, address, and phone number. Keep a list of luggage contents (for claims should your luggage be lost).

➤ If you are traveling by air, take any medications and important papers (passports) in a carry-on bag.

➤ Make sure you have homeowner's or renter's insurance on your wedding gifts before you leave home.

➤ If traveling overseas, convert some cash to the foreign currency to cover initial expenses (transportation, tips, and more) *before* you leave. You really don't want to go out on your wedding night to convert currency!

➤ Overseas, it is best to use a credit card for purchases. The conversion rate usually is better than you'll get at a bank, which is much better than you'll get in stores and hotels.

If you travel to a sunny climate or to a climate with lots of snow, be sure to take and use your sunscreen. Nothing can ruin a romantic getaway faster than a painful sunburn.

Most of all, remember that your honeymoon—whether it's two weeks on a remote island or two days in the local hotel—should be a special time for the two of you. Plan ahead and make every minute count. Relax, get some much needed sleep, and get your marriage off to a great start. (Use the Honeymoon Worksheet at the end of this chapter to make this special trip everything you've always dreamed it would be.)

The Least You Need to Know

➤ Plan early. It takes a good travel agent and advance planning to get the best prices and accommodations.

➤ Be realistic about what you both want and what you can actually afford. Don't overstep your budget.

➤ Put a lot of thought into how you want to spend these first days as husband and wife. Choose a location you are both comfortable with and then pick activities that you both enjoy.

THE HONEYMOON WORKSHEET

Activities to include: _____

_____

_____

Travel agent: _____

Telephone: _____

Budgeted amount: _____

Destination: _____

Hotel: _____

Mode of travel: _____

Meals included?: _____

Extra expenses: _____

_____

Documents required: (Passports, ID) _____

Luggage needed: _____

_____

_____

What to pack: _____

_____

_____

PLANNING CHECK-OFF LIST

Six to Twelve Months Before the Wedding

_____Announce your engagement.

_____Plan the engagement party or make the announcement to the rest of your family and friends.

_____Attend bridal shows.

_____Talk with a bridal consultant/wedding coordinator. Make an appointment for a consultation.

_____Together with both sets of parents, discuss wedding plans, including formality.

_____Determine a budget.

_____If you are sharing expenses, decide who will pay for what.

_____Select a date and time for the wedding.

_____Call the church or synagogue for an appointment with the officiant.

_____If it will be a civil ceremony, call the officiant.

_____Meet with the officiating person.

_____Ask friends and family to serve as wedding attendants.

_____Start comparison shopping for services, such as florist, caterer, photographer, and videographer.

_____Select wedding rings and make arrangements for engraving.

_____Begin writing your guest lists.

_____Gather ideas for reception: menu, beverages, entertainment, favors, and so on.

_____Call the reception site and reserve it.

_____Reserve your service providers: caterer, photographer, videographer, florist, musicians, limo, and so on.

_____Shop for your wedding gown and headpiece. Also look at attendants' dresses.

_____Begin to plan the wedding ceremony and reception music.

_____Register with department stores for bridal gift registry.

Five Months Before the Wedding

_____Select and order your gown, headpiece, and attendants' dresses.

_____Discuss honeymoon plans with your fiancé, and send for travel information.

_____Check samples of wedding invitations, announcements, and enclosure cards.

_____Begin shopping for wedding cake.

_____Reserve a block of rooms at hotels for out-of-town guests (include this information with invitations).

Four Months Before the Wedding

_____Select and order your wedding stationery: invitations, announcements, enclosures, informals, scrolls, napkins, and thank-you notes.

_____Get necessary travel documents (passport, birth certificate).

_____Draw maps with directions to the ceremony and reception site for out-of-town guests.

_____Make an appointment with the caterer or banquet manager to discuss your reception menu.

_____Make an appointment with your bridal consultant to "touch base" and get your questions answered.

Three Months Before the Wedding

_____Decide on honeymoon destination, and call for reservations.

_____Begin shopping for your going-away outfit and honeymoon clothes.

_____Finalize your guest list, check for duplicates, and correct spelling and addresses.

_____Review musical selections with your musicians.

_____Arrange for an engagement picture for the newspaper.

_____Make an appointment with the florist to discuss floral budget and floral decorations.

_____Check with local authorities about requirements for marriage license and blood test.

_____Make an appointment with your doctor for a physical.

_____Begin addressing the inner and outer invitation envelopes.

_____Complete honeymoon plans: buy air or cruise tickets.

Two Months Before the Wedding

_____Order the wedding cake and groom's cake.

_____Have a physical examination, blood tests, and any required inoculations for foreign travel.

_____Accompany groom to the formal wear shop and choose formal attire for the male attendants.

Seven Weeks Before the Wedding

_____Meet with the caterer or banquet manager and firm up reception details. Ask for a banquet room floor plan.

_____Consult a party rental store if equipment is needed at the reception.

_____Schedule an appointment with the bridal consultant.

_____Talk with musicians and review your selections.

_____Make an appointment with your photographer for your formal bridal portrait.

Six Weeks Before the Wedding

_____Call the church or synagogue and confirm rehearsal date and time.

_____Discuss music with the church organist and soloist.

_____Plan the rehearsal dinner with the caterer.

_____Visit the church and reception site and do a floor plan (if not done earlier).

_____Have the males in the wedding party, including the fathers, rent their formal wear at the same store.

_____If there are out-of-town male attendants, have the local store send them the tux information and a postcard to return with their measurements so they can order the tuxes.

_____Order wedding programs.

_____Order favor items (if using).

Five Weeks Before the Wedding

_____Mail all the invitations.

_____Select and buy gifts for all attendants.

_____Get swatches of attendants' dress fabric and have shoes dyed in one lot.

_____If attendants live out-of-town, arrange for their dresses to be sent to them for fittings and alterations.

_____Meet the florist and order your flowers. Take samples of fabric and pictures of your gown and attendants' gowns.

_____Purchase bridal garter, guest book, pen, cake knife, and toasting glasses, or borrow some of these items.

Four Weeks Before the Wedding

_____Prepare the wedding announcement for the local newspaper.

_____All invitations should be in the mail.

_____Make an appointment with your hair stylist and a makeup artist to try out makeup and hair styles for your wedding day.

_____Finalize arrangements for the rehearsal dinner.

_____Finalize arrangements for the reception.

_____Check with attendants' regarding their accessories.

_____Wrap attendants' gifts and have them ready to present.

_____Make an appointment for the final fitting of your gown.

_____Begin recording invitation acceptances and regrets.

_____Begin addressing announcements envelopes.

_____Select wedding gifts for each other.

_____Arrange for transportation of the wedding party to the wedding and reception.

_____Discuss the ceremony with the officiant.

_____Make a seating plan for the rehearsal dinner and reception.

_____Write place cards for the reception.

_____Decide whether you will use a receiving line.

_____If you are moving to another town after the wedding, call the movers and make arrangements.

Three Weeks Before the Wedding

_____Have your final fitting.

_____Notify all participants of rehearsal date, time, and place.

_____Have your formal portrait taken.

_____Check on honeymoon tickets and reservations.

_____Set up a table to display your wedding gifts.

_____Record gifts and continue to send thank-you notes.

_____Get marriage license.

_____Confirm transportation to ceremony and reception.

_____Attend showers given in your honor.

_____Arrange for bridesmaids' luncheon.

_____Ask a friend to handle the wedding gifts at the reception.

_____Make arrangements for gifts to be taken from the reception to your home or to storage.

_____Hire a "housesitter" for the rehearsal and wedding day for your home, your parents' home, and your fiancé's home.

_____Ask someone to be guest book attendant.

_____Check with cleaners about preserving your gown.

_____Assign someone to take your gown to that cleaners.

_____Pick up tickets and confirm reservations for honeymoon.

Two Weeks Before the Wedding

_____Finalize hotel arrangements for out-of-town guests.

_____Plan a "Welcome" package for out-of-town guests to be in their hotel rooms when they arrive.

_____Send your photograph and wedding announcement to the newspaper.

_____If you are changing your name on documents, do so now.

_____Check on accessories for the groom and male attendants.

_____Make an appointment with your hair stylist, makeup artist, and manicurist.

_____Give addressed and stamped announcements to someone who will mail them the day after the wedding.

_____Follow up on guests who have not returned their response card. You *must* have an accurate count for the caterer.

_____Meet with your bridal consultant to go over all the details.

One Week Before the Wedding

_____Eat right and get plenty of rest this week!

_____Give the caterer a guaranteed count for the reception.

_____Double check *all* service providers: florist, photographer, caterer, church, and so on.

_____Pay balances due on services required before the wedding.

_____Have money or checks in envelopes for your consultant to hand to organist, soloist, musicians, minister, and anyone who needs to be paid the day of the wedding.

_____Host the bridesmaids' luncheon.

_____Remind everyone of the date and time of the rehearsal.

_____Pack for the honeymoon.

_____Give gifts to attendants (if not planned for rehearsal dinner).

_____Spend some quiet time with your family.

_____Have "something old, new, borrowed, and blue" ready.

_____Explain any special seating to your bridal consultant.

_____Attend the bachelorette party (not the night before the wedding).

Two Days Before the Wedding

_____Check the weather conditions for the wedding day and make adjustments if needed.

_____Lay out everything you will need to dress for the wedding in one place at home.

_____Your bridal consultant should provide a CARE package: safety pins, thread, bobbi pins, hair spray, soft drinks, juice, crackers, and more for your use.

_____Make sure the cars involved have gas.

One Day Before the Wedding

_____Attend the rehearsal.

_____Make sure you and your groom are comfortable with the rehearsal and have no questions.

_____If you are leaving for your honeymoon directly from the reception, place your luggage in the car you will be driving and lock it.

_____RELAX—take a hot bath. Have a glass of warm milk or hot tea and get a good night's rest.

THE DAY!!

_____Have your bridal consultant get your gown, veil, and/or brides maids' gowns from the bridal shop and take them directly to the ceremony site (if the shop doesn't deliver).

_____Eat a good breakfast—something that will last—you want to include protein items and some bread items (for energy). You might be too nervous to eat closer to the wedding time.

_____Give yourself *plenty* of time to get ready. Don't rush! Enjoy this time. You may even indulge and have a makeup artist and hair stylist come to the ceremony site to apply makeup and do your hair.

_____Your consultant should make sure that anything belonging to you that needs to go from the church to the reception will be taken there.

_____ENJOY THIS DAY! You've planned well and now you can relax!

BEST WISHES FOR A LIFETIME OF HAPPINESS!!!

Part III
Spending Wisely—How to Find the Best Vendors

In Parts I and II, I discussed searching for various wedding vendors and service providers you have to work with during the planning stages for your wedding. I suggested some questions you can ask vendors as you try to figure out which vendors can provide the services you want at a price you can afford. I also talked about the order in which you must reserve facilities and book vendors. In Part III, I'll review some of this material, but there is additional information to help you on your wedding planning journey, such as how to interview vendors. Check out the worksheets that will help with the details of this task.

LESSONS IN READING THE FINE PRINT:

NUMBER TWENTY-SIX

IDIOT...

THE MELTZERS AND "THE GROUNDHOG DAY" WEDDING SPECIAL...

WWICK©

Chapter 10

Let Them Eat Cake!

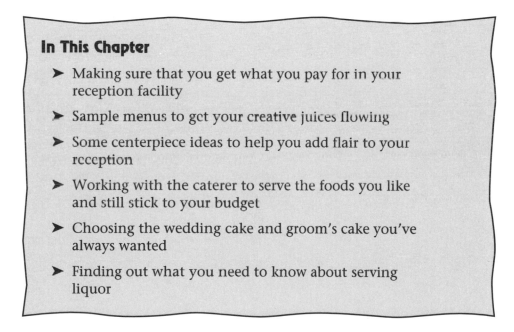

In This Chapter

➤ Making sure that you get what you pay for in your reception facility

➤ Sample menus to get your creative juices flowing

➤ Some centerpiece ideas to help you add flair to your reception

➤ Working with the caterer to serve the foods you like and still stick to your budget

➤ Choosing the wedding cake and groom's cake you've always wanted

➤ Finding out what you need to know about serving liquor

The Reception Site: Getting What You Pay For

The reception (facility rental and catering costs) will account for about 30 percent of your total wedding bill. When planning your wedding reception, make sure you pay close attention to all the details so that you get your money's worth. Remember to book early. The prime reception sites will be reserved as far as 18 to 24 months in advance in the larger cities. (Be sure to turn to the Reception Site Worksheet at the end of this chapter.)

One Size Doesn't Fit All

Your biggest consideration is whether the facility is large enough to accommodate your guests. There is nothing worse than being cramped in a facility that is too small with far more guests than you imagined. Make sure that it can hold your guests comfortably with the activities you want to include. Are you including dancing in your reception plans? Is there room for the wedding party to stand and be introduced or to enter from an outside area as they are introduced to the guests? Will you be having a receiving line at the reception? How does the traffic flow pattern of guests usually work?

Deal with the Details

Make doubly sure you get what the facility will and will not provide IN WRITING. The little things, such as linens, table skirting, microphone hookups (or the microphone itself), napkins, and dance floors are items you need to know about before the day of the wedding. Most reception sites provide those items as part of their contract, but that is not always the case. Just know what you're getting when you pay your deposit.

Book the reception site early! Get the details in writing of the items that the facility provides, and make sure that you feel comfortable with the manager.

Ask questions of the manager. Remember what I said earlier, if the manager's only comment is "we can't do that," see if you can't find another facility that is more accommodating. The manager works for you—not the other way around.

Working with the Caterer

Whether the facility provides an in-house caterer for you to work with or you bring in someone of your choice, what's your next step? Remember when we talked in Chapter 5 about the differences between an in-house caterer and others? In-house refers to a caterer that provides the food for functions within a particular facility. An outside caterer, as it implies, is an independent caterer you hire on your own, from outside the facility.

What's on the Menu?

After you have decided which caterer you will be working with, choose your menu carefully. Make good use of your food choices. If you are on a limited budget for the reception (and who isn't?), then make sure you thoroughly consider the time of day you choose for your wedding and reception. (Refer to Chapter 3 for more information about when to hold your wedding and reception.) The time of day your reception occurs has much to do with what your menu will be and can help determine how much money it's going to cost you. The following paragraphs explain in greater detail the various kinds of receptions that I touched on in Chapter 5. I also provide some sample menus to help get your creative juices flowing.

Food, Glorious Food

Where did all this fuss come from about serving food to your guests at the reception? The custom actually dates back to the ancient Greeks who had the bride and groom share a quince (fruit). The quince actually has a bitter and sweet taste. The Greeks thought that by having the couple eat this fruit, they were accepting the good and bad times that come with the marriage. Other cultures also have used the tradition of consuming food on the wedding day as a prerequisite to a good marriage. The ancient Brittons drank "marriage ale" for thirty days following the wedding. Those native to the South Sea islands, such as Bali, feasted on fruits and flowers for thirty days. At the end of that time period, the couple was considered to be married. Food has always played an important part in the wedding festivities.

Cake and Punch

Obviously, the simplest type of menu is a cake and punch reception. You can serve a lovely wedding cake with some delightful fruit or champagne punch, or maybe champagne all by itself. With that menu, you can include assorted nuts and mints (either chocolate or candies in other colors). The only supplies needed would be plates, cups or glasses, napkins, forks and the table linens, a few nice serving bowls or plates for the mints and nuts, a cake knife for the cutting ceremony, and some friends to help serve. This is one type of reception that you can take care of yourself or with the help from family and friends.

Hors D'Oeuvres

An hors d'oeuvres reception is another popular menu selection. Food items for this type of reception include various "finger foods," which can be eaten with the fingers instead of requiring utensils. Normally, the caterer places fancy wooden picks in attractive little cups by each food item so that guests don't have to use their fingers if they don't want to. Some hors d'oeuvres may require a fork, and if they do, a basket of forks is placed next to the food.

Be sure to check with the caterer about floor layout if you want to use the food station concept. Traffic flow here is crucial. If your facility does not lend itself to this type of layout, you probably should stick to a more basic setup. You may opt for dividing up the food into two areas and offering the same items in both places. This helps to move guests through the lines without so much delay.

You can serve hors d'oeuvres to your guests for relatively the same price as a buffet. The biggest advantage to having an hors d'oeuvres reception is that it allows for a more relaxed atmosphere than a formal dinner or even a formal buffet. Guests can help themselves throughout the evening from a variety of foods. You would want to include some foods from several food groups. For example, offer both hot and cold food choices and get a mixture of textures, colors, and presentation. (Presentation means how well they look on the serving plate and also how well that particular item holds up after several hours on a serving plate.) The chef or caterer should be able to answer your questions and guide you in selecting a well-rounded menu. If there are any ethnic foods you want to include, be sure to ask if they can be incorporated. Some caterers do allow you to bring in some food to the reception but may not allow it to be served on their table. (Something about health laws). Just do yourself a big favor and check with the caterer ahead of time.

The *food station* concept is becoming quite popular for receptions around the country. This setup enables you to offer different types and styles of food as various "stations" throughout the room. In different areas, you may have a seafood table, a fruit and cheese table, a pasta table serving several types of pasta and sauces, a carving table with roast beef for small sandwiches, some tables set with other types of hors d'oeuvres, and then a table set for sweets, which can include your wedding cake.

Buffet

A buffet reception means that the guests help themselves to the food. The difference between a buffet and an hors d'oeuvres menu is that the buffet is generally more of a complete meal. You can serve a variety of items on your buffet: some simple sandwiches and salads for an informal reception, or several entree choices for a more formal reception. Guests serve themselves and may return as often as they want for refills. The reason this is usually a less expensive meal than the served dinner is due to reduced labor costs. Your labor costs are much lower with a buffet for 200 than at a served dinner for 200 because fewer workers are required to serve the meal.

If you attempt a buffet reception on your own without the help of a caterer, you have to provide plates, serving pieces, chafing dishes, napkins, linens, silverware, glasses, and back-up help to replenish the tables as they become empty. It's a big undertaking. Be very sure you have competent people who can handle pressure and understand the meaning of the word *work*. Serving a meal—even buffet style—is lots of work.

Formal Dinner Reception

A formal dinner reception consists of several courses, with each course served to the guests at their seats. This is the most formal type of wedding reception meal and the most expensive. Again, the main reason is that more labor is required in the form of servers.

A formal dinner usually is served in courses. The meal normally begins with an appetizer, followed by (depending our your region) either a fruit course or a salad course. The entree, or main course, is served next. Sometimes at very formal dinners, your guests can choose between several entrées. They must specify their preference on the response card included with the invitation. Dessert is the last course and is served with assorted coffees and teas. You may want to offer wine with dinner and also serve champagne during the dessert.

You can limit the dessert portion of your reception to wedding cake, or you may decide to set up a sweet table. Several different types of sweets are available on a sweet table, and guests can help themselves to whichever dessert they prefer. The wedding cake would be the main attraction for the dessert table, but you can also include some petit fours, heart-shaped cookies, mini-cheesecakes topped with various fruit toppings, chocolates, or whatever your sweet tooth dictates. Consult with your caterer to find out what your options are.

111

So, What's on the Menu?

Here are some sample menus provided by several of the professional caterers I work with. These menus should get you thinking and give you some ideas about what you might want to serve.

Cake and Punch Reception

Wedding cake

Champagne punch

Fruit punch

Assorted chocolates

Mixed nuts

Hors D'Oeuvres Reception

Shrimp cocktail served in an ice sculpture

Assorted cheeses and crackers

New potato skins filled with a mixture of cream cheese, sour cream, herbs and dill

Roast turkey and beef tenderloin mini-sandwiches

Banana Rumaki

Fresh fruit and cheese kabobs

Bacon stuffed cherry tomatoes

Buffet Reception

Fresh fruit salad

Spinach salad

Carved tenderloin of beef with sour cream and horseradish sauce

Chicken Mandarin with puff pastry shell

Pear potatoes

Fresh cold vegetables vinaigrette

Glazed baby carrots

Assorted rolls and butter

Formal Dinner

Hors d'oeuvres served before dinner with cocktails

Pea pods with smoked trout; artichoke hearts with curried egg or chicken salad; cucumber slices with herb cream cheese and shrimp

First Course

Fresh pasta with sauteed vegetables, topped with fresh basil and a choice of salmon or black caviar

Second Course

Raspberry Sorbet

Main Course

Filet of beef tenderloin, mushroom turnovers with thin mushroom sauce, fresh asparagus with slivered almonds

Fourth Course

Fresh green salad of bibb and watercress with sliced strawberries and purple onions with poppyseed dressing

Individual loaves of french bread, whole wheat and rye

Butter rosettes

Dessert Course

Pears Cranbrook (pears poached in white wine, peeled, cored, and stuffed with cream du macaroon; then served on a bed of whipped cream and chocolate fudge sauce)

Wedding cake

Champagne

Assorted coffees and teas

Thinking Through Your Food Options

Suppose that you are going to have an hors d'oeuvres reception with a limited bar. Your test now is to make good use of your money as far as food selection goes. Offering liquor always means you must serve some substantial food. You don't have to serve meat and potatoes—especially for an hors d'oeuvres reception—but you do need to provide something filling so guests don't drink on empty stomachs. You might opt for some pita triangle sandwiches (pita bread cut into triangles and filled with various fillings). You may add a fruit tray with a yogurt dip. To that you can add some water chestnuts wrapped in bacon and cooked in a brown sweet and sour sauce (ummmm, one of my favorites), and so on. The catering manager should sit down with you and your groom and find out what your favorite foods are and how to incorporate them into the menu.

Bet You Didn't Know... One of the most famous champagnes in the world is Dom Perignon from France. Champagne was discovered by a monk in a northeastern region of France called "Champagne." This monk found that by sealing wine in a bottle for several years, the wine would begin to ferment and sparkle. That monk's name was Dom Perignon. Today, Dom Perignon is a very famous and very expensive addition to your wedding reception.

One of my favorite catering managers always asks for family recipes to duplicate and serve at the reception. Clients are thrilled to have someone who cares that much and wants to make the reception special for them. One recent wedding reception combined a Spanish family with a German family. The catering manager took treasured family recipes from both sides and duplicated several dishes. Then, for an added touch, the couple used menu programs and added side notes about the family recipes and their origin.

When talking to the caterer about how much this wonderful menu will cost, ask if the cost includes add-on items, such as tips and gratuities. If the linens aren't part of the reception hall billing, then they may be included in the catering bill.

Also, ask to see pictures of the caterer's previous receptions. Often, the way the caterer displays the food can mean the difference between a good reception and a wonderful reception. Will the caterer garnish the serving tables with ivy or other greenery to make it more appealing? Do they have access to votive candles or colored linens if that is what you want?

Can you taste the food prepared by the caterer? Many times, you can either make an appointment to come for a tasting or sampling of the foods prepared, or caterers may offer a tasting at certain times of the month. This is usually not a concern if the caterer is with a hotel or restaurant that serves meals consistently to the public. You can simply go out for dinner to sample the menu.

Playing the Numbers Game

Talk to the caterer some more about what the guaranteed numbers mean. (Refer to Chapter 5 for more information about guaranteed numbers.) Find out what percentage the caterer will go under and above for the guest count that you provide. Make sure that you understand how this process works and what it means for your reception.

At a recent wedding reception I coordinated, the mother of the bride had given the caterer a guaranteed number of 125. She "guesstimated" the number of expected guests. When the guests at the church only numbered 70, I was concerned that her count was going to be high and that we would have many extra places at the reception. I was right. She was very upset that guests hadn't shown up when she thought they would. She was stuck with a bill for 50 extra guests (at $25.00 per person) because she had not taken the time to get an accurate response count.

As another example, at one wedding in Boston in the late 1980s, 50% of the guests who said they were coming didn't—leaving the bride with an extra 130 dinners that she had to pay for.

These stories illustrate how important it is to have an accurate count for the caterer. DO NOT GUESS. So many times brides will say, "Oh, I know they're coming to the wedding" or "I think we'll have about 150

Never guess at numbers for your reception count. Guessing can destroy your food budget and may leave you feeling angry, disappointed, or even embarrassed. Even the best caterers cannot afford to supply your reception with unlimited amounts of food.

people." Hey, save your guesses for the lottery or the racetrack. "I think" and "I guess" are two phrases you don't want to use when it comes to guaranteeing your guest total for the caterer. This number equates to money—at times, LOTS of money. (Turn to the Catering Worksheet at the end of this chapter when you are planning the food for your reception.)

Centerpiece Ideas

For any type of reception besides a cake and punch reception, you will need to provide tables for your guests to sit during the event. The layout of your facility, the time of day and style of the reception, the table size, and the number of guests you want to seat are all things you must consider before you decide what to use for centerpieces.

Simple or Sensational?

If you are on a tight budget, but you still want something on each table, consider using simple votive candles in votive holders, some greenery, and maybe a sprinkle of glitter or confetti. The greenery adds a soft, natural touch to the table. The candlelight gives off a soft glow, and the confetti and glitter add some sparkle and a party atmosphere. You can rent the votives from your florist and he also can provide the greenery. You can probably get friends to help set up the centerpieces for the day of the wedding, which helps reduce the labor cost in the florist's bill.

If you want something more elaborate, the sky is the limit. One bride rented beautiful five-point silver candelabra and asked the florist to place ivy and lilies and babies-breath intertwined along the stems. With tall white candles, it was a lovely setting for an hors d'oeuvres reception. While not too expensive, it was very elegant. Some of the most elaborate centerpieces are floral arrangements created on pedestal stands. The stem of a pedestal stand extends up about 3 feet, and at the top there is a section that can hold a large arrangement of flowers. These are very elegant yet practical because you don't have to peer around a centerpiece to be able to talk to the guest across the table. If budget is not a problem, then let the florist have full reign with the flowers. If money is a concern, use the less expensive flowers in the pedestal vases. No matter what flowers you use, you can create a very elegant centerpiece.

Other Table Ideas

Using other forms of "decorations" can add to the overall look of your tables. Most of the time when the menu calls for hors d'oeuvres, the table decorations can be much simpler. Tables for hors d'oeuvres receptions are usually only set with cloths and centerpieces. Sometimes, there may be champagne glasses present—but not always. So, if you want to add a little zest, consider using some form of favor which can double for added decorations.

One of the best kinds of favors is individual candy wrapped either in boxes or papers that correspond to the color scheme of the wedding. For example, one couple's colors were black with accents of gold. They were having an hors d'oeuvres reception and for centerpieces used tall candlesticks with greenery, baby's breath, and gold confetti scattered on the white linen. The caterer used black and white napkins tied with a gold ribbon. Then at each place, the bride placed a small shiny gold box containing two truffles for each guest. The candlelight, greenery, and gold confetti created a lovely atmosphere. Because they were able to keep decorating costs down, they had more money to invest in their food choices.

Other ideas for centerpieces that are simple and cost effective are colored ribbons down the center of the tables accented with either votive candles or tall candlesticks and some selections of greens.

Balloon bouquets on the tables are in order for the more informal reception. Balloons can create a party atmosphere and cover a multitude of blemishes at the facility.

Even small things, such as using a decorative napkin fold or a flower placed inside a napkin, can add a nice touch to an otherwise simple table. If the caterer has choices of colored linens, ask to see samples. You may find something that coordinates nicely with your color scheme.

That Fantasy Creation: The Cake

Perhaps one of the creations given the most thought during the wedding planning stages is the wedding cake. Maybe you've dreamed about a five-tier creation with fountains and lights or a simple, stately, stacked cake with fresh flowers being the only color. When you are

shopping for your wedding cake, be sure to ask for suggestions and recommendations from family and friends who have recently married. The caterer you are working with may also offer a wedding cake service, or he may be glad to provide you with names of competent bakers if you just ask.

So Many Choices...

Today, you can select a wedding cake in a variety of flavors and fillings—again, another way to make a particular wedding unique.

You may want a carrot cake with cream cheese filling, a layer of chocolate cake with raspberry filling, or maybe even lemon cake with an orange flavored filling. Mix different flavors on different layers so all guests can have a choice. The sky is the limit when it comes to choosing flavors and fillings for your wedding cake. Gone are the days of only a white wedding cake.

Bet You Didn't Know... The first wedding cake goes back to ancient times when the cake was actually a mixture of sesame seed meal and honey. As Western Europe developed, the cake consisted of a small, unleavened biscuit. In the 1600s, a French chef tried an experiment with small cakes he stacked together and held in place with a white sugar icing. And before the Civil War in this country, the wedding cake was actually a fruitcake.

Maybe you love the look of rolled fondant icing. It's pure elegance. It consists of a layer of icing that is literally rolled over the cake layers. It is completely smooth all the way around. When you meet with the baker, ask to see pictures of his creations. Take pictures with you of cakes you think are particularly pretty or that have caught your eye. Ask if he can duplicate these. When my parents celebrated their 35th wedding anniversary, I took a picture of their wedding cake and gave it to the baker with a description of the flowers my mother had used. The baker created almost perfectly their wedding cake complete with cake top. They were thrilled.

*Tiered cake decorated with a combination of icing flowers and real roses.
Photo by Wyant Photography, Inc.*

Bargaining with the Baker

Ask whether the baker bakes fresh or works from frozen cakes. Some
bakers bake early in the week and then freeze their cakes and decorate
them on Friday, with finishing touches the day of the wedding. I
personally prefer fresh because I think the cake tastes better, but that's
something you will have to decide for yourself. Get all the information;
it never hurts to ask questions. Wedding cakes are usually priced per
person, and your locale determines what that per person charge will be.

Ask whether the baker will deliver the cake or if you have to
arrange to pick up the cake. Is there an extra charge for delivery to the
reception site? Trust me, picking up a wedding cake and hauling it
across town is not a pleasant task. Every bump you hit makes you
wonder what the cake will look like when you arrive at your destination. I only do it for clients when we have no other choice.

Most bakers will deliver. They may charge for that service, but it's
probably worth it. Ask the baker if there is a deposit on the cake stands
and pillars? Finally, ask if they will cut and serve the cake for you.
Again, there may be a charge for that, but cutting a wedding cake is an
art. If they don't offer that service, the catering people most likely will
cut and serve the cake for you.

119

Also, check how the wedding cake pieces (plastic pillars, the layer pieces holding the cake together) are to be returned. Find out whether the caterer will take care of that for you or if you are responsible. You don't want to have to play with icing and cake pieces as you are trying to leave for your honeymoon, so take care of this item before your wedding day arrives. Designate a family member or friend to help. (Be sure to use the Wedding Cake Worksheet at the end of this chapter.)

The Groom's Cake

The groom's cake, which was once a part of every wedding reception but slowly lost its popularity, is beginning to make its way back into many weddings. At the turn of the century, the groom's cake was similar to a fruit cake, heavy and rich with dried fruits and nuts. A small piece was served in small white boxes and guests took a piece as they left the reception. Unmarried females guests placed the box under their pillow and supposedly, as legend goes, the man they dreamed of would be their husband.

 Bet You Didn't Know... The wedding cake chosen by Luci Baines Johnson and Patrick Nugent in 1966 weighed a whopping 300 pounds and was 14 tiers high. The icing posed a problem as the couple tried to cut the first piece. They couldn't cut through it. Finally, the President himself had to step in and make a stab at it.

Today, groom's cakes are appearing in all kinds of shapes, sizes, flavors, and themes. Grooms have used basketball and football themes for their cakes. One groom who loved to play bridge had his groom's cake designed like a huge hand of cards. Remember the red velvet Armadillo in *Steel Magnolias*? That was an original (if not odd) groom's cake. One couple, heading to Florida for their honeymoon, chose a groom's cake made like the island they were going to visit. Complete with sugar "sand" and blue icing "water," a doll-sized hotel and people, and a toy red convertible, it was the focal point of the lobby area. They didn't want to take away from the elegant, stately wedding cake in the ballroom, but they did want their guests to view the creation and have fun enjoying it.

Chocolate seems to be a very popular flavor with grooms, but I have also seen cheesecakes served with luscious fruit toppings as a groom's cake. Experiment and have fun with this. If your budget will allow it, and you want some creative way to express yourselves, consider having a groom's cake.

A groom's cake displayed next to the wedding cake. Photo by Wyant Photography, Inc.

Those Luscious Libations

One of the hardest questions for folks to answer when planning their wedding reception is, "Do we want to serve liquor?" Sometimes the answer to that is an overwhelming "yes." Sometimes the answer is "no," but there are many fence-sitters on this issue.

Traditional etiquette says only that you must offer your guests something to eat and something to drink at the reception. (Remember the bread and water theory from a previous chapter?) Well, that applies to alcohol at your reception, too. It is your choice, and yours alone.

Look at All Your Options

If you decide to offer alcohol at the reception, you can choose from the following methods:

➤ *Open bar.* You may offer a full bar outfitted with the liquor you choose. The bar consists of mixed drinks, wine, beer, and soft drinks. You may also choose to serve some after dinner liquors. You pay the bill.

➤ *Limited bar.* You limit what you serve your guests. You may choose to serve wine, beer, and soft drinks only, or a combination (wine and soft drinks or beer and soft drinks). You can limit the time the bar remains open. For example, if your reception is scheduled to start with cocktails at 6:30 and dinner served at 7:30, you may decide to have the bar open from 6:30 to 7:30, close it from 7:30 until 9:00, and then open it again at 9:00 until one-half hour before the reception ends. You pay the bill.

➤ *Cash bar.* A bar service is available, but guests pay for their individual drinks. Many families have trouble with this concept, but, as I said, if you meet your obligation with "something" to drink, then don't worry about it. Another option is to offer wine and beer as a "freebie," and then have a cash bar on top of that. Then guests, if they choose, can have a mixed drink, but they pay for it themselves.

Remember, you do not have to offer liquor at all. That is a personal choice. Some couples may only offer champagne for the toasting part of the festivities. You can have champagne served to guests or place open bottles on each table. There are many ways to serve liquor at your reception. (Turn to the Liquor Worksheet at the end of this chapter for help in this area.)

Don't Take Your Responsibilities Lightly

Make sure you have a reputable liquor dealer serving the alcohol. Liability laws differ from state to state. If you hire a liquor dealer to come in and serve your guests, some of the liability which could otherwise fall to you, falls to the dealer.

Over the past five or six years, I have observed a much more conscious society as far as drinking habits go. When I first started out in this business, it was not unusual for some guests, provided with all that free-flowing liquor, to drink too much and dampen the party. I haven't had as many problems in the past few years that I had early in my career. People are just more understanding of the responsibilities that go along with serving alcohol, and guests are more conscious of their responsibilities, too. Certainly, the potential for abuse is still there, and you need to be aware and watch out for possible problems at your reception (or appoint a responsible friend or family member to watch the guests for you). Our society on the whole, however, does seem to have matured a little in this area. Always make sure that if you do offer liquor, you have someone assigned to watch for those individuals who may need help returning home. Be sure you have adequate designated drivers.

The Least You Need to Know

➤ Have your questions for each vendor written down; you want to appear in control.

➤ Get referrals from family and friends of the vendors whose services they have used recently.

➤ Ask about "add-ons" with the reception site and caterer.

➤ Ask the catering manager and the baker if sample tasting of cakes and the reception food is available.

➤ Always give an accurate count to the caterer. Never guess at numbers for your guaranteed count.

➤ Give careful consideration to whether you want the expense and responsibility that accompanies the serving of liquor at your reception.

RECEPTION SITE WORKSHEET

Reception site: _____

Contact person: _____

Telephone: _____

Time for reception to begin: _____

Time for ending: _____

What the facility will provide:

(Linens, skirting, mike hook-ups)

_____

_____

_____

_____

Fee for site: _____

Deposit made: _____

Floor plan layout:

_____

_____

_____

_____

Appointments with manager: _____

_____

CATERING WORKSHEET

Caterer: _____

Telephone: _____

Menu format:
- ❏ Buffet
- ❏ Hors d'oeuvres
- ❏ Sit-down dinner

Menu ideas:

_____

_____

_____

Cost per person:_____

Deposit made: _____

Next appointment with chef:_____

WEDDING CAKE WORKSHEET

Baker: _____

Telephone: _____

Price: _____

Delivery fee: _____

Deposit on cake pieces: _____

How to get items back to baker: _____

Number of servings: _____

Description of cake and fillings:

_____

_____

Groom's cake description:

_____

Flavor and fillings:

_____

_____

Price: _____

Number of servings: _____

Questions for the baker:

_____

_____

LIQUOR WORKSHEET

Dealer: _____

Telephone: _____

Address: _____

Contact: _____

Requested:
- ❏ Open Bar
- ❏ Limited Bar
- ❏ Cash Bar

Method of accountability:

_____

Liquor requested:

_____

_____

_____

Number of bartenders needed: _____

Time for setup: _____

Questions:

_____

_____

_____

_____

Snapdragons, Snapshots, and Song

> **In This Chapter**
>
> ➤ Understanding photographers and videographers
>
> ➤ Making sure you have the flowers you want and that they fit your budget
>
> ➤ Getting your money's worth in your invitation order
>
> ➤ Understanding the musical choices for your wedding

Focusing on Your Photography

In the discussion of the items you need to reserve first in Chapter 6, I talked about some of the questions you need to ask the photographers you are thinking of hiring to make sure that you find someone competent and affordable. In this section, we review those questions and add some additional ones. It's important for you to have a good understanding of how to hire a photographer so that you can ask intelligent questions and be happy with the final results.

Photography is a large wedding expense, and when all is said and done, you want to make sure that you have good pictures to help you remember the day. What you don't want is a lot of disappointment. Taking the time to do some smart shopping now will pay off when the proofs come back.

What's in a Picture?

You may encounter several different styles of wedding photography from which you will have to choose. The type of wedding photography that a particular photographer offers depends on his ability, experience, and personal choice, but if you at least know the differences and can understand the terminology, you will be better off.

Soft Focus

When we were married, I remember fondly the photographer pulling out these wonderfully romantic pictures from his samples and waving them tantalizingly in front of my eyes. They were dream-like and romantic with soft lighting. That type of photography is called *soft focus*. The photographer uses a special lens to give a romantic look to the pictures. You wouldn't want your entire album in this style, however, because after a few shots, the romantic look loses its effectiveness.

Portraiture

Portraiture is probably one of the most common types of photography, although you may not know it by this name. This refers to the formal posed pictures at the church or synagogue, ceremony site, and reception. There isn't much spontaneity here, but the pictures can be almost perfect, depending on the photographer. The time element here is what you need to understand. Yes, your pictures can be quite lovely, but if it's going to take the photographer five hours to accomplish that task, maybe you should think of other alternatives.

Natural Light

This type of photography does not use artificial light. In other words, there is no flash used with the camera. The photographer takes what light is available naturally and uses that to create the image. When done well, a natural light photograph reminds you of a fine work of art, but it is very difficult to arrange.

Photojournalistic

Wedding photography done in the *photojournalistic* style takes its technique from the news media. The photographer, through pictures, tells the story of your wedding on film. Instead of posing pictures trying to create a mood, the photographer follows the people and mood of the event and captures it on film as it happens. This can be a fantastic way to show emotions, highlights of the day that have special meaning, the people involved, and anything special you want to include.

In one wedding I coordinated, the groom's mother had passed away just six months before the wedding. He wanted to do something special in her honor at the service. When the parents were to be seated, he appeared in the back of the church and walked by his father's side down the aisle. They went to the altar rail and lit a candle in memory of his mother. It was a very touching moment, and one which the photographer really couldn't pose. By using the photojournalistic approach, the photographer got a wonderful shot to capture this special moment.

Contracts

It's very important to understand the kind of contract the photographer uses and exactly what the price includes. Make sure you understand this. Does the contract include albums? Does it include a charge for the proofs?

As I mentioned in Chapter 6, one very important feature to consider is whether the contract includes a time limit. When you buy a package, is there a time limit on how long the photographer is available? Suppose that your wedding is at 5 p.m. You don't want to see the groom before the service, so you have some pictures taken with your bridesmaids and family. Your groom has similar shots taken with his groomsmen, ushers, and family. The majority of the pictures, however, must be taken after the service. Then, of course, you want the photographer to go to the reception and get some shots there: the cutting of the cake, the toast, your first dance, your dance with your dad, and so on. If your contract has a four-hour time limit and you start pictures at 4 p.m., that means that at 8 p.m. that photographer is either finished shooting your wedding or he goes into overtime. That's what you want to avoid if at all possible. I've been quoted $150 per hour overtime for photographers in the Midwest. That's a lot of money. So, check on whether the contract contains a time limit clause. It may be cheaper for you in the long run to get a package with more time than you think you'll need just to save you from having to pay overtime.

When All Is Said and Done

Good wedding photography is meant to last a lifetime. You want to choose a photographer who can help you capture on film all the wonderful emotions of your big day. You want someone who treats you with respect and sensitivity, and you want all this without even noticing that the photographer is in the room. (Use the Photography Worksheet at the end of this chapter to determine your photographic needs.)

Finding Value for Your Videography Dollars

The basic questions you ask of the photographer also apply to the videographer. The biggest question is whether the tape you receive will be edited or unedited. Too many times, the couple is disappointed with the video because they expect it to look just like a TV production. Always ask to see a demo tape of the video- graphers work. That's the best way to make sure that the finished product is what you expect it to be. Check for the quality of the tape both in coverage of the event and how the tape flows from event to event. Does he use fade-outs?

Always check with the officiant to make sure you are permitted to have your ceremony videotaped. That is your responsibility, not the video company's. Nothing is more embarrassing than having the video company all set and ready to go when the officiant announces that his church or synagogue does not permit videotaping. Check ahead of time.

Ask if you have choices in music (if the tape is edited). Ask about including special effects, such as incorporating your baby pictures into the video or using animation. Will there be a cordless mike on the groom to pick up the vows segment of the ceremony? Ask if the videographer will attend the rehearsal to get a feel for placement at the ceremony site and to meet the officiant. (Turn to the Videography Worksheet at the end of this chapter.)

Nipping Your Floral Bill in the Bud

Your florist bill can consume a significant portion of your wedding budget. You can make the most of your wedding dollars, however, by using your imagination and finding a good florist to help you stretch your dollars. (Use the Floral Worksheet at the end of this chapter to help you with your planning.) References here are crucial. Ask those same friends and family members who have recently had weddings who they used and how they liked a particular florist. Don't ask if the flowers were pretty; ask how the florist was to work with. Was he reliable? Did he show up on time? Did he label the flowers? There is nothing worse than having a box of 30 boutonnieres and no idea who they go to.

Ask about the choices you have with aisle cloths. If you can, rent real cloth, not the plastic type. If you can't find the cloth type, then look for the aisle clothes that are heavy paper-type fabric, but are still disposable. Will the aisle cloth be taped or pinned and will the florist do that? I once had a florist who just dropped off the flowers and aisle cloth and ran. I had never secured an aisle cloth before that day, and boy, did I learn a few things. Now I ask that question early on. Always make sure the aisle cloth is secured to the flooring. One bride didn't know she needed to secure the aisle cloth and as she started down the aisle, the cloth rolled up under her gown. By the time she reached the end of the aisle, there was a huge white "thing" wrapped around her gown—not a very nice picture.

A good florist should be willing to assist you with ideas and ways to make your floral dollars go farther. Is the florist familiar with the ceremony site? Has the florist previously provided flowers for your reception facility? How can you make your reception hall pretty without spending a fortune on centerpieces? It can be done, but you'll need help.

If you want silk flowers, what quality of silks do they use? You want to make sure you use a good quality silk flower. There is nothing worse than cheap looking silk flowers. And speaking of silk flowers, be very sure that none of your guests are allergic to the odor of some silk flowers. They can sometimes, literally, stink.

Taking Stock of Your Invitations

I've learned a lot about invitations over the past few years, and I now offer invitations and accessories to brides at a discount. Rule number one: Never pay full retail price for invitations. I can hear the invitation companies screaming right now, but there is so much competition out there for your invitation order that you should never have to pay full price. You can always get something discounted.

You can find selections for your wedding invitations at many stores and bridal shops. Most times, if you open the Yellow Pages and look under "invitations" or "wedding services," you can find a whole

range of retailers that offer invitations. Many bridal consultants and bridal salons offer invitations. Card shops, or party-goods stores offer invitations and other accessories you will need for the big day.

Your wedding invitation is the first item your guests will see about your wedding. It sets the whole tone for the wedding and reception to follow. It gives the guests the first glimpse of the type and formality of your wedding. Whether it's an engraved, ivory colored, formal invitation or a pair of kissing frogs (there really is such an item), your invitation tells your guests something about the style of your wedding. (Turn to the Invitations Worksheets at the end of this chapter for help with invitations.)

Selecting Your Invitations

Engraved invitations involve a process where the paper is stamped with a mold, leaving an indentation in the paper. The ink is added to fill in the indentation and then it is dried. If you look on the back of an engraved invitation, you will see indentions. It takes six to eight weeks to order engraved invitations. A newer technology, *thermography*, is more popular today than engraving. It is the opposite of engraving. In this process, the words are written out in glue and the ink color sprinkled over the glue. Then it is heated, so the lettering is raised. If you run your fingers over the invitation, you can feel the lettering. Thermography is much less expensive than engraving and still has an elegant look.

The first thing you want to do when choosing invitations is to find the proper paper. When you look through all those books of invitations, remember that the paper is the only thing that can't be changed. Feel the paper quality. Is it heavy enough for your tastes? A good, cotton bond paper is the best choice. Everything else that goes with the invitation is "fill in the blank." You can change the script, the ink color, the wording, and some companies will even change the format. Don't think that just because the invitations you like are shown in navy ink and you have your heart set on gold ink that you have to find other invitations. Chances are you can change the ink color.

If you are having invitations engraved, be sure to allow at least six weeks for the delivery of the order.

You should order your invitations at least three months before the wedding. That will give you one month for the order to be delivered (plenty of time) and one month for you to address them and get them in the mail one month before the wedding.

At holiday times or other busy times of the year, you may need to order your invitations four months in advance. Just be sure that everything is solidly booked with the ceremony site and the reception facility before you order your invitations.

When ordering your invitations, be sure to check with the store about what will happen if there is a mistake in the order. Do they guarantee their work? To ensure that your invitations will be correct, I would recommend working face-to-face instead of discussing your invitation order over the phone.

Make sure you take the finished invitation to the post office and have it weighed to determine the correct postage. What you don't want to happen is for all your invitations to come back stamped, "Return for postage." One bride I worked with recently had taken her invitations to the post office three different times to have them weighed. Each time the invitation was under one ounce. The day she took all 250 invitations, with postage, to the post office to mail them, the clerk informed her that they were oversized and would have to have additional postage. I don't know why she wasn't give the correct information on her three previous visits, but when I checked the book from which she had ordered her invitations there was a disclaimer on the page that said it was oversized and would require additional postage. The moral of this story is that just because the invitation weighs less than one ounce doesn't necessarily mean it won't require additional postage.

> Always order 25 more invitations and enclosures than you think you will need. It is much cheaper to order the extra 25 than to have to order more later on.

Wording your wedding invitation can be a simple task, or it can be very complicated. Located in the front of most invitation books (where you will select your invitations from) are wording suggestions for almost every known circumstance. You can find the traditional, formal wedding invitation issued by the bride's parents to the wording used when Uncle Fred is sending the invitations for his niece's wedding. From those samples and from the samples you see on the following pages, you should have the help you need to make the wording for your wedding invitation an easy task. Most times, salespeople are standing by to help with details that are complex or unusual.

Mr. and Mrs. James Rodney Miller
request the honour of your presence
at the marriage of their daughter
Cynthia Elizabeth
to
Mr. John Robert Kolb
Saturday, the ninth of November
nineteen hundred and ninety-nine
at half after six o'clock in the evening
Memorial Baptist Church
2324 South Seventh Street
Cleveland, Utah

Formal invitation issued by the bride's parents.

Mrs. James Rodney Miller
requests the honour of your presence
at the marriage of her daughter
Cynthia Elizabeth
to
Mr. John Robert Kolb
Saturday, the ninth of November
nineteen hundred and ninety-nine
at half after six o'clock in the evening
Memorial Baptist Church
2324 South Seventh Street
Cleveland, Utah

Formal invitation issued by the bride's widowed mother.

Mr. and Mrs. James Rodney Miller
request the honour of your presence
at the marriage of his daughter
Cynthia Elizabeth
to
Mr. John Robert Kolb
Saturday, the ninth of November
nineteen hundred and ninety-nine
at half after six o'clock in the evening
Memorial Baptist Church
2324 South Seventh Street
Cleveland, Utah

Formal invitation issued by the bride's father and stepmother.

Mrs. Elizabeth Ann Miller

and

Mr. James Rodney Miller

request the honour of your presence

at the marriage of their daughter

Cynthia Elizabeth

to

Mr. John Robert Kolb

Saturday, the ninth of November

nineteen hundred and ninety-nine

at half after six o'clock in the evening

Memorial Baptist Church

2324 South Seventh Street

Cleveland, Utah

*Formal invitation issued by the bride's parents,
who are divorced.*

Mr. and Mrs. Collin James Whitney
request the honour of your presence
at the marriage of Mrs. Whitney's daughter
Cynthia Elizabeth Miller
to
Mr. John Robert Kolb
Saturday, the ninth of November
nineteen hundred and ninety-nine
at half after six o'clock in the evening
Memorial Baptist Church
2324 South Seventh Street
Cleveland, Utah

Formal invitation issued by the bride's mother, who is divorced and remarried.

Miss Cynthia Elizabeth Miller

and

Mr. John Robert Kolb

request the honour of your presence

at their marriage

on

Saturday, the ninth of November

nineteen hundred and ninety-nine

at half after six o'clock in the evening

Memorial Baptist Church

2324 South Seventh Street

Cleveland, Utah

Formal invitation issued by the couple.

> *Mr. and Mrs. James Rodney Miller*
> *request the honour of your presence*
> *at the wedding reception of their daughter*
> *Cynthia Elizabeth*
> *and*
> *Mr. John Robert Kolb*
> *Saturday, the ninth of November*
> *nineteen hundred and ninety-nine*
> *at half after seven o'clock in the evening*
> *Meadow Brook Country Club*
> *Cleveland, Utah*

Formal invitation issued by the bride's parents to the wedding reception only. Ceremony is private.

All the Little Extras

Invitation companies offer all sorts of extra accessories to complement your wedding invitations, such as reception cards, response cards, informal notes, napkins, thank-you note cards, at-home cards, scrolls, or Within the Ribbon cards for guests.

Reception cards are cards enclosed with the invitation that invite the guest to the wedding reception. Sometimes, guests are only invited to the ceremony and not the reception. Usually, guests are invited to both. Most formal invitations include a reception card enclosure. An "at-home card" was used more in the mid-century when couples would take extended honeymoons and guests would be told that "After January 8, Mr. and Mrs. Smith will be at home," meaning you could visit after January 8. Today, this is all but forgotten but is still used in some parts of the country.

Scrolls are small pieces of paper, usually a fine paper, with a verse or message from the couple printed on them. These scrolls can be handed out at the ceremony or saved and used as a favor at the reception. Within the Ribbon cards are those cards enclosed with the invitation that give guests special seating "within the ribbon" or in a reserved spot. Within the Ribbon cards are usually used for very large and very formal weddings where many guests are expected and seating special family members is a must.

Be careful about the wording on your invitation if your wedding time falls around a meal time. For clarity, list on the reception card what type of reception this will be: "Hors d'oeuvres Reception" or "Dinner Reception." That way, guests know what type of food service to expect.

One suggestion I make to brides is to not print the wedding date on their napkins. If you leave the date off your napkins, for example, you can use them after the wedding in your new home. You may consider printing just your names or even the initial for your last name on the napkins. I worked with one bride who wanted something different for her napkins. She wanted to use only a large initial of her new last name. It took a special dye cut to make the initial (which she had to pay for), so she ordered not only napkins but informal notes to use for thank-yous and some larger stationery, too. She made good use of the special dye cut and had some unique stationery to show for it.

Making Beautiful Music

In Chapter 6, I talked about the importance of shopping around and then reserving the musicians early for your ceremony and reception. You may want to review that material and then consider some of the additional suggestions in this section. (Also, use the Musicians Worksheet at the end of this chapter to help in your planning.)

Waltzing Down the Aisle

Unless the couple comes from a musically inclined background, music is often a largely overlooked aspect of the wedding ceremony. If you use your imagination, however, the opportunities for unique musical touches are endless. For your ceremony, you may want to consider some of the more common choices: piano, organ, string group (either a trio or quartet), harp, violin, harp with a violin, trumpet, or perhaps even a choir. There are several wonderful music pieces written solely for trumpet and organ that are especially grand for processionals. "Trumpet Tune" by Purcell and "Trumpet Voluntary" by Clarke are two of my favorite pieces. They are majestic. The wedding march song from *The Sound of Music* is a magnificent piece for a processional, which goes best with a long aisle. One bride wanted the organ and trumpet to play for her attendants' entrance but she only wanted trumpets for her grand entrance. She hired three trumpeters who played a wonderful fanfare followed by a very majestic version of "Bridal Chorus." It was fantastic! I can still hear all the guests say "Ahh."

A choir adds a very nice touch for the wedding service. One couple who were both members of a professional choir hired the group to sing several songs during the prelude and the lovely piece "One Hand, One Heart," from *West Side Story*, during the lighting of the unity candle. It was very moving, and it meant so much to that couple to have the choir and their friends be part of their service.

I have worked with several couples who have sung to each other either before the service or during the service. One bride this summer surprised her groom at the altar after they had finished their exchange of vows. The soloist stood up as if to sing and instead the bride, a music educator, started singing "When I Fall in Love." The congregation just melted in the pews. It was wonderful—so romantic and personal. The groom was totally surprised and delighted. But beware. Unless this sort of thing comes very easy to you, don't try this at home. Leave the singing to the professionals. You will be emotional enough on your wedding day; you don't want to have to worry about performing for 300 guests.

One bride I know had the honor of having several songs written for her as a wedding gift and played during the service. She listed that information on the program and it was a very personal touch for her to remember.

When planning your ceremony music, remember that you can use a variety of songs as long as the officiant is comfortable with your selections. Depending on your officiant, he may have the final say about which music is acceptable and which isn't. Make the music mean something to you and your groom.

Visit the musician in charge of your ceremony music. If you are having the ceremony in a religious setting, that person will most likely be the Minister of Music, the Director of Music, or the organist or pianist. Talk with him about your likes and dislikes and what you would like to hear on your wedding day. Ask for ideas. Many times, if you meet in the facility, he can play a few bars of a certain piece so you can hear the music. If you don't have access to a musician who can accommodate you, visit your local music store and purchase some tapes of wedding music. I have several tapes I loan to brides so they can be more active in choosing their wedding music.

Taped music is nice, but it can also be very risky. At a recent wedding, the young man running the tape machine missed his cue. He then got so excited that he jumped up, knocked over the music stand for the soloist, and turned on the microphone all in one fell swoop. The congregation found it humorous, but the bride and groom did not. When you deal with tapes and tape players there is a possibility of problems—either human or mechanical. Be very careful if you decide to use taped music.

Music to Relax By

Although certainly not mandatory, music is a nice addition to the reception. It can be very simple or very elaborate. A pianist playing soft background music is nice for the simple cake and punch reception, or you may choose to have a 20-piece orchestra in the ballroom playing the sounds of Glenn Miller for a formal dinner and dance reception. It goes back to your personal tastes and what style of wedding you and your groom want.

At one wedding I coordinated, the bride's name was Amy. During the evening, the groom had the band play "Once in Love with Amy."

Bet You Didn't Know... The first gift registry was founded in 1901, much by mistake, at a store named China Hall in Rochester, Minnesota. A poor, stressed clerk (see, they even had stress back then) couldn't remember the local brides' china patterns and which pieces the townspeople had purchased for which bride. He decided to write each bride's name on an index card along with her china pattern and which pieces had been purchased for the couple. Somehow it caught on, and now we have gift registries all over the country.

The couple danced around the ballroom to that tune and everyone applauded. It was a very special moment for them. Another couple took ballroom dance lessons in order to have a wonderful first dance. They even went so far as to have that dance choreographed by a professional choreographer. It was great to see a young couple so very poised glide around the ballroom with their bends and dips. Fred and Ginger, eat your hearts out.

When you discuss your reception music with the vendor, ask for a tape of the musician or group if you are unfamiliar with the music. Check the contracts. How many breaks do they require and how often do they take those breaks? Do they have access to taped music to play during those breaks? It's nice for the guests to hear some soft music playing in the background rather than dead silence. Will they announce you or help with the garter and bouquet toss? How long will they play? Will they stay past their end time if you request them to do so, and how much is the extra time going to cost? What is their professional dress for the event? If you are lucky enough to see them perform before you book them, look at the poise and composure they have with the crowd. Your dance floor should be active most of the evening, which is usually a sign of a good reception. In order for that to happen, a band must be able to "read" the crowd. If a style of music isn't working, will they try something different? Again, check with family and friends who have used this particular musician or group before and get those references.

Music can add a wonderful aspect to both your ceremony and your reception. Make wise musical choices for both situations. Music can help you complete your wedding picture. Your musical choices can "frame" your wedding day and set the mood for all to enjoy.

Gift Registry

This is the time in your wedding planning when you may want to consider taking your groom and visiting some retail establishments in your area to register for wedding gifts. This is a rather painless process but one that is very necessary. Unless you don't care whether you get 42 sets of glasses or 16 toasters, then get yourself down to the local department store and register. Usually the store will have someone assigned to help couples register. In larger department stores, you can register for household items, china, silver, glassware, linens, furniture—whatever they happen to sell. Register for the items the two of you will most likely be needing. It helps both you and your guests.

Some larger chains across the country offer computerized registry for brides and grooms. Meeting the needs of our scattered society, stores such as Service Merchandise, Marshall Fields, and L.L. Bean have adopted the computer system for nationwide registry. Other locally owned store chains (within a given region) have the computer up and running to keep track of the items you request and to tally those as they are purchased.

Never, I repeat, *never* send a list of the stores where you are registered with your wedding invitation. You can spread the word through family and friends, but it should not go out with the invitation.

The Least You Need to Know

➤ Make sure you feel comfortable with the photographer who will be taking your wedding pictures. You will be spending a significant amount of time together and need to have a good rapport.

➤ Ask the officiant if your wedding may be videotaped.

➤ Ask to see a demo tape of a videographer's work before you make a commitment.

➤ Before you sit down to discuss your floral needs, ask the florist to visit the ceremony and reception sites if he isn't already familiar with them.

➤ Always ask about getting a discount on invitations. You should never pay full price. Always order 25 more invitations than you think you will need.

➤ If at all possible, try to see the musicians at work before you put down a deposit.

PHOTOGRAPHY WORKSHEET

Photographer: _____

Address: _____

Telephone: _____

Referred by: _____

Type of photography (portraiture, candid, photojournalistic, soft focus, natural light): _____

Deposit: _____

Package Plan (including time limit, overtime charges, charge for proofs, number of pictures, albums included, and so on):

_____

Next appointment: _____

VIDEOGRAPHY WORKSHEET

Company name: _____

Address: _____

Telephone: _____

Contact: _____

Referred by: _____

Type of video requested (edited or unedited): _____

Attends rehearsal: _____

Number of cameras needed: _____

Music selection: _____

Provides cordless microphone for groom: _____

Special effects used: Baby pictures? Credits? Animation? Fade in or out? _____

_____

FLORAL WORKSHEET

Company name: _____

Address: _____

Telephone: _____

Type of flowers desired: _____

_____

Wedding colors: _____

Ceremony site flowers: _____

_____

Aisle cloth: _____

Secured by florist? _____

Floor plan for ceremony:

Floor plan for reception:

Ideas for reception flowers: _____

_____

Centerpieces: _____

_____

Cake table flowers: _____

Rentals (palms, ferns, trees): _____

Personal flowers: _____

Bride's bouquet: _____

Bridesmaids' bouquets: _____

Boutonnieres: _____

Mothers' corsages: _____

Flower girl basket: _____

Servers: _____

Delivery time: _____

Deposit made: _____

Rehearsal dinner flowers: _____

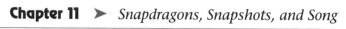

INVITATIONS WORKSHEET

Company name: _____

Contact: _____

Telephone: _____

Discount available: _____

Paper size: _____

Color ink: _____

Number needed: _____

Traditional vs. contemporary: _____

Enclosures

   Reception cards: _____

   Response cards: _____

   Maps: _____

   Within the Ribbon: _____

Accessories

   Napkins: _____

     Sizes: _____

   Toast glasses: _____

   Place cards: _____

   Programs: _____

   Matches: _____

   Cake knife: _____

   Scrolls: _____

   Favor ribbons: _____

   Thank-you notes: _____

   Cake boxes or bags: _____

MUSICIANS WORKSHEET

Company: _____

Telephone: _____

Address: _____

Contact's name: _____

Referred by: _____

Type of music (band, DJ, single instrument): _____

_____

Do they provide song list to choose from? _____

What is attire for reception? _____

How long will they play? _____

How many breaks do they take? _____

What are overtime charges? _____

Will they help with introductions and garter and bouquet toss?

_____

Next appointment: _____

Chapter 12

Puttin' on
the Ritz

In This Chapter

➤ Some additional tips for shopping for your wedding
  gown

➤ Help in dressing your bridesmaids

➤ Decking out the men in your wedding party

➤ Creative ideas for your wedding transportation

Dressing the Part: Dresses, Dresses,
and More Dresses

Finding the right gown for the bride and then trying to outfit the
bridesmaids can sometimes seem like an insurmountable task. It
doesn't have to be if you take it one step at a time.

Cinderella for a Day

In Chapter 6, I encouraged you to shop for your wedding gown at
least six months before your wedding if possible. Many things can
happen in the process of having the dress made, shipped, and altered.

It's always better to have plenty of time built into your schedule, just in case something goes wrong. Purchasing a bridal gown and all that goes with it is a major undertaking. My best advice is to shop wisely. (For help in shopping wisely, turn to the Wedding Gown and Bridesmaids' Dresses Worksheet at the end of this chapter.)

As I mentioned earlier, be sure to make an appointment with the shops before you visit. It makes you appear more serious about buying, and if they know you are coming, they can give you the time and attention you deserve. If the shop doesn't accept appointments, ask them for the best time to shop. Saturdays, for example, are often very busy days for bridal shops; try to shop on another day of the week.

If you don't dress up for this wonderful occasion, at least take a pair of dress shoes with you. Have your hair fixed appropriately and add a little makeup. You want to look your best, and you want to get a realistic picture of how you will look on your wedding day in the gown. Somehow, trying on a bridal gown wearing your Nikes and your hair in a ponytail just doesn't seem to paint the appropriate picture.

Let me emphasize again that it's a good idea to take along only one or two people on your shopping excursion—not your entire wedding party. Too many well-meaning friends with too many ideas of what you should look like on your wedding day only add to your confusion. Shop at several different stores and get referrals from recent brides. Ask those brides how they were treated. Were all their questions answered satisfactorily? How did the gown look when it was ready to pick up or when it arrived at the ceremony site? Were the sleeves stuffed with tissue? Was a bodice form used? Was the train tied up or draped over the hanger?

A bodice form is a piece of cardboard shaped like a woman's upper body that the shop places in the bodice of your gown to keep it wrinkle-free and looking fresh. This protects the gown during travel time from the shop to your home or ceremony site.

Ask the shop how they will *bustle* the gown's train. Bustling the train means that either hooks and eyes or buttons are sewn onto the back of the gown at appropriate places. When the buttons are looped, the train is pulled up so that you can move more freely around during the reception. Bustling your gown is very important. Be sure to get answers to these questions. They may appear to be little things, but they can make a difference in whether your gown looks freshly pressed or as if you slept in it. Not a pretty sight.

Shop with an open mind. Just because you have your heart set on a sheath gown with detachable train, don't be afraid to try on the gown with the flowing skirt and cowl neckline. Don't rule anything out until you've seen yourself in the mirror. You may be surprised at how nice you look.

It's not a wise move to order your gown from a shop advertising that it is going out of business. If you can buy the gown off the rack, that's fine. But don't put down a deposit and allow them to order your gown. One bride I worked with learned this lesson the hard way. The shop called and said that the gown was in. When the bride went to get her gown, the shop had "lost" the gown and couldn't reorder. What really happened was that the shop sold that gown to another customer for more money.

Be sure to ask about alterations! This can become a major expense when ordering your bridal gown. Manufacturers all use a different set of guidelines for measurements. While you may wear a size 8 in ready-to-wear women's clothing, formal wear has a different set of measurement guidelines. Let the bridal shop explain how a particular manufacturer determines sizes. It will be different from your normal street clothes. Do not order a gown two sizes too small because you expect to lose that much weight before the wedding. Bad idea. If you want to lose weight before your wedding (and many brides do), explain that to the shop so they are aware, but order the gown using your present measurements. They can always take a dress in, but letting it out can be more difficult, and sometimes impossible.

Pretty Maids All in a Row

When shopping for your bridesmaids' gowns, try to take only your honor attendant and/or your mother or a close friend. Do not, I repeat, *do not* take your whole wedding party with you. Most bridal shops cringe when they see an entire wedding party march through the door. If you are asking only one or two friends to be in the wedding, then you can take your whole party; otherwise, it's best to take only a select one or two.

It is the bride's responsibility to choose what the attendants will wear. You should take into consideration their physical size and coloring, and you don't want to force them into bankruptcy, but the final choice is yours. You also need to make sure that the style and color of their dresses complement your gown. You don't want to have your six

Alterations can be very expensive; always know up front what the shop will charge for alterations. Your best bet is to try to remain approximately the size you were when you ordered your gown. If you are expecting a large weight loss, either have your gown made locally or wait until you are closer to the desired weight before you order.

bridesmaids dressed more elaborately than you. Horror stories abound in the wedding world of brides and bridesmaids getting into real shouting matches while deciding on the attendants' dresses. It doesn't have to be that way.

I've worked with several brides in the past couple of years who have said to their bridesmaids, "Wear a black dress, no satin or sequins, but other than that, I don't care." When the first bride told me this, I was a little skeptical. The final picture, however, was rather pleasing. Each girl got to pick a dress that complemented her figure, and because each chose her own dress, it was probably something she would wear again. I've also had brides purchase material and then have their bridesmaids choose their own patterns. So, although they dressed alike in color and fabric, the dress styles were individualized. Again, each girl got the dress she wanted and would most likely wear it again.

Try to choose a dress with a reasonable price tag. If your attendants are coming to your hometown, buying you a gift, providing their own transportation, paying to stay in a hotel (although it would be nice if you could either pay for their hotel or find them a room in Aunt Laura's home), along with all the other expenses that go with being in a wedding, their calculators will be running overtime. Help them out by keeping the cost of the dress reasonable.

Accessorize to the Max

Several items are often considered as bridal accessories: veil or headpiece, shoes, jewelry, bra, and slip.

You want to be sure to choose a headpiece that complements your gown and the way you plan to wear your hair for your wedding. You have the following choices in veil lengths:

➤ *Finger tip veil*   Just brushes the shoulders and frames the face.

➤ *Elbow length veil*   Brushes the elbow.

➤ *Chapel length veil* Measures three yards long (9 feet).

➤ *Cathedral length veil* Measures four yards long (12 feet).

If your gown doesn't have a long train, you may want to consider having a longer veil. Try on different styles to be sure you get the best match for both your gown and your hair style.

Bet You Didn't Know... Lady Diana Spencer's wedding gown included a 25-foot train.

You also need to pay close attention to your shoes. Remember, you will be on your feet for hours. The last thing you need is a pair of shoes that makes your feet hurt. If your feet are complaining, you won't relax and enjoy the festivities. Brides often choose a lovely pair of formal shoes for the ceremony and then slip on a pair of ballet slippers for the reception. Their feet are exceptionally appreciative.

Jewelry is an accessory that can add to your total look. Don't overload yourself with jewelry, though, especially if your gown is heavily beaded. A pair of pretty earrings and a simple pearl necklace may be all that you need. You should remove your watch and any other everyday jewelry.

What goes underneath your gown is just as important as all your other accessories. The type of bra and slip you choose to wear with your gown are very important. First, you want a bra that is comfortable and gives you the support you need with your particular gown. Most bridal shops carry bras and slips. The slip, whether your gown is a sheath or a southern belle style gown, helps give your gown the proper shape. If your gown is a slim sheath, you may decide not to wear a slip. Make sure, however, that you cannot see panty lines through your gown.

Dressed to Kill: Formal Wear for Men

The groom and his men want to look handsome just as the bride and her attendants want to look beautiful. Take some time to look through bridal magazines to get a feel for what is available for the men in your wedding party. (Be sure to use the Tuxedo Worksheet at the end of this chapter.) Prints and paisleys as accents in ties and cummerbunds are appearing more frequently these days. Of course, the white tie is still considered very formal and is a most appropriate look for a formal

wedding after six o'clock in the evening. Many times, for a hint of color to coordinate with your bridesmaids, the groom may choose to have colored handkerchiefs in the men's breast pockets. The groom may chose the traditional cutaway coat with gray-striped trousers and an ascot.

If your wedding leans more toward semiformal or informal, a nice dark suit and a white or pastel shirt is always a good choice. Make sure that the men have formal shoes. You don't want the men, dressed to the hilt in a wonderful tuxedo, to arrive wearing cowboy boots or tennis shoes. They need to have a pair of black or gray (depending on the color of tuxedo) leather or patent leather dress shoes. Also, white socks just don't complement the ensemble for someone wearing a dark suit or tuxedo. Make sure that the groomsmen have black socks to go with their formal shoes.

Bet You Didn't Know... One ancient tradition was to dress the bridesmaids and groomsmen like the bride and groom so that the evil demons would be confused should they try to put a curse on the couple.

The men should order their formal wear about two to three months before the wedding. Look in the Yellow Pages under "wedding services and supplies" or "formal wear" for listings of those retailers that offer tuxedos (formal wear) for rent. You can also purchase tuxedos, but they are expensive; unless you plan to use one extensively, it is cheaper to rent a tuxedo when you need it.

Many stores offer some kind of special or discount on tuxedo rentals. "Rent six tuxedos, get the groom's free," or maybe, "Rent your tuxedos from us and you receive your limousine rental free." Always ask about specials.

Select the style and brand of tuxedo that will complement the wedding theme, the time of day, and what the bridesmaids are wearing. If the bridesmaids are in very casual street length dresses, you wouldn't want the groomsmen dressed in a formal black tie and tails. The salespeople at the tux shop should be able to help you determine just what style you need and what will go well with the wedding theme.

Your rented tuxedo is a "package deal." In other words, you will receive the jacket, trousers, choice of shirt, tie, and vest or cummerbund for one price. You can incorporate some color with the outfit by choosing ties and vests or cummerbunds in colors that either match the color scheme or coordinate with it. Shoes may be rented also, but that is usually an extra charge. Sometimes, colored handkerchiefs are included to add color to the outfit (they go in the breast pocket, not your back pocket).

Alterations are usually kept to a minimum. Jacket sleeve length and pant length are always altered, but unless you have a specific concern, shops try not to get bogged down with alterations.

If you have out-of-town men in your wedding party, then the task is relatively simple to get them fitted. When you go to the shop to select your formal wear, give the names of the men who need to be fitted to the shop. They will provide postcards with the brand name and style number of the tuxedo included. Send those postcards to your out-of-town men and have them take the cards to their local tux shops. There, they will be measured and can try on the same brand jacket to check for fitting. That shop will also

It's a good idea to carry collar extenders in your emergency kit in case the shirt is too tight around the neck. This little contraption can add an inch or so to make your life and breathing a little easier.

take other measurements to ensure a correct fitting. Then, have your men return the cards to the local tux shops. Now, their tuxedo orders can be placed. When the men arrive in town for the wedding, have them go to the tux shop and try on their tuxedo completely (or at least the jacket and trousers). Last minute alterations can be made if something doesn't fit properly.

Arriving in Style

The mode of transportation you plan to use for your wedding day is one little detail that is easy to overlook. With a little planning, however, this item can add a unique flair to your special day. (The Special Transportation Worksheet at the end of this chapter can help you in this area.)

Many couples use special transportation to take them from the ceremony to the reception. Other couples use special forms of transportation from the home to the ceremony, and some couples use special types of transportation to take them from the reception to their wedding night destination. It's a personal choice; be creative, but stay within your budget.

That Luxurious Limousine

Couples enjoy using special transportation to take them from the ceremony site to the reception. The most common form of transportation is, you guessed it, the limousine. Elegant and classy, the limousine can make you feel like a true king and queen. When choosing a limo company, be sure to ask for references from family and friends. Most companies offer either hourly prices or package prices. Ask what services are included. Will the driver be uniformed? Nothing looks tackier than a beautiful bride and handsome groom exiting the church to an awaiting white limo with the driver decked out in jeans, a dirty tee shirt, and tennis shoes. Ugh! I have seen it happen, so be sure to ask the right questions so it doesn't happen to you.

In most states, the limo company employees cannot furnish champagne or wine unless they have a liquor license. If you purchase the liquor, however, they usually are willing to serve it. With any luck, they will even use some lovely crystal stemmed glasses.

A limousine ready to transport the couple. Photo by Wyant Photography, Inc.

Make sure you get all the specifics in writing: pick-up time, where you are to be delivered, and any extra services you may require. I recall one nightmare story that drives home the importance of using reputable limousine companies recommended by friends and family who have had positive experiences. This particular driver turned to the bride as I closed the car door and said, "Hey, babe, where are we headed?" Now mind you, I had just reminded him where he was to take the couple, but I guess it was just too much for him to comprehend. Anyway, the bride was upset but told the driver where the reception was being held. The driver didn't have a clue how to get to the reception, got lost, had to stop for gas, and was an hour late in getting the couple to the reception. To top it all off, he had the audacity to walk into the reception and approach the mother of the bride and demand more money because he had gone into overtime! Do you think I've ever hired this bozo again? I don't think so. Make sure you get those referrals from people you trust. Don't let something like this happen to you.

If you need to have your luggage taken from the ceremony site and transferred to a vehicle at the reception, get those specifics in writing now so that you don't have to worry about that on the wedding day. You want to get everything in order before the big day.

It Was Good Enough for Cinderella

If a limousine isn't in your plans, there are other options you can consider. Many cities have horse-drawn carriages that can transport you on your big day. I worked with one bride who was having an outdoor wedding and whose dream was to arrive at the ceremony site in a horse-drawn carriage just as the processional was beginning to play. Guests turned their heads to witness the bride arrive in a white carriage pulled by two white horses. It was lovely and she was extremely pleased. That is also the only time in my business career that I've had to cue a horse.

When looking for information on horse-drawn carriages, look under "wedding services" or "carriages" (in larger cities) in your Yellow Pages. Make sure they carry liability insurance. This is very important. Expect to pay some big bucks for this luxury. The reason it is costly goes back to the liability insurance. Ask about uniformed drivers. Ask what happens to your deposit if Mother Nature doesn't cooperate and it rains. Ask your questions now and avoid disappointment later.

Horse-drawn carriage waiting for the couple to emerge. Photo by Wyant Photography, Inc.

Other Options to Consider

Some cities boast trolley cars that you can rent for special events. They are trackless but still remind you of simpler times. You usually can rent these for a half day or full day depending on your locale. Couples sometimes use them to transport the entire wedding party from the ceremony to the reception. You can decorate these cars to coordinate with your wedding colors or theme and have a lot of fun.

Over the years, I have coordinated some larger weddings in which the couple rented buses for their wedding party. The buses not only transported the wedding party from the ceremony to the reception, but they also shuttled family members and some out-of-town guests. The buses returned to the reception site later and took the guests back to their cars. If your budget allows, you can go one step further and have the bus pick up the out-of-town guests at the hotel, deliver them to the ceremony site, take them to the reception, and finally deliver them safely back to their hotel. Wow! What a deal. No worry about getting lost in a strange city or drinking too much at the reception—just a lot of happy, well cared for guests.

One wedding I coordinated had a groom from New Jersey and a bride from Indiana who took the bus idea one step further. The wedding was held in Indiana, so the groom's family rented a Turner Coach to transport 60 of their relatives and close friends to the wedding. They had a wonderful time on the trip. Each guest paid for his or her share of the bus ride, and although it probably wasn't cheaper than driving a personal car, it was much cheaper than flying, and more relaxing and enjoyable!

Bet You Didn't Know... When Prince Charles and Princess Diana left their wedding reception for their honeymoon, the prince's brothers, Edward and Andrew, borrowed a lipstick and wrote *Just Married* on a piece of cardboard and attached it to the carriage.

Be Creative

Perhaps my trophy for the most unique mode of wedding transportation I have ever witnessed goes to a couple I worked with several years ago. They had a beautiful garden wedding following by a lovely garden reception. The home was in the country, and we were surrounded by trees, flowers, and the beauty of nature. When I asked them if they were going to leave from the reception in any special form, they assured me they had nothing in mind and would just leave in their car. When the time came, the bride's brother appeared with a small Ford tractor (yes, I said *tractor*). It had a box on the back for hauling. The couple took one look at the tractor, hopped on board, and off they rode into the sunset (or the field, or wherever their car was parked). The picture that scene created was fantastic and still remains in my mind today.

Parents of one bride surprised the couple with a helicopter ride from the reception to the airport. So be creative, and if possible, try to tie in the season, location, and interests of the couple.

Use your imagination. Make your grand exit in style, but make it in *your* style. As always, remember to ask many questions of the various vendors and get referrals.

Happy Trails to you.

Arriving in style, this couple emerges from a Rolls Royce. Photo by Wyant Photography, Inc.

The Least You Need to Know

➤ Try to allow at least six months for the ordering and receiving of your wedding gown. If you don't have that much time, you may find that it will cost you a bit more.

➤ Take only your mother or a friend or two with you to shop for you gown. Too many opinions can make your decision all the more difficult.

➤ Try to choose bridesmaids' dresses that won't break the banks of your attendants. Think about their physical attributes and coloring, as well as what they can reasonably afford.

➤ Help your groom choose formal wear that complements the style of wedding you are planning and that works well with your gown.

➤ Be creative when you are deciding on the transportation you will use for your wedding day. Use your imagination and have fun with this decision.

WEDDING GOWN AND BRIDESMAIDS' DRESSES WORKSHEET

Shops to visit: _____

_____

Referred by: _____

_____

Date of appointments: _____

_____

Contact at shop: _____

Telephone number: _____

Style of gown: _____

Color selection: _____

Budgeted amount for gown & veil: _____

Budgeted amount for accessories

Bra: _____

Slip: _____

Shoes: _____

Jewelry: _____

Deposit paid (date): _____

Payments to be made (dates): _____

Bridesmaids' dresses

Color choices: _____

Style of dresses: _____

Cost of dress: _____

Cost of alterations: _____

Number of attendants: _____

Attendants' names, phone numbers, and addresses:

1. _____

   _____

   _____

   _____

2. _____

   _____

   _____

   _____

3. _____

   _____

   _____

   _____

4. _____

   _____

   _____

   _____

(Add more paper if needed)

Next appointment: _____

   _____

Questions to ask: _____

   _____

   _____

   _____

   _____

TUXEDO WORKSHEET

Name of store: _____

Address: _____

Telephone: _____

Salesperson: _____

Price: _____

Style number: _____

Color: _____

Tie/cummerbund/vest/shirt color: _____

Accessories

    Shoes: _____

    Gloves: _____

    Hats: _____

    Other: _____

Deposit made: _____

SPECIAL TRANSPORTATION WORKSHEET

Mode of transportation desired: _____

Contact name: _____

Telephone number: _____

Referred by: _____

Contract used: _____

Contract/deposit returned (date): _____

Hours needed (time of day): _____

Special instructions/directions sent: _____

Add-Ons (Those Neat Little Extras)

In This Chapter

➤ Adding that personal touch to your wedding

➤ Sending a wedding newsletter to friends

➤ Designing a wedding program

➤ Choosing a favor for your guests

➤ Selecting gifts for your attendants

➤ Using disposable cameras at the reception

By now you've covered the biggies, and the dollars are starting to add up. However, you still want your wedding to have a uniqueness, but how can you make your wedding unique when you're on a tight budget? If you have no budget (yes, Virginia, there really are brides without a budget), what kind of ideas can you incorporate to give your wedding some dazzle?

There are several items that many couples want to include as part of the festivities. The more money you have budgeted for these items—called *add-ons*—the more of them you can add to your wedding. If you do a little research now, you'll discover that you can include some of these add-ons in your wedding budget.

Start Spreadin' the News

One new trend sweeping the country is a wedding newsletter the couple sends to members of the wedding party, family, and close friends. Especially for couples who have family scattered around the country, this friendly, chatty newsletter is an ideal way to introduce people to each other before they meet at the rehearsal. Make these newsletters relaxed, informative, and fun. "My maid of honor is Debbie Jones, my best friend since we were five-year-olds. John's best man is Tim Smith, a fraternity brother from the University of Wisconsin."

Introduce all the members of the wedding party and tell a little about each. Talk about your family members. Go over the preliminary wedding plans (depending on how far in advance or how many times you are planning to send these newsletters). Talk about hotel accommodations, the rehearsal place and time, the rehearsal dinner, other activities planned for the weekend, airport shuttle information, and other information that can make your wedding party and out-of-town family members feel more comfortable. It will make them all feel a part of this great time.

Simple computer printing and your old friend the photocopy machine are the cheapest way to produce these newsletters. You can spend more and have them printed, but that is certainly not a necessary expense.

Here's a sample opening paragraph from a newsletter:

We've started the countdown… we now have less than four weeks until Jim and I take that big walk down the aisle. We thought we'd give you an update on what's happening that weekend and introduce you to the other members of our wedding party.

And so on. As I said, make it chatty, newsy, and informal. There will be plenty of formality in your other wedding activities. Use this newsletter to help the "cast" know where they need to be and at what time, and to help those in your wedding party who don't know each other begin to feel a part of the group.

Just Follow Along, Please

Wedding programs are a nice addition to your wedding service. They can be simple or elaborate. The whole purpose of a wedding program is to enable the guests to participate in the ceremony by displaying the

Photograph courtesy of Wyant Photography, Inc.

Many churches and other ceremony facilities are no longer allowing birdseed or confetti to be thrown, so couples are trying to be more creative in ways to make their grand exit special. Some couples are giving their guests balloons to release as they exit the ceremony.

"Ask [your caterer] about the little extras, such as immaculate service staff with white-glove presentation, petite strawberries in the guests' champagne glasses, butler-style hors d'oeuvres, carving stations with chefs in white jackets, and flaming Crêpes Suzettes prepared at each guest table."

Jacquelynne T. O'Rourke, Edelweiss Caterers

Gold accents add simple elegance to this stacked wedding cake.

Simple table setting in which elegance is enhanced by use of all white linens and spring flowers for the centerpiece.

"Be very honest with the banquet manager regarding your budget. A good banquet manager is capable of saving you money if you are truthful with him."

Jerry Green, The New Savory

A simple food display with ice sculptures.

A swan ice sculpture.

Often, the way your food is displayed can mean the difference between a good reception and a wonderful reception. Ask your caterer to decorate the serving tables with flowers and greenery to make it more appealing.

In moving between the ceremony site and a separate reception facility, you often lose three things: time, money, and guests. Finding a facility that can accommodate both events can keep costs down and make all your wedding details seem more manageable. In this photograph, the area for the ceremony is shown in the upper-left corner and the reception area is in the front.

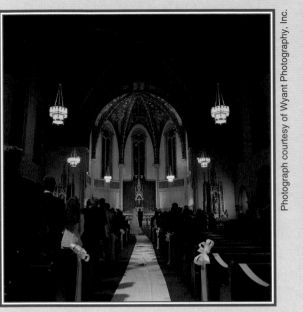

A beautiful church lends itself to a beautiful wedding.

Aisle decorations create a lovely effect.

Work with your photographer to pose some unique pictures that can help you capture the true romance and beauty of your special day.

Cakes today are limited only by your imagination and your pocketbook. A skilled baker can turn your dream cake into reality with such special touches as icing flowers accented by real roses.

Choosing elaborate wedding transportation, such as the Rolls Royce chosen by this couple, can add class to any wedding.

Horse-drawn carriage for transportation to the reception.

A trolley car transports this couple to the reception.

Traveling to the reception in a vintage car.

Treat yourselves like royalty for the day. Allow room in your wedding budget for special transportation so you can arrive in very distinctive style.

Photograph courtesy of Wyant Photography, Inc.

With a little imagination, you can tie all aspects of your wedding together to reflect a central theme. For a wedding planned around a Victorian theme, for example, you could offer a Victorian-style wedding cake similar to the one shown here.

You can add elegance and beauty to any reception facility by paying attention to the linens and centerpieces you use on the tables. An elaborate table setting might include two layers of tablecloths reaching to the floor and very large and elegant floral centerpieces.

Today, wedding cakes are being offered in so many flavors and styles that the cake you choose is limited only by your imagination. Virtually gone from today's wedding cakes are plastic flowers and a plastic bride and groom. Instead, fresh arrangements and greenery are the order of the day, as illustrated by this stunning basket-weave tiered cake that uses only fresh flowers and ribbons.

Even the traditional elements of a wedding ceremony can be treated with elegance and grace. In this photograph, the customary Jewish wedding canopy (chuppah) has been created from tulle and enhanced with fresh flowers.

"Choose your wedding colors before talking to your florist about flowers. Coordination of dress colors and flowers will be much easier if the bride provides small swatches of dress material."

Jack Sitarski, Poplar Flower Shop

Jewish wedding ceremony showing the placement of the groom's parents (to the far left of the couple).

An example of a chuppah.

Ceremony using the church's layout to its best advantage for positioning the wedding party.

A food display using greenery only and with the food trays on various levels for added dimension.

Simple cake under a balloon arch.

Having your wedding invitation affixed to the unity candle creates a lovely display and is a wonderful keepsake of your special day.

Couple being released by a "bubble blow."

"Hire a photographer who will make the day *your* day and not his or her day. The photographer is there to make your day worry-free as far as the photographs go. You should be able to trust this person and let him or her guide you through the photographic moments."

Don and Madeline Wilson, Studio 2 Photographics

Couple being released with a rose petal toss.

A release of swords at the end of a military wedding can add grace and dignity to the occasion. Leaving the ceremony under an the arch created from swords adds pomp and circumstance to your grand exit.

order of the service and identifying the members of the wedding party. It's something like a playbill at the theatre. Guests do enjoy seeing who the cast members are. Sometimes, the couple will list next to the wedding party member's name "friend of the bride," "cousin of the groom," or whatever is appropriate. Other couples have listed the attendant's hometown. It's interesting sometimes to see just how far your wedding party has come to be part of this day.

Use Your Imagination

Some couples write notes of thanks or appreciation to their parents and guests in the program. Other couples list their new address and telephone number on the program back. Some programs even explain a part of the service that is out of the ordinary. One couple married on the bride's parents' 30th wedding anniversary in the same church. The groom's parents had, during that same year, celebrated their 35th wedding anniversary. In the program, the couple wrote a short letter to their parents congratulating them and thanking them for giving them (the couple) good role models for a long and happy marriage. Mentioning that point in the program made the guests more aware of that fact.

A sample wedding program cover. Photo by Wyant Photography, Inc.

Another couple who had been to "hundreds" of weddings, as they told me, decided to put some wedding trivia in their programs. This way, they reasoned, their guests would have something to do besides

171

listen to music or make grocery lists. It was a clever program and the trivia actually tied in some of the customs they were carrying out in their service. Make these programs as unique as the two of you.

Keep It Simple... or Go to Extremes!

Many brides try to coordinate their programs with their invitations. The trick here is to order blank stock to match your invitation paper when you order your invitations. Then take this paper to a local printer to have your program produced. It is much cheaper than having the invitation company produce your program, and you have more control over the outcome.

Programs can be as simple as a single sheet of colored paper printed on a computer and duplicated. Roll it up and tie it with a coordinating ribbon and you have a simple, inexpensive program. For an elaborate look, have your programs printed on several sheets of paper covered with a heavy outer paper, emboss or engrave monograms on the front, and then tie it with coordinating ribbons.

One of the most elaborate wedding programs is a missal. It is used in a Catholic service and includes, verbatim, everything the priest says. This type of program is especially nice when the majority of your guests are not of your faith. At a Greek Orthodox wedding I coordinated last fall, the couple was very considerate of the fact that many of their guests were not Greek Orthodox. They included in the program explanations of each of the three parts of the worship service. This gave all the guests insight into the meaning of the service and made it much more enjoyable. This type of program is more costly simply because of its length, but you can still produce it economically.

Favoring Your Friends

Favors, at least in the Midwest, are making a big comeback. A favor is a little gift you give your guests as a "thank you" for attending your wedding. You can select expensive and elaborate favors or very inexpensive and simple favors. The idea is not to dazzle your guests with great favors but to make them feel special and appreciated.

Some of the more expensive favors may include a silver picture frame with the guest's name framed inside (this can double as a place card). The guest can take this frame home and replace the name with a small picture. You can also give other types of picture frames, such as those covered in fabric, or porcelain or wooden frames. These are beautiful additions to your reception table.

Another rather elegant favor idea one bride used was a glass candlestick with a small votive candle. The glass was etched with pink roses and the stem tied with a matching pink bow. She had purchased enough for each female guest to take one home, and it was a breathtaking sight as guests entered the reception hall with all those individual candles glowing. I still remember all the "ahhs." It was beautiful!

Candy is another elegant, although not as costly, favor idea. Many candy makers use a mold that says *Thank you for sharing our joy,* and finish by wrapping the chocolate bar in clear paper and tying it with a coordinating ribbon. Place these chocolates at each guest's place to add to the table decoration, or place them in a pretty basket or on a large silver tray near the exit. Guests can then each take one as they leave.

Another variation on the candy idea is to have truffles made and boxed in a pretty fashion. Use a white or ivory box, top it with your initials or monogram, and tie it with a ribbon. I've also seen some gorgeous gold boxes used for individual candy pieces; these also can enhance the table decorations. Again, you can place these at each guest's plate or leave them by the door on a large silver tray. I know of some couples who have taken this favor one step further and have tied a small printed note to the box.

Here are some other simple favor ideas:

➤ Golf tees with the wedding date or your initials imprinted.

➤ A single silk rose tied with a ribbon and placed at every female's plate.

➤ A small tulle bag containing rose petals or potpourri.

➤ A scroll printed with your favorite verse or poem and tied with a ribbon or enclosed within a gold ring.

➤ Seedlings that guests can plant and nurture to maturity to represent the growth of the marriage.

You can go wild with seasonal favors during the holidays. For Christmas weddings, I've worked with couples who have ordered ornaments printed with their names and the wedding date, and each guest takes an ornament home to hang on the Christmas tree. I also know one Christmas bride who took the time to make individual

wreaths for each guest. The wreaths were tied off with Christmas ribbon and a small gold bell.

Make sure you have enough favors to go around. Nothing would be worse than having more guests than favors and having to decide who gets one and who doesn't.

Another rather innovative idea for more established couples is to make a donation to a favorite charity and leave a nicely calligraphied card at each place setting, which lets the guest know that a donation was made in his or her honor. The card may read "A donation from Jenny and Matt has been made in your name to Habitat for Humanity."

Here are some additional tips to get you thinking about possible favor ideas:

➤ Purchase small wicker baskets (check out some of the wholesale houses) and place a small arrangement of silk flowers, assorted candies, or small decorative soaps inside.

➤ Cluster your favors to make the table centerpiece. For example, small individual pots with flowers or plants in them arranged in a circle in the center of the table make a lovely centerpiece. You may even take some tulle and drape it around the base of the circle or tie some ribbons around the pots. As guests leave, ask that they each take a pot with them.

➤ Check craft stores in February for heart-shaped items and ideas. A mug with a heart and your initials makes a nice favor. A heart-shaped magnet for the refrigerator or heart-shaped candies all make small, inexpensive favors.

➤ If your wedding has a theme, try to stick to the theme when you plan for favors. A Mexican theme wedding, for example, may have small sombreros or piñatas for favors. For a Hawaiian-themed wedding, floral leis were handed out as guests arrived at the reception. It was a fun way to say, "Glad you're here."

Smile, You're on Candid Camera!

One fun way to help capture your special day from many different angles is to provide disposable wedding cameras at every table at the reception. (You can now purchase these cameras in white boxes made to resemble lace instead of the standard Kodak yellow.) It's usually wise to include a little note of explanation with the cameras to let your guests know that they are provided for the guests.

Some brides wrap the cameras like gifts (to complement the wedding colors) and use them as part of the decorations. You can purchase as many cameras as your budget will allow. Some couples put cameras at every table while others spread them out to every other table. Make sure there are instructions as to where guests are to deposit the used cameras. Many times a large basket at the exit is sufficient.

Recently I've noticed friends and relatives pocketing the cameras and walking out the door of the reception with them. I've also heard this complaint from other bridal consultants in the Midwest. This is not the intended use of these cameras. Be sure you clearly spell out for your guests the purpose of these cameras; you may want someone to survey the reception room and collect the used cameras.

Attending to Your Attendants

The gifts you choose to give to your attendants (a nice way of saying "Thanks for putting up with my irrational behavior for the past six months") need to be custom designed for your wedding party. I'm not saying go out and have something custom designed for each and every member of your wedding party. I just mean that you should try to make the gift truly special—not just another mug or string of pearls. Do you know how many sets of pearls the average 24-year-old woman accumulates? Probably more than you or I would dare to count and certainly enough to open her own jewelry store. So when it comes time to look for gifts for your attendants, think about who they are and what they like. There is nothing carved in stone which says you must buy them all the same thing. I know that is usually easier, but with a little planning you can come up with some unique gift ideas for these special friends.

Have fun selecting these gifts. For the sports nut, how about a new racquet or a membership to a health club? For the traveler, an overnight bag and travel alarm clock are good ideas. For the new home owner, maybe wind chimes, a brass doorknocker or a stained glass sun catcher. Books are also great personal ideas.

What about a gift certificate? One bride knew her matron of honor was on a very tight budget, so for her gift, the bride gave her a gift certificate to her favorite restaurant. Do you have any collectors in your wedding party? How about a glass piece, a Hummel figurine, or maybe a Precious Moments figurine?

 **Bet You Didn't Know...** The idea of a bridal shower goes back many centuries to the Netherlands when a poor Dutch miller fell in love with a rich maid. The maid's father disapproved of the marriage and refused to provide a dowry. The miller's friends got together and "showered" the couple with items that would help them establish a household. Thus, the bridal shower was born.

Any item that you can have engraved or monogrammed is just that much more personal. Beer steins, basketballs, footballs, and Swiss Army knives are some ideas for the men. For the women, try picture frames or lingerie. (I gave all six of my bridesmaids different forms of lingerie according to their personalities—some slips, some bras, some teddies.) Of course, you can always give jewelry, especially if you want them to wear the same necklace or earrings for the wedding. I've known some brides who have given their attendants the hose and shoes they needed for the wedding; others have given them gloves to wear. One bride chose a different book for each of her bridesmaids according to her individual tastes, and then the bride wrote a personal message on the inside cover.

You don't have to spend an arm and a leg on gifts for your wedding party, but you need to offer at least a token for supporting you on this special day.

Some other wedding party gift ideas include the following:

For men

➤ Cuff links

➤ Monogrammed wallet

➤ Engraved money clip

➤ Travel kit

➤ Engraved calculator

For women

➤ Jewelry box

➤ Basket with soaps or perfumes

➤ Charm bracelet

➤ Bud vase

➤ Music box

➤ Lingerie

For children

➤ Mug with name

➤ Charm bracelet

➤ Games (checkers, chess, backgammon)

➤ Stereo headset

➤ Classic edition of *Mark Twain*

➤ T-shirt (*I was a ring bearer in Matt and Cathy's wedding*)

For either sex

➤ Anything monogrammed in crystal or pewter

➤ Silver picture frames

➤ Personalized stationery

Bridal Showers

Bridal showers are wonderful parties given in the bride's honor. Friends and relatives "shower" the bride with gifts for her new married life. Gifts can be either for personal use or for her new household. Anyone can offer to host a shower in the bride's honor, but generally speaking, the bride's mother or sisters probably should not be the hostess. Aunts, and certainly a good friend or the mother of a good friend, may host a bridal shower.

Bridal showers come in all types these days. You may find a kitchen shower appealing, or maybe a linen and lingerie shower (think about those lovely teddies and nightgowns) would be a real plus. You may opt for a couples shower so that the guys can get in on the act, too. Couples can bring items that you each can use.

When Floyd and I were married, my cousin hosted a surprise couples shower for us. Guests brought me kitchen items and staples, while they brought Floyd tools and blueberry muffin mix. Blueberry muffins are his favorite food in the world, and I think we received 35 boxes of muffin mix.

Someone may even throw a "Round the Clock" shower. Each guest is given a specific hour of the day and is told to bring a gift appropriate for that time.

Showers are entertaining and are a good way to spend some time with those you care about. Above all, remember to keep up with your thank-you notes. You do need to write each guest a personal thank-you note and send an especially nice note to the hostess.

➤ Candle holder

➤ Pen and pencil sets

➤ Bar set

➤ Crystal ice bucket

The Least You Need to Know

➤ Consider some of the little extras, such as newsletters and wedding programs, that you can add to your wedding to make it more unique and personable.

➤ Send a newsletter out to the wedding party and close family to alert them to times and dates of pre-wedding functions. Make it newsy and entertaining.

➤ Think about using a wedding program for your ceremony. It's a nice way to outline the service and who is in the cast of characters. They can be as simple or as elaborate as your budget dictates.

➤ Say "thank you" to your guests for helping make your day so special by presenting them with favors. Again, they do not have to be expensive. Something as simple as a bag of Hershey kisses at each place may be a nice touch.

➤ Providing disposable cameras at the reception is another way to add to the festivities and capture the moments on film.

➤ Try to choose gifts for your attendants that have some special or personal meaning to the person. If possible, have the gifts personalized.

PROGRAMS WORKSHEET

Type of program desired: _____

Method of producing:

❑ Self

❑ Printer

❑ Invitation company

Contact: _____

_____

_____

Telephone number: _____

Deadline for production (date): _____

Deposit paid (date): _____

Suggested wording: _____

_____

_____

_____

_____

_____

FAVORS WORKSHEET

Ideas: _____

_____

_____

_____

_____

_____

_____

_____

_____

_____

_____

Cost per person: _____

Contact: _____

Telephone number: _____

Chapter 14

Making the Most of Your Dollars

In This Chapter

➤ How to stretch your wedding dollars

➤ Ways to cut some costs from your budget

➤ Understanding contracts and agreements

Saving Your Pennies for Priorities

So far, I've suggested some questions for you to ask the vendors you are considering using. I've told you what to expect from these vendors, and you have started spending some of those precious wedding budget dollars. Before you blink and all those dollars have disappeared, it's time to look at ways that you can trim some costs from your wedding bill.

Smart wedding shopping techniques begin with not being an impulsive buyer and having patience. Time is your friend when you're in the wedding market. As you shop with the various vendors, give yourself the time you need to make sure you're getting the best product for the best price. A lot depends on the importance you place on

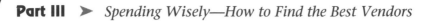

each. If that photographer is very important to you, then figure out a way to incorporate his fee into your plans. One bride I worked with found the perfect gown for her wedding. The gown was an original and very expensive. Her parents told her she had a choice: the gown or a dinner and dance reception. She chose the gown; it was a higher priority for her. It doesn't matter what your cousin Shelly did for her wedding. This is *your* wedding and you need to decide which items are most important to you.

The following sections give you some ideas of specific ways you can cut wedding expenses and stretch your wedding dollars.

Finding Ways to Cut Your Floral Bill

Check with the church to see if another wedding is scheduled on the same day as yours. If there is, ask the other bride about sharing the expense for ceremony site flowers. The florist can make arrangements in neutral shades of white or ivory and can add colored ribbon to make each bride's arrangement more coordinated with her specific colors. You could luck out and find a bride who shares your color scheme. This can save you half on the floral bill for the ceremony site. A good friend of mine found out the church was booked for another wedding the same days as hers. Karen called the other bride, they met with the florist, and they were able to split the bill in half. Each bride had truly beautiful church flowers at only half the cost.

At the ceremony, have the pew markers designed so they can double as centerpieces at the reception. I recommend this frequently to brides and they all love the idea of having wonderful pew markers and equally wonderful centerpieces. Transporting the pew markers can be a problem, but it's nothing that your florist and wedding coordinator can't handle.

Transport any flowers you use at the ceremony to the reception. Why spend all that money on flowers for guests to enjoy for only 30 minutes? Have those bouquets transported to the reception and plan to use them there. Again, your florist and wedding coordinator can take care of this detail, or you can ask a trusted friend.

If you are being married in the spring or summer, you can eliminate the cost of a large, expensive bridal bouquet by gathering wildflowers the morning of your wedding and tying them with a lovely ribbon to coordinate with your colors.

If you live in a large metropolitan area, check to see if there is a local floral design school. Many times, students at these trade schools will gladly produce your wedding flowers for the cost of materials so that they can gain the experience and a letter of recommendation.

If your reception facility needs some "plastic surgery" to cover flaws in the room (marks on walls, exposed pipes, ugly pictures that cannot be removed), use balloons instead of flowers or greenery. The balloons are cheaper, will cover more, add a festive party look, and can be assembled the morning of the wedding.

Select flowers grown locally and use only flowers in season. Instead of carrying a bouquet of roses, you can carry a single rose or a small floral arrangement on a family Bible or prayer book.

Some of the prettiest arrangements I've seen in churches have been assorted greenery mixed with candles. There were no flowers present, just an assortment of greens, palms, ferns, and plants, intertwined with votive candles. This type of arrangement should be less expensive than using all flowers.

Check with your florist about the possibility of renting centerpieces. One couple on a tight budget had 20 tables to decorate for the reception. They found a florist whose daughter had recently married, and he rented his daughter's silk arrangements to them. The arrangements were lovely, and no one was the wiser.

> Don't ever be afraid to ask if an item can be discounted or rented. What more can someone say than "no"? Many times, you will find yourself pleasantly surprised by the answer. Just because you've never heard of doing it this way doesn't mean it can't be done. Ask if the florist has suggestions on how something can be done less expensively.

Dressing for Less

If you sew or have access to a good seamstress, make your gown and veil. You can save some big bucks here. I've had brides find wonderful seamstresses who produced the gown they had always wanted for a fraction of the price they would have paid in a shop. Just be sure to examine other gowns produced by this seamstress before you secure her services.

Here are some additional ideas to help you save money on your wedding attire:

➤ Check out the bridal discount stores, but be very careful! If you can buy a dress off the rack at one of these stores, you probably will come away with a bargain. If they have to order a gown for you, be sure that you understand their terms completely. With many stores of this type, the gown that arrives in the box is what you take home—rips, tears, stains, and all. The store usually will not send it back if it is damaged. It's yours! Just be sure you know what you are agreeing to.

➤ Look for a ready-to-wear tea-length gown that requires very little alteration.

➤ Look for sales at the bridal shops. You can often find truly lovely gowns on the sale rack for one-third to one-half off the original price.

Several companies offer gown restoration services, which can make your mother's or grandmother's yellowed gown beautiful again. The Yellow Pages in larger cities can lead you to companies who offer this service.

➤ Consider wearing your mother's gown. Many times, these gowns from days gone by are actually back in style or will blend with the theme of your wedding. My sister, Kim, wanted to wear our mother's gown for her garden wedding. (Mother had also had a garden wedding.) The seamstress had to take a tuck here and there, but otherwise, it was perfect for Kim. Instead of wearing a veil as mother had, Kim wore a garden hat with fresh flowers and veiling. My dad said there was a huge lump in his throat as he walked Kim down the aisle and thought about his bride of 30 years.

➤ Consider wearing your grandmother's gown. A friend of mine used a Victorian theme for her wedding and wore her grandmother's gown. She even wore the high-buttoned shoes to match.

Even if you can't physically get into the gown, see what can be done to remake it. You may be surprised at what a good seamstress can accomplish.

➤ Don't overlook resale shops. These stores are springing up all over the place in the Midwest. Many gowns that have been worn only one time end up here. You can pick up a lovely gown for a fraction of its original cost.

➤ Order your bridesmaids' dresses from national catalogs. One bride ordered all seven of her bridesmaids' gowns from a catalog and saved half of what she would have paid in a shop.

➤ Rent your gown and your bridesmaids' dresses. This is a great idea when you do not have a lot of planning time for your wedding.

➤ Borrow shoes from a friend or buy inexpensive ballet slippers. I wore white slippers that cost only $2.95, and no one knew the difference.

➤ With tuxedos, always look for package deals, such as, "Rent five, get the groom's tux free." Try to rent the tuxedos from stores that have a local warehouse. Then if there are problems, you stand a much better chance at getting the problem resolved.

All bridal discount stores are not created equal. Try to buy off the rack, because ordering from these establishments can be risky. Before you put down a deposit, make sure you understand what you are buying and what they will do about flaws or mistakes.

Regulating Your Reception Expenses

If you are trying to watch your reception dollars, plan your reception outside a meal time. You can save quite a bit of money by having a morning or early afternoon wedding and reception.

Here are some additional ideas to help you pinch those reception pennies:

➤ Watch for sales on liquor or paper goods. Ask about discounts when buying by the case.

➤ Use paper products instead of renting crystal or china.

➤ Use carafes of wine on the table rather than bottles. Open wine bottles can be wasted, especially if the guests at a table do not drink alcohol.

➤ Rent a champagne fountain instead of using champagne bottles on the table, or have individual glasses of champagne served to guests.

➤ Instead of offering an open bar, limit your guests' choices to only wine and/or beer, or serve a champagne punch instead of other liquor.

➤ Use only house brands of liquor. Most of your guests will not notice, and the cost difference between house brands and premiums is tremendous.

➤ Check local vocational schools for students or recent graduates in food service or decorating who would be willing to produce the food or decorations for your reception in exchange for the experience and the exposure. Many times, those just starting out will offer their services.

➤ Cut down the size of your guest list. Remember the cost of the reception equals about 30% of your total budget. If you can't feed a crowd of 500 a sit-down dinner, cut that number to what you can handle. You can even do two receptions. Immediately following the service, have the cake and punch at the church social hall for the larger crowd. Then, later on that day, offer your close friends and family the dinner and dancing reception.

➤ If you are having a "do-it-yourself reception," take all the offers you can from family and friends who volunteer to bring in items. Although this is risky because someone may not follow through on a promise (yes, it does happen), it can save you many dollars.

➤ Borrow as many items as you can. Don't rent or go out and buy a brand new punch bowl, cake servers, or toasting glasses. Some friend or family member who has married recently may have these items. Ask to borrow them.

➤ If you need extra help with serving, check with a local sorority or fraternity. Many times these groups, for a donation to their philanthropy project, will send several people to help serve your reception.

Managing Your Music Dollars

Check into using local high school or college student musicians instead of paying union wages for experienced musicians. The students are often thrilled with the extra money and the added experience.

Ask a reliable friend who has some experience and understanding of what makes a good DJ to play some tapes for you at the reception. He'll need a good sound system.

Hire the musicians for a minimum amount of time. One couple wanted a string quartet to play for their service and part of their reception. They couldn't afford to have the group for more than two hours, so they used them for the ceremony and then used them an hour for the beginning of the reception. The crowd loved the soft music for the opening of the reception. When the musicians left, the couple had a friend play CDs for dancing music.

Economizing on Those Extras

As I mentioned earlier, borrow any items you can. Don't buy a ring bearer's pillow, cake servers, or toasting glasses. Unless you get these items as gifts, there is little reason to spend extra money on them.

Have the ring pillow made. It's fairly simple and will mean even more to you. One bride asked her grandmother to make some of the "extras" for her wedding. The grandmother felt so much more a part of the planning. She made the ring bearer's pillow, the bride's two garters (one to throw, one to keep), crocheted hankies for each bridesmaid to carry, and a table cover for the cake table with the couple's initials embroidered on it. She also crocheted "pew bows" for the ceremony. It meant so much to the bride that her grandmother was part of the wedding preparations, and the grandmother was so proud.

Don't have a date stamped on your wedding napkins. That way, you can use the extras in your new home after the wedding.

Paring Down Photography Costs

Hire a professional photographer to shoot the formal wedding pictures, and then have a trusted friend who has some skill with a camera take the candid shots at the reception.

Check out colleges and trade schools for an advanced photography student to shoot your wedding for a set fee and then give you the negatives for processing.

Contracts and Agreements

During the course of your wedding planning, you will most likely be required to sign several contracts or agreements with the various vendors you are hiring. If you are not accustomed to a contract and its terminology, take someone with you who is familiar with the legal mumbo-jumbo.

Never, I repeat, *never* sign anything—contract, agreement, letter of intent—if you do not *completely* understand its meaning.

Most contracts are written by an attorney who wasn't hired to make legal jargon understandable to the uninitiated. If you aren't sure what the contract means, if you need a point clarified, or if you want to be sure you understand what is required of you, ask the vendor to explain the contract in layman's terms. If you're still not sure what it means, ask to take the contract out of the store to share with your family, with your attorney, or someone else who can help you. Most vendors don't have a problem with letting you take the contract out of the store. If they do, maybe you should wonder why. The contract is for both your protection and that of the vendor's. While it can contain many legal terms, it does have a legitimate purpose during the wedding planning.

Always keep your contracts in a safe, easily accessible place. When you need to look at your contracts, you won't want to spend hours trying to find them.

The Least You Need to Know

➤ There are many ways to cut costs from your wedding budget.

➤ Never be afraid to ask for discounts or to inquire about renting items instead buying them.

➤ Always read and make sure you understand what you are signing when you put your signature on a contract or agreement. If you do not understand the document, find someone who can explain it to you before you sign on the dotted line.

Part IV

Help! My Mother's Driving Me Nuts!!

If you are already well into the wedding planning stages when you stumble on Part IV, do yourself a favor. Stop! Read Part IV from start to finish. It can make all the difference in your emotional state for the remainder of your planning. If you have turned to this part before you begin any actual planning, you are taking a good first step in having as stress-free a wedding as possible. Part IV deals with the emotional side of this whole wedding thing. It examines what goes on emotionally—and mostly subconsciously—with some of the people around you as the process unfolds. I will talk about marriage as a rite of passage and why some decisions are so emotional for those involved. Then, I'll offer some practical tips that may help smooth things over. I will also examine the wedding stress factor (what is normal, what is not), working with divorced parents and blended families, and where you can turn for help.

So now, into battle... .

And in This Corner...

This Could Happen to You!

On April 9, 1970 (yes, this really happened before many of you were born), my husband-to-be asked my father for my hand in marriage. For you younger readers, I don't mean to imply that my father took an axe and whacked off my hand for my intended groom. Floyd, my fiancé, was simply asking my Dad for permission for us to marry. Back in 1970, this ritual was still considered proper behavior.

I will never forget that day as long as I live. Daddy and Floyd were in the living room for the longest time. When they finally emerged, my dad had the biggest smile on his face. He hugged me and told me how happy he was for me. My mother was working in the den. She taught school and, as was usual on a Sunday evening, she was grading papers. When Daddy went into the den to tell her the big news, there was silence. Lots of silence. I mean absolute silence. The kind of silence that cuts right through you. This was not a good sign. Dad left the den, still grinning from ear to ear. (Hey, being one of four children, my marriage meant one less mouth to feed—just joking Daddy.) As he walked out, my mother just looked up at me from her chair and said, "Why?"

"Why what?"

"Why are you marrying him?"

"Because I love him."

"That's not a reason. It will never work. You're too different."

And she started to cry. She cried from April 9 until December 27. On December 27, my best friend Karen hosted a lovely bridal shower for me. I think it was then that mother realized that her oldest daughter was going to get married with or without her consent. She stopped crying, and Floyd and I were married on January 30, 1971.

I was totally unprepared for the confusing emotions my mother and I were about to experience. I didn't know something as wonderful as making plans for my wedding could cause so much stress in a relatively normal family. None of the wedding planning books I bought mentioned anything about the emotional side of getting married.

I remember wondering why, if this was supposed to be the happiest time in my life, I was feeling so miserable. I would ask my mother a question or ask her opinion about some detail, and she would respond by crying. She would look at me and start crying. It began to feel more like I was planning my funeral instead of my wedding.

Mother did little to help with the wedding plans. It was a combination of my being organized and her being reluctant even to acknowledge that the upcoming wedding was really going to take place. I think she believed that if she didn't help, things might not get done and there would be no wedding.

It wasn't so much that my mother objected to Floyd. Yes, we were of very different backgrounds, but this wasn't a problem for me. (As this book goes to press, we are celebrating our 24th wedding anniversary.) We had dated for more than three years, we were both college graduates, and Floyd was established in business. Mother's reluctance was actually due to the fact that she didn't want to believe she was old enough to have a daughter of marrying age. One of her "babies" was old enough to leave the nest. That is a traumatic moment in a mother's life. Believe me, I know from personal experience. I now claim a 21-year-old son.

Marriage: A Rite of Passage

Over the years, I've had brides and their mothers explode into major battles in my office. I've had brides and mothers burst into tears. I've had mothers so upset with their bride-to-be daughters that they have walked out in the middle of a consultation. I've seen the tension so thick you could cut it with a knife. This mother-daughter tension is not a pleasant experience, and it isn't one you will see much written about in wedding planners. You and your mother may experience some of this emotional tension, so it is something you both need to understand. I know that if you can understand why all of this is happening, maybe, just maybe, you will find some peace in what can be a very hectic and stressful time in your life. Gaining the knowledge and understanding of why these emotions are exploding may make your wedding planning go a little more smoothly.

Brides and their mothers may disagree on many topics during the wedding planning stages—even the choice of mate. Something I didn't understand at 23 years of age, but have come to understand through my work with brides and their families, is that a marriage is a *rite of passage*. You are passing from one part of your life into a new part; you are leaving the primary role of the daughter and taking on the new role of wife. This universal rite demonstrates to a community that one of its own is old enough, responsible enough, and mature enough to take a mate. There are three basic rites of passage: birth, marriage, and death. Of these three, marriage is the only one you choose. With this rite of passage comes a whole slew of emotions. These emotions are what get you and your mother into trouble.

The Emotional Roller Coaster: What to Expect

Let's talk about your emotions for a minute. Keep in mind that most of what goes on with your emotions during this time is subconscious. You don't know why you feel the way you do; it's just how you feel. Right

Part IV ➤ *Help! My Mother's Driving Me Nuts!!*

now you are engaged to a wonderful man. You're excited; you're scared; you're happy; you worry about how well his family will like you; you wonder if your parents will get along—all kinds of things are running through your head. Now throw in the fact that your mother insists on beef for the entrée, and you and your groom both want chicken; or she thinks pink is a terrible color for the bridesmaids' dresses, while you've had your heart set on pink for years. You have the makings for some major fireworks, but what is really going on here? Is it about beef and chicken? Is it about the ten different shades of pink you want to incorporate? I doubt it. It's about the bonds between parent and child, it's about power and control, and it's about growing up.

Mother and Me

At this point in your life, you may be torn between yearning for independence and yet not being ready to leave the nest. You want to make your own choices and decisions, but you may be reluctant to give up the security of having someone take care of you.

Your mother also may be feeling torn. She has reared you to be an independent woman, but she's not really ready to lose her little girl. She wants you to be strong, but she wants to make sure you make the right decisions (which often translates into the decisions she would make). Your mother is afraid that the marriage will break the bonds between the two of you. And that makes her sad. So while she may be perfectly willing to argue over beef or chicken, or your choice of colors, you can be fairly certain that's not really what she's upset about. She's afraid the marriage will change your relationship with her. She's afraid your new husband will replace her, and you won't need her anymore.

She's also afraid of the aging process. She's afraid of "losing" her baby. She's afraid of many things, most of which she can't explain to you, nor does she understand. She wants to be your friend and let you have your way, but in doing so, she loses some of her control. Her mothering abilities are on display now and she wants a great "report card" to show when all is said and done.

Don't be too hard on her. Had I understood what I know now about what my mother was really experiencing, I think we could have talked some and made each other feel so much better. Try not to let these subconscious emotional issues get in the way of your planning, fun, and excitement.

Daddy's Little Girl

Much is written about the pre-wedding tension between mother and daughter. What about dad? Where does he fit into the plan?

Fathers are generally very interesting creatures when it come to making plans for their daughter's big day. He's proud of the woman you've become and he wants only the very best for you. On the other hand, he may be somewhat jealous of your groom, the man who is going to take you away. Dad has been your protector; now he's giving up that role, and he does so with a little sadness. It doesn't matter how he feels about your groom, his little girl is growing up.

Dad also may feel left out of all of the planning stages. At times, it does seem like a solely mother-daughter planning frenzy. Kind of like a marathon of planning. If he seems grumpy or on edge from time to time, he may just want to be part of the process, too (other than writer of the checks), but he just doesn't know how to ask. When you ask if he would like to help, he may gruffly tell you that you and your mother are doing just fine with the planning, but he may not tell you that he feels better just that you asked.

Ask Dad how, or if, he wants to be involved in the wedding planning. If he gives the go-ahead, offer him some task that he will feel comfortable handling. Ask him to arrange for the limos for the day, or ask him to talk with the bartender about the brands of liquor you plan to serve.

Always try to keep Dad informed about the decisions you've made. Try to ask his advice and counsel. This will make him feel close to you and needed. It wouldn't hurt to give him some extra hugs along the way either.

Who's in Control Here?

One point of battle that may creep into your plans is the "who's in charge" theme. You, the bride, see this wedding as *your* wedding and rightly so, it should be. You know what you and your groom want and don't want for this day. You've taken every precaution to check out references with vendors. You've read articles, been to bridal shows, and interviewed tons of vendors. You know exactly what you want this day to include down to the last piece of wedding cake.

The only problem is that your mother may not have read the part that says you're in charge. You mother wants to be in charge, too.

Okay, so you're the bride, the princess, the star, but your mother seems to be making all the decisions. Your mother may hold the checkbook, and the checkbook may have strings attached. It's her one last chance to show her stuff. Your mother may be having a tough time giving up her dominant role. She's taken care of you for all these years and made decisions with your best interests at heart. How could you not want her to make all the arrangements for your wedding, whether you like them or not? Control, power (whatever you want to call it)—that's what this is all about. She's afraid of losing her power.

Another factor that may determine what kind of a role your mother wants to have in your wedding is how much control she had over her own wedding. So many times, the mother who had a small, simple wedding wants to re-create through her daughter the wedding she never had. She wants the control she didn't have. Your invitations will be the ones she didn't have. Your gown will be the one she wanted. Your entrée choice will be beef because her own mother, or her circumstances at the time, did not allow her to serve the food she really wanted to serve. If your mother wants to make this the big production she never had, while you have a small, simple wedding in mind, you may have some big problems. If you can't go along with your mother's desire to have the wedding of the year, then be prepared for the fireworks because I can guarantee you that they'll be there.

If this sounds like what you're going through, or what you think may happen, try talking to your mother. Sit down with her in a quiet setting; talk calmly and rationally about the wedding plans *you and your groom* have been planning. In your most adult, mature voice, let her know (very delicately) that this is your wedding, and while you want her help, it needs to be for items you and your groom want included. There are more practical tips later in this chapter.

Tension Between Parents

Something else that I have come to recognize (often on sight) is tension caused by two sets of parents vying for the couple's allegiance. You are no longer dealing with just your parents. All of a sudden, you've got another set of parents to worry about. Your groom wants his parents' names on the invitation because they are paying for the liquor at the reception. Your mother says no way, that tradition dictates that only the bride's parents' names appear on the invitation.

Well, dear reader, your parents are battling out (subconsciously) their fear of losing your loyalty. How many times have you heard married friends say, "Oh, our parents are driving us nuts. They both want us to spend Christmas with them. How can we choose?" Well, you have to make a stand, and the sooner the better. It's nothing more than a power struggle over you, the new couple on the block. Your parents are arguing over who will have more control over you after the wedding. They want to make sure you still have allegiance to them. You and your groom need to have a heart-to-heart early on and decide what limits you will set. Your primary allegiance needs to be to each other.

Just remember that your parents aren't creating all this turmoil intentionally. Often, they do not understand why they behave like they do. Once you understand what is going on, you can learn to work around it or work with it. How I wish someone would have told me some of this back in 1970. It certainly would have made my life a lot easier just understanding what my mother was experiencing. I know if we could have talked openly about the emotions we were both experiencing and the fears we shared, she and I would have had an easier time with my whole wedding process.

It is best to decide very early on what limits you will set as a couple regarding the expectations of your respective parents. Floyd and I agreed before we were married that I would handle concerns/ problems with my parents and he would deal with his. So far (24 years), it has worked out very nicely.

Practical Tips

You and your mother are driving each other nuts, and the closer your wedding day gets, the thicker the tension. Hey, I said I would tell you why it is probably happening. I didn't say you'd stop arguing. Okay, now what? Well, let's talk about it. Here are some practical ideas that may help.

➤ Work on your attitude. Attitude makes all the difference in the world. Don't think of this wedding as solely you and your groom's. Think of it more as a family affair. It's still your wedding, don't get me wrong, but if you can focus your attention away from yourself, you may be more open to others' suggestions and be willing to compromise.

➤ Remember, above all else, it is the *marriage*, not the wedding, that is really important. Which gowns are worn, flowers are carried, and entrées are eaten doesn't matter in the end. What matters is

197

Part IV ➤ *Help! My Mother's Driving Me Nuts!!*

the marriage between two people who care, trust, love, and like each other enough to spend the rest of their earthly lives together. That's commitment folks, with a capital C.

➤ Put all the cards on the table. Know what you're dealing with and whom. As a united front, you and your groom should approach your family with your wedding desires. See what they are willing to contribute and take it from there. At least you'll know where you stand. Trying to second guess your parents is not only time-consuming but also not at all practical. Many couples would rather know what amount of money they have to work with than to guess at what they "think" they may be working with. You need to know what's what. The same philosophy applies to the marriage in general. If your parents are opposed to the marriage, listen to their views and explain your position. In my situation, my mother made it quite clear that she did not approve of the wedding. I listened to her views, explained my feelings, and kept moving forward. I knew almost from day one the resistance I was up against.

➤ Decide which items about the wedding you must have control over and which items you could turn over to your mother. Don't let her feel left out. That only spells trouble and makes her feel even more insecure. You want to prevent your mother from feeling insecure, if possible. Insecurity sometimes leads to irrational behavior, and you sure don't need that now. The same advice goes for the mother of the groom. One of the fastest ways to make an enemy of your future mother-in-law is to keep her guessing about the wedding plans. Unless she is helping financially, she doesn't have a real decision-making role, but asking her opinion, her advice, and which colors she likes best will only help make your relationship stronger and make her feel more a part of the process. Keep her informed and ask for advice.

Make time for your physical needs; eat right, exercise, and get enough sleep. You can't possibly keep up with the physical drain of wedding planning, plus all the raging emotions, if you are exhausted.

➤ If you and your mother have a huge argument and you hang up the phone or slam the door on her, take a deep breath, count to 100, and call back or walk back in the room. It may be very hard to do, but it will help you in the long haul. Explain that it's the wedding stress that has you bummed out and not her. Try to start fresh. Forgive and forget. In ten years, no one will remember.

198

➤ Send her a card or flowers and tell her you love her. Mothers love that mushy stuff. And please, make it sincere. So many times, mothers just act the way they do because they are mothers. (It's in our contracts we sign when our babies are born, really it is.) If she feels appreciated and loved, and still knows you care about her, that will go a long way towards mending fences.

➤ Try to get enough rest and exercise, and eat properly during the wedding planning. Stress depletes the body's reserves. If you aren't physically able to handle all the ups and downs, you will be more stressed.

Be patient with each other. It's normally a stressful time, just given the nature of all that goes on. Don't let a relatively small item ruin the fun and excitement of planning for one of the most important days of your life. If you argue, take a deep breath and count to ten or 100, or even to 1,000 if necessary, and start over.

➤ Above all, try to stay calm and be patient. Keep the lines of communication open. Always be willing to listen. Good luck.

The Least You Need to Know

➤ Just understanding that arguments naturally happen during this planning process (and that those arguments are normal) may make this time easier to get through.

➤ Try to take into consideration the emotions your parents are experiencing. They don't understand, at least consciously, why they are acting as they are.

➤ Marriage is one of the basic "rites of passage." You are leaving a familiar role and assuming a new role, and it's normal to experience uncertainty and tension on this journey.

➤ If you get into an argument with your mother, take a deep breath, count to ten, and try to start over.

➤ Remember that in the end, it is the marriage that counts, not the wedding. They are very different. Don't get so lost in planning the details of the wedding that you forget about the marriage.

Chapter 16

I Think I'm Losing My Mind

In This Chapter

➤ Understanding normal wedding stress

➤ Finding ways to control the stress

➤ Dealing with divorced parents and blended families

➤ Getting help if you need it

Is This Normal?

"I'm stressed to the limit. I just can't take any more." During the wedding planning stages, you'll find yourself saying this more times than you can count. You'll be saying it to family members, to friends, to yourself, even to perfect strangers.

Yes, by their very nature, weddings are stress-producing events. The escalation of your emotions stemming from the added burdens and worries associated with wedding planning can cause pre-wedding stress. It is an emotional time. Much of the stress comes from all the details you have to be involved with, along with a sense of not having control over all that's going on. As the bride, you may feel pulled in many directions. You have too many advice-givers and not enough supporters. At times, you may even wish you had just chosen to elope. Relax; all these feelings and emotions are in the normal range of wedding stress.

You may be angry one minute and feel relaxed and energized the next. You may be smiling, and then all of a sudden, you burst into tears. You and your groom may fight over little things. He may feel overwhelmed with the planning and may not want to be included in it. You may feel as though you haven't a friend in the world. Just understand that all of these feelings and emotions (the ups and the downs) often accompany this time in your life.

Not every bride or every couple experiences pre-wedding stress. I have talked with brides and their families who thoroughly enjoyed the wedding-planning process. However, if you're like the majority of harried brides in the months before the wedding, you are likely to feel some added anxiety. Let's look at some of the reasons for this stress.

It Costs What?

Remember when we talked in Chapter 3 about the budget and trying to determine what is important to you and your groom and how much you have to spend? Remember when I suggested that you try to stick to that budget? Well, one very good reason for sticking to a budget is to help prevent all the negative emotions that can accompany spending more money than you have allotted.

Going over your budget is one of the biggest stress factors in wedding planning. It's like extending the limit on your credit cards; it's like running a tab for every friend and distant relative at the local pub. It just keeps adding up. You buy something here and something there. You order your flowers and when the estimate comes, it is twice your budget. Instead of getting the violinist for the prelude music, you've decided to add a string quartet. How much more can three little musicians be? What started out as a simple affair has now escalated into a complex and expensive affair. Your wedding budget may resemble the national debt, and the price tag keeps right on climbing. Then there are all the little extras: garter, guest book, welcome packages at the hotel, parking fees—the list goes on and on. Not expecting the add-on costs and not getting an accurate estimate for a service can leave you drained financially and emotionally. This is why keeping your expectations reasonable and setting realistic goals is so important.

Friends and family can get rather edgy when dealing with money matters. Your dad just doesn't understand why everything costs so much or why you are having the quartet instead of just the violinist. Add in a family crisis and you have the ingredients for a stress-filled event. One couple, who was paying for the wedding themselves, had carefully budgeted what they expected to pay for their outdoor wedding. Down to the last penny, everything was right on track. Unfortunately, their new puppy picked up the Parvo virus and spent nine days at the vet's with IVs and medication. Suddenly, the couple had an $850 expense they had not planned on. Emergencies and crises happen; that's just part of life. Take into consideration normal living expenses during your wedding planning, but also try to set aside some money for surprises.

Too Much Advice from Too Many People

When you become engaged, it's like you are suddenly wearing a sign that says, "Advice Needed Here!" You are deluged with all kinds of advice from all kinds of people. In Chapter 1, I suggested that you seek advice from those who had recently married; this is always a good idea, but be prepared for a lot more than you bargained for from other advice-givers.

All of a sudden you get to hear the details of every wedding horror story, of every wedding planning detail problem, and countless hours of "I did it this way." You will be filled to the limit with too much advice. Here's a scene that just may happen to you.

Scene: Coffee shop. You run into a friend you have not talked with for several months.

"Oh, Sally, good to see you."

"Say, Cindy, I heard you're getting married next month."

"Yes. Jim and I finally set the date."

"Well, tell me about your plans."

"Oh, we just want a simple wedding, nothing too fancy."

"Where did you get your gown?"

"At Bitsy's Bridal Boutique."

Silence. Then, "Bitsy's Bridal Boutique?"

"Yes, why?"

"Oh, nothing… it's just that they ruined Jane Owen's gown. Ruined it, I tell you. They didn't hem the dress, left a huge hole in the side seam, and then, would you believe it, the gown came back with a big pink stain on the front. They said they didn't do it, but who else did? I tell you Cindy, you're a fool to work with them."

At this point in the conversation, you are sweating; your pulse is beginning to beat rapidly. You're starting to breathe heavily; your head is spinning. And you are wondering… did I do enough homework on Bitsy's Bridal Boutique? I checked with other friends who have used them; they seemed competent. So far, they are completely on schedule. Have I made a big mistake? I don't want pink stains on my wedding gown.

Don't get bogged down with too much advice from the advice addicts. Yes, they may have your best interests at heart, but if you've done your homework, you should be fine.

Get a grip! Do a reality check! You have just experienced what I fondly refer to as listening to the "advice addict." If it happened, the advice addict knows it, they know why it happened, they know who it happened to, and they know what to do about it. Take what that person has to say with a big grain of salt. While you do need advice from many friends, especially those recently married, you eventually will reach a saturation point. You will become the proverbial sponge that can no longer soak up any more advice. Your cup will begin to overflow.

Relax! Take a deep breath. Let the advice addict's message go in one ear and out the other. Use what you can and discard the rest.

This too shall pass.

Trying to Please Everyone

Another potential point of certain stress is trying to please everyone. "Everyone" meaning the entire western hemisphere. "Everyone" meaning your family, his family, both sets of parents, grandparents, aunts, uncles, cousins, second cousins, second cousins two times removed, all your friends, and your boss (you probably *do* still have to work for a living).

We've talked about this being you and your groom's wedding. Don't lose sight of that now. You cannot possibly please everyone. There will be someone, somewhere, who doesn't agree with what you are doing, the way in which you are doing it, what you are serving, wearing, saying, singing, playing, or handing out. With weddings, it's just a given—you can never please everyone.

If you have done your homework, then just go with the flow. Worry about what you and your groom feel is necessary and what you want to include. Do take into consideration your family and their desires or wishes, but the bottom line here is that this is still *your* wedding. You will drive yourself nuts if you try to meet the demands of the entire family.

If you run into resistance with family members, be calm, be tactful, be diplomatic, and be firm. Don't alter your plans just to please someone else unless you can make the change without compromising your basic plans. One bride wanted a very simple floral design for her wedding ceremony site. Her mother insisted that the church had to be filled to the ceiling with flowers and candles. Not wanting to call in the fire department, the bride made her point with the florist, and thought the matter was completed, but the mother changed the flower order and did not tell her daughter. When the flowers were delivered and being set up in the church, the bride noticed a change in the order. She was upset, to say the least, but she calmed down enough to talk with the florist. They worked out the details. She let her mom have some additional floral pieces, but sent back the six sets of candelabra. She decided, at that point in time, she could live with some additional flowers but not all the candles. She wasn't particularly partial to the idea of the sprinkler system going off in the middle of the "Wedding March."

Divorced and Blended Families

Where do I begin on this topic? Divorce happens. It happens frequently in this country. It may have happened to your parents or your groom's parents or someone in your family. With divorce and remarriage of parents comes *blended families*—you know, "yours, mine and (sometimes) ours." If your parents are divorced and have remarried, you have a step-parent and probably some stepbrothers or stepsisters and extended aunts and uncles and grandparents. This is what we, in the wedding industry, refer to as a blended family. And the sheer numbers added to your family tree can provide plenty of additional stress. Divorced family members don't necessarily bring any additional problems to your wedding planning. If the divorce was particularly nasty, however, and the parties involved are still relatively hostile, you have the potential for some wedding fireworks. Some extra precautions may be in order.

 If your parents are divorced and not on friendly terms, never assume they will put aside their differences long enough for you to walk down the aisle. Always use caution, courtesy, and compassion when you discuss your wedding plans with them and how you see their individual roles.

I have been hired in several situations because there were less-than-amicable divorced members in the family and the hiring party wanted me to help keep the peace. I know from first-hand experience how Matt Dillon must have felt back in Dodge City. With the divorce rate so high in this country anyway, you may encounter this problem. If you are faced with divorced family members, particularly parents, you need to proceed with caution.

When Divorced Parents Are Talking

Let's assume your parents are divorced. They have been divorced for many years and are on good speaking terms with each other and you. Both have remarried and you feel comfortable with the stepparents. When you announce your engagement and sit down to discuss plans, be sure to include both sets of parents, that is, both sets of your parents and your groom's parents. If there is physical distance between all of you, make sure you keep both parties informed as to what you discuss and decide, and ask for opinions from all sides. Never put the two sides at odds with each other. Don't compare them to each other. Please don't say to your mother, "Well, Daddy's wife is going to take me to see Vera Wang about designing my gown." (FYI: Vera Wang is a big-time designer who creates some fantastic gowns with hefty price tags.) You'll only create a distance between parties that doesn't need to be there.

I know what it feels like to be a negotiator. I've been asked many times to make a stepmother who feels left out and wants to be included feel good about being involved in the wedding. It's not easy. So many times, just a matter of having more open communication between the parents is all that is needed. You must make very sure that all your communication between your divorced parents is accurate and complete. Don't expect them to assume anything.

As for finances with divorced parents, let me offer this tip. Open a checking account to be used solely for wedding expenses. Have each contributor (your mother, your father, and so on) contribute equal amounts of money to the account. As the wedding bills are paid, each party contributes additional equal amounts to cover other costs. Any money left over might be given to the couple for a nest egg. This helps greatly in alleviating the "But I paid for this" syndrome.

It is also helpful to chart out who is going to be responsible for each aspect of the wedding expenses. Take a piece of paper, and make four columns. One column is for the item, and the three others are for each set of contributors (you, your father, and your mother). Then, go through the list and decide who will be responsible for each item. You've got it in black and white. Give each parent a copy of the plan.

What I just described is the ultimate situation when dealing with divorced families. Unfortunately, there are more situations where we pray for peace among the parents just long enough to get through the day.

When Divorced Parents Aren't Talking

If your divorced parents want nothing to do with one another, accept that fact and work around it. For seating purposes, your mother should be seated in the first row and your father in the second. I have had brides request that their divorced parents be seated together in the first row. It is a truly an unselfish act for divorced parents to put aside their anger and support their child, and it is not too much for a child to ask.

Part IV ➤ *Help! My Mother's Driving Me Nuts!!*

I know of one wedding that had an unusual twist to the divorced parents' situation. The groom's parents were divorced, had been for many years, were both remarried, but were still not speaking to each other. As the mothers (all three) were being seated, the young usher seating the groom's stepmother and father seated them in the first pew where the groom's mother and stepfather were to sit. When the groom's mother realized what had happened, she demanded that they be moved. Not wanting to cause any more of a scene than there already was, a friend suggested that certainly for 30 minutes they could all sit together in the same pew for the son's sake. Reluctantly, they did. They managed to control their frustration with each other long enough to get through the service.

One wedding many years ago involved a wonderful couple who extensively planned their wedding. We'd spent time covering all the little details. The bride's parents were divorced and her mother had remarried. When we had finished the final consultation a few days before the wedding, I asked the bride if there was anything else I should know. She paused and replied, "Have I mentioned that my father hasn't spoken to us in five years?" Well, no I hadn't picked up on that. I asked her who was going to escort her down the aisle and she informed me that she had asked her brother. So that is the way we practiced at the rehearsal.

I received a late phone call after the rehearsal was over. The bride was very upset and crying. Her father had called her and demanded that he be the one to walk her down the aisle. She didn't know what to do. We talked about options and decided that she should probably let him do the honors. He showed up right before the ceremony, appropriately dressed in a tuxedo. He was very uncomfortable standing in the church lobby, obviously a fish out of water. When the processional began, his daughter came up to him and took his arm. They marched down the aisle and before she left him at the altar to go to her groom, she reached over and gave him a hug and a kiss. Here was a family who had not spoken to each other in five years. And with this one simple act, the ice had been broken. Since then, the other two sisters have married and Dad has been at each of their weddings. While I'm sure those parents are still not best buddies, they have put aside their differences long enough to give their children a happy, peaceful day.

Each wedding with divorced families has a different set of circumstances which have to be addressed. You have to be sensitive, to a point, to the wishes of your divorced parents. Be supportive and try to be understanding. If you are faced with dealing with divorced parents and family members during your wedding, try to accommodate their requests. For example, don't put your mother at the same table with your father and his twenty-two year-old new wife. Even if they get along great, the fact that your new stepmother is younger than you may wear a bit on Mom. Use some common sense when dealing with divorced parents. They are still your parents. Hang in there, keep your chin up, and move forward.

Where to Get Help

All right, I'll admit it. Sometimes, these delicate issues can cause some hairy situations. What do you do if you need some objective help and guidance? There are several options open to you.

Officiant

One of the best places to gather some strength and advice is from your minister, priest, or rabbi. These trained professionals deal with all kinds of stressful situations, including parents who hate each other and are going to be forced to spend three hours in the same room at your wedding.

For additional help in dealing with divorced family members, you may find some helpful suggestions in *Planning a Wedding with Divorced Parents*, by Cindy Moore and Tricia Windom (Crown Publishers, 1992).

If you are experiencing some difficulties with your wedding planning due to the circumstances of the divorced members of your family, make an appointment with your minister, priest, or rabbi. He should be familiar with your family situation. Explain what has happened and how you are feeling, and ask for some guidance. Sometimes, I think that by just expressing our concerns, fears, and uncertainties, we feel better, even if the situation hasn't changed. You may still be faced with the same problems as before, but just being able to vent your feelings and have your concerns heard can reduced the stress level. Sometimes, too, if you get your fears out in the open, they aren't as frightening as they first seemed.

Your family may need a counseling session. If your family will have nothing to do with counseling, then go yourself. If your groom will attend with you, that's great. At least you should feel better and be better prepared to handle the other pressures of the wedding planning.

Bridal Consultant

Many consultants feel that through our experiences, we should at least have earned our Ph.D. in Human Behavior. Given how close we are to the individual situations that arise with families, there are many times when I've felt as though I could easily hang out a shingle, "Dr. T. M. Lenderman." I have learned many things about human beings and what we can do if pushed hard enough. Sometimes, if you are having some difficulties coping with the stress of accommodating divorced family members, your bridal consultant can be a great help. She's probably seen the same situation several times before. If nothing else, explaining why you are upset or how you can rearrange the reception tables so that your two sets of parents and their new partners won't be seated next to each other will at least get the frustration off your chest. Besides, she may have an idea or two you haven't thought of to help resolve the problem.

The more experience your bridal consultant has, the better off you are as far as dealing with divorced families. For one wedding I'll never forget, the couple hired four armed guards and stationed them at the church doors and at the reception to keep out an unwanted guest. As sad as it was, the unwanted guest was the groom's mother. I don't believe I have ever been more nervous and anxious at a wedding. The mother had threatened to come to the church and blow us all away. Now, I've been in delicate situations before with divorced parents and angry parents, but this one left me sweating bullets (pun intended). She was angry with her son for inviting her ex-husband to the wedding. She didn't show up, but the fear from that day still sends cold chills down my spine.

Trusted Family or Friend

If you aren't comfortable discussing your problems relating to your divorced parents with anyone outside your family, seek out a trusted family member or good friend.

If you choose a family member, be very certain that you can trust him or her to be discreet and not share what you have confided. What you don't need is one side of the family against the other side over the fact that you shared your concerns with Aunt Marilyn, and she told cousin Helen, and Helen told your sister Jane, and so on. No, you don't need that. What you need is someone who is reliable and is also a good listener.

The same policy applies to a friend you may confide in. Make sure that your friend will keep what you share in confidence. You need to express your feelings, and you need to know that it's okay to be feeling these things.

These challenges don't need to dampen your wedding planning or your wedding day. You know your family. If the groom's parents are experiencing the difficulties in dealing with divorced players, let him handle it. Just use some common courtesy, tact, and diplomacy. Keep your sense of humor and make the best of the situation. Remember, no family is perfect. You just have to work with the cards you are dealt and make the best of it.

The Least You Need to Know

➤ Don't be surprised if you feel overwhelmed and stressed during the planning stages for your wedding. These are normal reactions to this often hectic and emotion-filled time.

➤ Keep in mind that there are lots of folks out there who are just waiting to give you some advice, whether or not you ask for it. Take what you can use and let go of the rest.

➤ When working with divorced family members, be considerate of their feelings. Never compare the parents to each other.

➤ If your parents are divorced, it's especially important to try to work out potential financial problems before they happen. You might want to open a joint checking account, have each parent contribute equally to the account, and pay all your wedding bills from that account.

➤ If the situation demands, get some outside help. Many times, you will feel better just by talking to an objective listener about what you are feeling.

Part V
Special Weddings

Every wedding is a special wedding. Ask any bride-to-be and she will tell you just how special her wedding will be. What I am referring to here, however, are weddings that take on a special flair or a unique idea, or that follow a theme.

Part V talks about all these "special weddings." I will introduce you to theme weddings, including seasonal, outdoor, military, and Victorian. You'll find out what a "weekend wedding" consists of and how to plan one. I will tell you what a "destination wedding" is and offer some ideas for where you may want to hold one. I will also get down to the basics of the more traditional religious services.

What's in a Theme?

Weddings with themes are big these days. Brides and grooms want to create a unique atmosphere for their big day and are choosing themes around which they can build this atmosphere. Couples often select a wedding theme based on a particular season or date.

Seasonal Weddings

A seasonal wedding is one that takes place near a certain holiday or during a certain season of the year. Examples of holidays around which you may choose to hold your wedding include Christmas, New Year's Day, Valentine's Day, Halloween, and the Fourth of July. Each seasonal wedding can have as much or as little themed parts as you want. Have fun thinking up new ways to celebrate the season and your wedding.

Weddings around Christmas or on New Year's Day are popular and enjoyable. I've been involved with weddings for both these occasions and have found them to be delightful.

Christmas Weddings

Christmas weddings, in particular, can be wonderfully romantic. I don't know if it's the season, the snow (at least here in the Midwest), the decorations, or the soft glow of all the candles. The season itself just seems filled with more love, hope, and peace than other seasons, and those sentiments tend to shine through weddings held during this season. Most facilities and churches decorate for the holiday season, which can add a special and lovely touch to your wedding festivities.

If your hold your wedding in a Catholic church, be sure to check on exactly when the church will be decorated for the season. Some Catholic churches are decorated late. Even if your wedding is on December 20, don't assume that the church will already be decorated. A Catholic church cannot be decorated before the last Sunday in Advent. When in doubt, ask the priest.

Usually, the church is filled with wonderful Christmas decor, which can mean less work for you and a break for your budget. Candles are especially nice during the holidays, adding to the warmth and glow of the season. Lots of red ribbon and Christmas greens with pine cones are a wonderful natural touch. Poinsettias, the flower of Christmas, usually abound. In Chapter 4, I told you about the beautiful Christmas wedding in which the church had 500 white poinsettias. If you are thinking of being married at Christmas, you may want to "shop" for a decorated facility.

Here are some additional touches you may consider for a Christmas wedding:

➤ Consider having your musicians play Christmas carols as prelude music, or having a children's choir caroling among your guests either down the aisles before the service at church or between the tables at the reception. Have Christmas song sheets printed on parchment paper and tied with a red velvet ribbon and left at each place.

➤ Give guests a program tied with a Christmas plaid ribbon. Leave a small wreath tied with Christmas ribbon at each place setting. Have ornaments printed with your names and wedding date and hang on a large Christmas tree at the reception. As your guests leave the reception, they can take an ornament to hang on their own trees.

➤ Dress your bridesmaids in traditional black velvet tops and Christmas plaid skirts. Bouquets could contain silver bells or other ornaments among the flowers.

➤ Use touches of gold with red accents in the bouquets or centerpieces. Use different sized "presents" tied up with festive ribbons and stacked in the middle of the table for centerpieces. Small pine trees individually decorated with tiny Christmas ornaments could adorn each table at the reception.

➤ Drape white lights and garland around posts or in front of the cake or head table to give off a warm glow.

➤ Carry a white muff instead of a bouquet; pin silk poinsettias onto the muff for color. Serve hot mulled cider as guests arrive at the reception and add Christmas cookies to the dessert table.

New Year's Eve or New Year's Day Weddings

You can create a special atmosphere planning a New Year's wedding, whether on New Year's Eve or New Year's Day.

For the New Year's Eve wedding, the obvious is to have noise makers and confetti for your guests. Here are some additional ideas for New Year's weddings:

➤ In the center of the dance floor, have a huge sack of balloons tied up, ready to release at the stroke of midnight.

➤ Have guests make New Year's resolutions at their tables, seal them in envelopes, and leave them in a basket by the door. You will mail those out later in January to your guests as a reminder of the resolution and of your wedding.

➤ Consider providing a big-screen television or several smaller televisions spaced around the reception room for the football buffs, or consider providing a separate room with a television so that die-hard fans can get a glimpse of the games. This idea works best if your reception is small and informal. While probably not high on your list of things to offer for your wedding reception, this does allow for mingling and some fun for your guests.

Valentine's Day Weddings

Valentine's Day is a romantic holiday; add a wedding to the day and you have the setting for some special happenings. Here are some ideas you may consider for a Valentine's Day wedding:

➤ Consider a gown in a pale shade of pink, or wear a traditional white gown and dress your bridesmaids in varying shades of pink or the traditional Valentine's Day red velvet.

➤ Use heart-shaped everything at the wedding and reception. You can rent a heart-shaped candelabrum from the florist, and you can probably find unity candles with hearts on them and even a guest book in the shape of a heart. Have two intertwined hearts printed on the front of your programs. Use heart shaped chocolate mints at the reception. You can buy heart-shaped napkins; really, you can.

➤ Go with a red, pink, and white color scheme. Rich red tablecloths, touches of pink in the flowers, and white linen napkins can give a striking appearance to your reception. Add white votive candles and red or pink confetti sprinkled on the tables, and you have pure romance.

➤ Have place cards or table numbers written on heart-shaped cards. Obviously, don't forget the heart-shaped wedding cake. Top it off with a hand blown glass figurine of two hearts. Gifts for your bridesmaids may include heart-shaped jewelry either to wear at the wedding or for their personal enjoyment.

➤ Have your florist send a balloon bouquet, heart shaped, of course, to your groom on the morning of your wedding. Write a love poem and attach it with a pretty ribbon. What a romantic way to start the day!

Fourth of July Weddings

Talk about fireworks! As the ceremony ends and the officiant pronounces you husband and wife, what is more appropriate than to have a fireworks display go off overhead? (Try not to catch the facility on fire.) Here are some more Fourth of July theme ideas:

➤ Since it's July, why not plan for an outdoor reception with red, white, and blue tablecloths?

➤ Lead off the processional with a 1776 traditional drum and fife core. Consider using the "1812 Overture" for the Recessional. How majestic!

➤ Have your gown and those of your wedding party made in an 18th century style.

➤ Top off the cake with sparklers, and give children some sparklers to enjoy (with adult supervision).

➤ Right before you and your groom exit, gather the entire reception out on the lawn and have a fireworks display to bring your wonderful day to a dramatic end.

Halloween Weddings

I know it may sound a bit weird, but a Halloween wedding can be a real treat. One of the more outstanding weddings I have been involved with recently took place on Halloween night. The bridesmaids were dressed in black sequined dresses, complete with sequined shoes. The bride chose a white sequined gown with detachable train. It was elegant! She used lots of gold accents throughout the decorations at the church and at the reception.

We carried out the Halloween theme more fully at the reception site. When the bridal party was announced, each female attendant carried a hand-held mask (you know, the kind you see may see at a southern ball). The masks were lovely. Some were beaded, some were covered in a moire ribbon fabric. Some were sequined. The men in the wedding party each wore a half face mask. As each couple was introduced, they entered the ballroom, bowed and curtsied to the audience, and removed their masks. The bride and groom each had very elaborately designed masks. It was fun and certainly a unique idea.

Other Halloween weddings have held more to the tradition of Halloween and have asked guests to come in costume. Some of the traditional functions taken from Halloween have been included, such as candy apples as part of the food, black and orange color scheme, fall leaves, baskets of nuts and berries, corn stalks and pumpkins nestled together, and so on. For favors, have Halloween treat bags prepared and left at each place setting for your guests with a note from you and your groom.

Go with the Flow of the Season

Whatever your ideas for a seasonal wedding, don't try to go against the grain. If you choose to marry in December, for example, and you know the facilities will be decorated for Christmas, it makes no sense to take down all the decorations and put up something else.

One couple, planning for their December wedding, rented a church that was fully (and most beautifully) decorated for the holiday season. Every pew had a gorgeous red pew bow. Garland had been hung and a huge Christmas tree was aglow with white lights. The bride had chosen peach and blue for her colors, and she removed only the center aisle red pew markers and left all the other Christmas decorations in place. Those peach dresses in December looked a little out of place with all the Christmas decorations. Just use some common sense.

Outdoor and Garden Weddings

Outdoor and garden weddings are probably the most difficult to plan and the most risky to carry out. For some reason, people seem to feel that if they opt for an outdoor wedding in Grandma's lovely garden, it somehow that will be easier and cheaper than renting a facility and reception hall. Nothing could be further from the truth.

 Choosing an outdoor wedding does not mean it will necessarily be cheaper or less elaborate than an indoor wedding. A great deal depends on your geographic location. If you live in a climate such as California, where the weather is not a major risk factor, then an outdoor wedding is an easier task.

The only place in this country where it is not too risky to plan an outdoor wedding is California, where the weather—aside from the occasional earthquake or mud slide—usually cooperates.

Weather. Ah, Mother Nature. "It's not nice to fool Mother Nature." Well, trust me, you can't. I know; I've tried. She will do what she will do and there is nothing you can do about it. If bad weather crashes your outdoor wedding, you may be in for some big trouble.

The first thing to consider when scheduling an outdoor wedding is to have a back-up plan. Ask yourself where the events will take place should the weather not cooperate. This is an important agenda item. Never assume that it wouldn't dare rain on your parade.

Mother Nature can sometimes be downright mean. One of my most outstanding wedding memories is a lovely outdoor wedding that was held in a nature preserve. The couple owned property adjoining the preserve and more than anything they wanted to be married by the lake. We decided to have tents put up as our back-up plan. The tents arrived on Friday morning. The rain started Friday night. It rained so much that it washed out half the road leading to the property. The wedding was scheduled for 7:00 on Sunday evening. We had water everywhere; I mean everywhere. I don't think that even Noah himself encountered more water. The tents had "bowed" at the top from too much water. Two of the uprights came completely out of the ground. We had standing water in some places. You could literally float an air mattress inside the tent. It was a mess!

Bet You Didn't Know... Superstition says that if it does rain on your wedding day, it is a sign of good fortune.

When the wedding day arrived, it sprinkled and the clouds were dark and ominous, but at least it didn't rain. Right before the service, the minister came up to me and with a look of panic on his face and asked, "Teddy, what should I do if it starts raining during the ceremony?" I looked him right in the eye and said, "If they're little drops, read fast. If they're big drops, read faster." At that point, there is nothing else you can do.

Rule Number 1 for outdoor weddings: Always have a back-up plan for all the events of the day, including the ceremony.

Another hard fact of life with outdoor weddings is that you have to bring everything you will need to the outdoors; you need to be completely self-sufficient. For example, your caterer doesn't want to find out that she can't use the water in the well for cooking because it hasn't been tested. Depending on the size of your crowd, you may have to rent port-a-potties, lighting, tables, linens to go on the tables, markers to guide the guests to where you need them to go, a guest book stand, chairs, a valet parking staff (or at least help with traffic control), plus the normal wedding items: food, drink, and music.

You also want to make sure that you have the bug population under control in the area. Have a professional outfit come to the site several weeks before the event to determine what you need to have controlled. Always let the professionals deal with insecticides. Most professionals will spray early in the week and then again later, closer to the exact date. Just because you don't see bugs when you're out in the woods doesn't mean they don't see you. It's a pretty scary sight to see your lovely white wedding cake covered with a black trail of ants marching up the side.

Not only is it possible that you could have rain or cold to contend with, you may also run into excessive heat at an outdoor wedding. One June wedding I coordinated drove home the problems that heat can cause. June weather is normally fairly nice and mild in Indiana, but for this wedding, the thermometer kept right on climbing. After it hit 103 degrees, I stopped looking. The wedding reception was held in tents. Do you know how hot tents can get with temperatures in the 100s? The musicians were sweating profusely. I was sweating profusely. The guests were dying on the vine. They couldn't dance because they were afraid of heatstroke. Some guests actually had "water" in their shoes. That's hot, folks, any way you look at it. And it was very uncomfortable for everyone.

Okay, so you still want to have an outdoor wedding. Pay close attention to the physical site. Look for uneven places on the ground. Where will the wedding party enter from? Wearing high heels on soft ground is not pleasant and may even ruin your shoes.

The physical placement of your ceremony is extremely important. It helps if you can see the site at the time of day you plan for your wedding. For example, you and your groom do not want to be facing the west at 4 o'clock on a September afternoon. You will be blinded by the sun. Likewise, you don't want your guests facing into the sun for the same reason. So check lighting, sunshine, and sun position so you know what you're up against.

My sister opted for an outdoor wedding and was married in our grandmother's garden. We had put the chairs out that morning. It was a beautiful, sunny June day. The ceremony was scheduled for 2:00 in the afternoon. As the guests were escorted to their chairs, you could tell immediately which chairs had picked up the heat of the day. One quick sit and the guests popped up. Those chairs were hot! Be sure to pay attention to all the little details.

Since you'll have to make up your "aisle" at your outdoor wedding, try to fashion something that fits with your theme. At a July outdoor wedding held several years ago in a city park, the bride and her father arrived in a horse-drawn carriage as the processional began. She had made an aisle of clusters of balloons to coordinate with her colors, anchored by rocks covered with wrapping paper. The balloons gently blew in the breeze and as the string quartet broke into "Trumpet Voluntary," the bride stepped out of her carriage and marched radiantly down the aisle to meet her groom. It was a lovely entrance.

As I mentioned earlier, depending on your property and the size of your guest list, parking can be a major problem. Wherever you schedule the outdoor wedding, make doubly sure you have adequate parking facilities and attendants. What you don't want or need is someone parking sideways and blocking another car, either the next door neighbor's or a guest's. You're in big trouble should that person turn out to be your neighbor. Valet parking is a great idea, if the logistics can be worked out.

Checking Your Car at the Door

Valet parking is the type of parking you see at many larger restaurants and hotels or country clubs. You pull up to the front door, an attendant greets you, gives you a claim check, and lets you out. He then takes your car, parks it, locks it and returns the keys to the head valet. When you are ready to leave, you present the claim check to the valet who gets your car and brings it back to the front door. Wonderful service, and if you have a tight area to put lots of cars, it is a good idea to get help with the parking.

Another solution is to run a shuttle from a local parking lot (for example, a school or church) to the site. (Make sure that you check with local authorities in case you need a special permit.) Then, hire a company to operate a van or bus.

If you are planning an outdoor wedding, make sure the neighbors know what is taking place. You want to keep on good terms with them.

You should decide on one focal point for the service so your guests can focus their attention toward one area. You should try for something natural: a grouping of trees, a fountain, or the head of a garden. Since you are outside, you don't want to compete with Mother Nature, just enhance her.

One more thing to think about is your gown. If you're going to be outside, you probably don't want to haul around a gown with a long train on it. It will only get dirty and pick up every available grass clipping, leaf, and bug in the general vicinity. A tea length gown or a gown without a train may be a better choice than a long gown with a train.

You need to be somewhat of a risk-taker to take on and enjoy an outdoor wedding. If you are someone who likes to feel in control of a situation, I suggest you stick with a more conservative plan and stay indoors. Outdoor weddings can be beautiful, but they certainly are not for the faint of heart.

Military Weddings

The biggest differences between a military wedding and a civilian wedding are the invitation, the uniformed attendants or couple, and the arch of swords (or sabers) at the end of the service. Everything else is the same.

Bet You Didn't Know... The tradition of the arch of swords at the end of the wedding started in 1909 when an officer bridegroom and his attendants raised their swords to toast the bride. The idea caught on and has been formalized to be part of military tradition.

The wording on the invitation needs to be written precisely according to standard etiquette, your branch of service, and your rank. Be sure to check with your bridal consultant or the stationery store expert for the correct military wording on your invitations. There are many different correct forms to use.

Here's what happens at the end of the ceremony: all commissioned officers present form two lines opposite each other outside the church or right inside the foyer. As the couple exits, the head usher commands "Draw Swords" (Naval officers) or "Draw Sabers" (Army, Air Force, and Marine officers). Then, using their right hands, the officers draw out their swords or sabers to form an arch. The couple passes underneath the arch, and the officers return their swords or sabers to their sheaths.

A release of swords at the end of a military wedding. Photo by Wyant Photography, Inc.

Dress can be your dress uniform, full-dress uniform including medals, or merely ribbons. Badges may also be worn. Men or women in uniform do not wear flowers, corsages, or boutonnieres.

If your groom is a member or graduate of one of the academies, you may display its flag in the church along with the American flag. One wedding with a military theme that I coordinated used white braid rope for pew markers. The bride had the florist add some greenery creating a very nice setting. She had the florist use that same rope braiding at the reception hall on the stairways and at the entrance. Even the cake was draped with "rope" icing to coordinate with the overall picture.

Victorian Weddings

A Victorian wedding refers to the Victorian period in England when Queen Victoria ruled (1837–1901). It was during her reign that many of the customs we now think of as "Victorian" were established. A Victorian wedding makes us think of softness, beauty, lace, ribbons, and flowers.

For your gown, shop for a dress that features a high neckline, puffed sleeves, and a form-fitting bodice with a tight waistline. There are several patterns on the market that duplicate the Victorian look if you can't find one ready-made.

Bouquets in the Victorian period were small clusters of flowers held together by a silver, ivory, or gold holder called a *Tussy Mussy*. They are making a comeback in the Midwest. Many mothers, instead of having corsages pinned to their dresses, are choosing to carry a Tussy Mussy with their flowers. You can incorporate old pieces of lace and ribbon in your bouquets, and your bridesmaids can wear lace and ribbon in their hair. If their dresses have the appropriate neckline, you could have each maid wear a ribbon with an antique broach pinned on it. Very Victorian. For pew markers, use long pieces of lace and ribbons interspersed with pink roses and ivy.

 Another Victorian touch for your wedding cake is to have the baker enclose small charms in the top layer of your cake. Attached to the charms are ribbons. Gather your bridesmaids around you and have them each take a ribbon and pull out one of the charms. The charms, according to tradition, will tell the bridesmaid of her future, love, hope, good luck, who is next to marry, and who will be the old maid.

Make your Victorian centerpieces full and romantic with roses and lots of baby's breath. One added touch is to sprinkle rose petals around the table. Some florists will give you these petals. They have to pull off the outside petals of roses anyway (they tell me that the outside petals are not of high enough quality), and they just throw them away. It's a very nice touch. Chair bows are another nice touch for Victorian weddings. Tie large bows of lace and ribbon with rose buds and baby's breath to the back of your chairs at the reception. If you have a large floral budget, tie bows to all the guest chairs. If you're on a tighter budget, tie bows only to the wedding party's chairs or maybe every other chair. It is a wonderful sight to enter a reception hall and see all the ribbon and flowers accenting the table and chairs. To complete the Victorian look, consider placing a single baby rose bud tied with a thin ribbon at every female guest's place setting.

You can develop any type of wedding theme as much as you want. You may use only a hint of a theme or you may go all out and make it a truly thematic wedding, from start to finish. The choice is yours. Finding some books at the library on a particular theme you've decided on for your wedding can be some additional help.

The Least You Need to Know

➤ Seasonal theme weddings are a natural idea if you want to give your wedding a theme. You can have some fun picking a date to base your wedding around.

➤ Outdoor weddings can be beautiful and fun, but they are risky. Always have a back-up plan.

➤ Military weddings differ from civilian weddings only in the way in which the invitations are worded, the presence of uniformed attendants, and the arch of swords or sabers.

➤ Victorian weddings can be wonderfully romantic with the addition of lace, flowers, and candles.

Hey! What Are You Doing This Weekend?

In This Chapter

➤ What is a weekend wedding?

➤ Activities to include for your guests

➤ Some practical tips

➤ The DOs and DON'Ts of weekend wedding planning

Earlier, I talked about an important fact concerning weddings of the 1990s: the boy-next-door seldom marries the girl-next-door. Gone are the days when childhood sweethearts grow up and marry each other. We are a very scattered society. Travel is quick, efficient, and relatively inexpensive. In many aspects, our world has gotten smaller. You graduate from high school and move out into the real world—often far from your hometown. That world may include college, vocational school, the military, or the work force. Whatever a new environment brings, it is likely to offer you an opportunity to meet people from other parts of the country or even other parts of the world.

As you move out into the world, it's very possible that one of the people you meet will become your partner, and he or she also may live far from his or her family. Bringing that family across the country (or from halfway around the world) to meet with your family and help the two of you celebrate this union can be the springboard to a wonderful, fun-filled, romantic, and relaxing weekend wedding.

What Is a Weekend Wedding?

A weekend wedding is a wedding that offers your guests additional activities beyond the normal wedding festivities throughout the weekend. Instead of attending only the wedding and reception, your wedding guests, often coming from all over the country, may choose to participate in several pre-planned functions. The wedding and reception are the highlights of the activities, but you can plan other outings to help guests put aside their hectic schedules for a little while and provide them with a mini-vacation. It's a chance to meet new friends, a chance for your two families to do some bonding, and a chance for your friends and family to spend some quality time together.

 Check with the local officials about the legal requirements for the marriage license in the area. If either of you are from the area, it's not a big problem. If you are both from out-of-town, check early about exactly what and when you need to apply for your marriage license.

Weekend weddings have been around for hundreds of years. In ancient times, the Romans and Greeks celebrated weddings with very elaborate feasts and parties that lasted for several days. During the Middle Ages, the wedding festivities were often days, and sometimes weeks, long. These events were related to our modern fairs or carnivals and included storytelling, dancers, jugglers, various foods, musicians, and, of course, in King Arthur's time, jousting tournaments. Even in the American colonies, our ancestors brought family and friends from far and near to help celebrate in a wedding feast that lasted for several days. So while the term *weekend wedding* may be relatively new, the idea certainly is not.

As I mentioned earlier, the weekend wedding is becoming increasingly popular because we are such a scattered society. Many couples have been out on their own for quite a while before they marry, so they choose to make their wedding celebration a longer and more elaborate event, bringing together the people from all parts of their respective lives. Couples want their guests (the people most special to them) to get to know each other, to build memories, and to help make their wedding truly memorable.

Many times, the weekend wedding can bring a family back to an area where there is common ground. The University of Notre Dame in South Bend, Indiana, for example, houses a gorgeous cathedral where couples who are alumni may be married. Cyndi Basker of Celebrated Events in South Bend specializes in weekend weddings there. She provided much of the research for this chapter. The couples she works with come from all over the country to be married in the cathedral at Notre Dame.

Other colleges and universities have couples return to be married in their facilities. St. Mary-of-the-Woods, a women's college in West Terre Haute, Indiana, also permits alumnae to be married in its beautiful church. I've worked with several couples who have brought their guests to St. Mary's for their wedding day, and we've added activities in the area to fill out the weekend.

Coming back to a place that holds special memories is not the only reason for a weekend wedding. This kind of wedding also offers the couple the opportunity to include many people in many different activities and to make the wedding a truly memorable event.

Guest Activities

Your guest activities for a weekend wedding can be as unique as the two of you and the location you have chosen. You can arrange those activities around a theme or a time of the year. You should plan for a variety of activities: enough so guests feel special, but not so many that they become physically exhausted. Guests are invited to the activities, except for specific invitations (the rehearsal) and may or may not choose to participate.

Here's a sample weekend format to give you some ideas and to get your creative juices flowing:

THURSDAY, SEPTEMBER 5
(for guests arriving early)

6:00-10:00 a.m.	Continental breakfast in lobby
11:00 a.m.-4:00 p.m.	Shopping in the new mall (bus will transport to and from hotel)
7:00 p.m.	Notre Dame baseball practice at new stadium

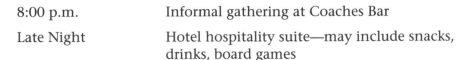

| 8:00 p.m. | Informal gathering at Coaches Bar |
| Late Night | Hotel hospitality suite—may include snacks, drinks, board games |

FRIDAY, SEPTEMBER 6

6:00-10:00 a.m.	Continental breakfast in lobby
9:00-10:00 a.m.	Golf tournament (see Jim to sign up)
10:30-11:45 a.m.	Campus tour—main circle
6:00-7:00 p.m.	Rehearsal—wedding party
7:00-7:30 p.m.	Musical ceremony at the Grotto
7:45-11:00 p.m.	Rehearsal dinner at The Commons
Late Night	Hotel hospitality suite

SATURDAY, SEPTEMBER 7

7:00-11:00 a.m.	Continental breakfast in lobby
8:30-9:45 a.m.	Campus tour—main circle
11:00-2:00 p.m.	Notre Dame vs. Michigan football game party in hospitality suite
3:00-11:30 p.m.	Wedding and dinner reception
Late Night	Hotel hospitality suite

SUNDAY, SEPTEMBER 8

| 7:00-11:00 a.m. | Continental breakfast in lobby |
| 8:45 a.m. | Mass in the Crown Room |

The preceding example shows activities for the weekend wedding where the hotel is the focal point for most guests. This is also an example of bringing the wedding guests to a point of interest other than the hometown location. In this case, the couple chose to bring everyone to the campus of Notre Dame.

This next example involves guests more with family, friends, and hometown activities.

FRIDAY, OCTOBER 8

10:00 a.m.	Van picks up guests at airport and delivers to hotel and guest houses.
4:00 p.m.	Hospitality time for guests at Aunt Helen's home. Those guests arriving may pick up their welcome packages and get the agenda for the weekend there.
7:00-8:00 p.m.	Rehearsal, St. Stephen's Church—wedding party
8:30-11:00 p.m.	Rehearsal dinner, the River House

SATURDAY, OCTOBER 9

10:00 a.m.	Brunch for all, Brown's Restaurant—Julia Miller, host
1:00 p.m.	Tour of art museum or Historical Society (see John for details)
5:00 p.m.	Wedding, St. Stephen's Church. Child care available at hotel (see John for details)
6:30 p.m.	Wedding reception, dinner and dancing, St. Mary's

SUNDAY, OCTOBER 10

11:00 a.m.	Brunch, Uncle Fred and Aunt Margaret's home
2:00 p.m.	Tennis and golf at the country club; games for the children included
5:00 p.m.	Picnic at the park—Jane and Jim O'Shea, hosts
9:00 p.m.	Fireworks display

MONDAY, OCTOBER 11

9:00 a.m.	Continental breakfast at Jane and Bob's home
After 11:00 a.m.	Guests depart

This sample showed us more local family members involved. With this type of weekend wedding, either the bride or groom probably lives in the area.

Depending on where your weekend wedding will be held and the time of year, here are some other ideas you may incorporate:

➤ Golf outings. These are very popular with both sexes. Include a breakfast or lunch and you have a great way to spend some quality time with folks.

➤ Softball game and maybe a tournament

➤ Trip to the local zoo

➤ Tour of a historical district

➤ Museums, including children's museums

➤ Shopping trips to malls

➤ Shopping trips to unique or quaint areas

➤ Day at a massage salon; treat your wedding party to the *works*: manicure, pedicure, and a body massage.

➤ Picnic or barbecue in a park or backyard

➤ Rent a bowling alley

➤ Go see a play

➤ Have a scavenger hunt through the city with prizes

Practical Tips

Whatever place you choose to bring your wedding guests for your weekend wedding, be sure to do your homework. Because you're including more activities in the weekend wedding, you'll need to do more research and get more help than if you were planning just for one day.

You can get help from various sources, including family and friends. If you are having a weekend wedding in a distant city, however, you may want to consider hiring a bridal consultant from that locale to work with you on the planning. It can save you time, money, and heartache.

Cyndi Basker of Celebrated Events offers some suggestions for early planning:

"When choosing your date for the weekend wedding, it is very important to check with the local Chamber of Commerce about other events that may be taking place on the weekend you have chosen."

Be sure to check with the local Chamber of Commerce for other events scheduled for the weekend. If you can stay away from busy times in the chosen city, you'll be better off.

Are there major trade shows in town? Is there a big sporting event? What about a festival? A convention?

"It will be impossible to book hotel rooms, and navigation around the city will be difficult for your guests if there are other major functions going on," says Cyndi. "Weddings on busy weekends will turn out to be a frustrating experience for your out-of-town guests who are not familiar with your city."

Booking a Hotel for a Weekend Wedding

After you have decided on a weekend and have checked out the date with the local Chamber of Commerce to make sure it doesn't conflict with another major event, your next step is to find a good hotel. Depending on your circumstances, this can be the gathering place for the majority of your guests.

When choosing the hotel, there are several items to consider. Is the hotel easily accessible to the church and the reception? If the hotel offers a ballroom, will it accommodate your reception? That makes things extremely easy for guests. They just walk up to their room following the reception. No drinking and walking laws apply in most states.

Choose a hotel with as many amenities as possible. Does it have an indoor pool? A sauna or whirlpool? Tennis courts, jogging tracks, weight rooms, and fitness areas are very popular for many people these days. Some hotels in downtown areas offer shops with a distinctive flare. Does the hotel have shuttle service from the airport? This is a big point if you have many guests arriving at the airport. Will the hotel provide a shuttle from the hotel to the local mall? Will the hotel help you offer a hospitality room for your guests? Many times, you may

After meeting with the hotel manager, if you detect a "bad attitude" or if you are treated poorly, see what other facilities you can find in your area. With a weekend wedding in which the hotel is a primary focal point, you need the hotel's full cooperation.

have to rent a room for this, but it is a nice gesture. Can you bring your own snacks to the hospitality room or are you be required to use the hotel's food service?

How "wedding friendly" is the hotel? This is a term used by Cyndi Basker. She explains that it is "very important that the hotel you choose for your wedding weekend have a good attitude." How much are they willing to go above and beyond the call of duty? For example, say you have 75 rooms reserved at the hotel for your guests. When each guest or couple registers at the front desk, they are to receive a balloon bouquet with the weekend agenda tied to it. Will the hotel instruct its front staff to make sure to present the balloons to your guests? Cyndi stresses that "the front staff needs to be helpful and friendly, and make all of your guests feel welcome." After all, the staff is probably the first contact your guest has with your weekend wedding.

Ask the hotel about reduced rates for large blocks of rooms. Many hotels will discount your room costs if you book a block of rooms. Does the hotel have good banquet facilities? Does the food have good reviews? Your guests may be eating here quite a bit over the weekend, and you want their tummies to be happy.

Finally, what is the overall appearance of the hotel? Is it well kept? Does it have a good reputation in the area? Is the manager accessible, and does he answer your questions fully and in a timely manner? There is nothing worse than being put on hold for days while waiting for an answer to a seemingly simple question.

Travel Advice

With many of your guests arriving from various parts of the country and by all modes of transportation, good information to them early on will help alleviate all types of problems.

Make sure that you investigate discounts on travel for a number of guests coming from the same locale. Often, your bridal consultant or travel agent can negotiate discounted airfare for travel. Be sure to ask.

Let guests know the basics of your weekend plans well in advance. You don't have to send them an entire agenda with times and places, but sending them the information that yes, you are getting married on July 5, in Madison, Wisconsin, will give them the opportunity to plan around that time. Maybe they were thinking of taking a vacation later in the summer. Receiving early information, they may include your wedding in their vacation plans. We talked in Chapter 13 about newsletters. This is a prime example of one of the benefits of using newsletters to alert your guests of what's going to take place, where, and when.

Newsletters are great ways to let your intended guests know about your upcoming wedding plans.

Make sure you have shuttle transportation or vans and/or cars lined up to pick up your guests as they arrive. You should know their travel plans, so you can get all those details coordinated in advance.

Make sure all your guests have a map of the area clearly marked with the sites where activities will be taking place. Also, make sure the map clearly shows one way streets or any construction that may be going on during that time.

Consider how guests will move from event to event. If the majority of your guests arrive by plane or train, they will not have access to cars. What kind of shuttle service can you work out with the hotel or a rental company? Here is where a bus is ideal. It can hold large numbers, and as the old commercial goes, "take the bus and leave the driving to us."

Consider walking as a mode of transportation. As long as your guests are not expected to walk vast distances in sub-zero temperatures while carrying your fourteen-tier wedding cake, they may find a nice walk to the mall or museum refreshing. Of course, should you have guests who are physically challenged, you need to make appropriate arrangements for them.

DOs and DON'Ts

When planning for the weekend wedding (whether you are having it in your home city with family and friends coming in from all over or you have made arrangements for it in another location, there are some DOs and DON'Ts to follow.

Always think of your guests' comfort and enjoyment during the weekend. Make sure you take care of their needs. They may be coming from great distances to help share in one of the most fun, exciting, and romantic times in your life. Here are some additional things to help make everyone's visit more pleasurable.

➤ Get the word out early about the wedding date and location so guests can begin to think how they can incorporate your wedding into their plans.

➤ Send a newsletter closer to the wedding date, describing parties, events, weather conditions, hotel information, hosts for parties, and the attire for the events.

➤ Update the schedule and let guests know of major changes.

➤ After the invitations go out, you may, if you need a count for a particular event, send out response cards (postcards will do) so you can get an idea of the number of guests you're expecting for certain events.

One of the more elaborate weddings I've worked with was a weekend wedding with the majority of guests coming in from out of town. In the invitation, a response postcard was included that asked guests when they were arriving, which hotel they were staying at, their choice of entrée for the reception, and if they had any special needs, dietary or otherwise. To this day I'm not sure why, but the response rate for those cards was 100%. Ask any consultant, bride, or mother of the bride today, and they will tell you that generally the response rate on receptions is terrible. We, as a society, are often very lax either in our knowledge or our expression of proper etiquette when it comes to responding to an invitation. Many of us don't know what R.S.V.P. means, or we choose to ignore it.

R.S.V.P. is French for *rèpondez s'il vous plaît* and means, simply, *please respond.* If you see it written on an invitation, it means you are to call the hostess or return a response card to tell her whether or not you can attend the function.

➤ Make guests feel welcome when they arrive. Place some kind of welcome package in their hotel rooms. It doesn't have to be fancy or expensive but it needs to be from you and your groom (or your parents). Your guests have traveled far to help you celebrate this wonderful day. Make them feel that much more special by having some kind of greeting in their rooms.

Wrapping Up Your Welcome

In a welcome package, include an agenda or itinerary of all the activities for the weekend. On the agenda, make sure you include the time, place, and date of the event, the dress for that event (casual, dressy, black tie), the hosts for the event (David's parents are hosting the wedding breakfast), a shuttle schedule or transportation schedule from the hotel or home to the event, the phone number of the event site (in case of emergencies), and a map of the area with the events marked (numbers work well, such as "#7 on map is wedding site"). Also in the package, include something to eat (maybe some homemade cookies, a small basket of fresh fruit, or some chocolates beautifully wrapped to coordinate with the wedding colors).

If you want to splurge, you also can include a split of champagne or wine with a couple of cheap wine glasses or some plastic wine or champagne glasses. In every basket, be sure to include a personal note from you and your groom welcoming your guests and thanking them for being with you on your wedding weekend.

➤ Leave copies of the wedding weekend agenda at the front desk of the hotel, in the hospitality room, and with both sets of parents. That way, if a guests misplaces his or her agenda, another one is readily available.

➤ Provide a list of baby-sitters or have sitter arrangements made for those guests who are bringing small children for the weekend. There will be activities that the adults want to participate in that are not children-friendly. Your guests will certainly appreciate your thoughtfulness in finding reliable sitters for the children. Sometimes, hotels can provide names of qualified sitters. If you're in a college town, check with the Education department for names of students who would be willing to sit.

➤ Think about your guests. Are they the athletic type? Are they sports fans? Do they drink? What kinds of activities would most of them enjoy? Plan your agenda around your guests' likes and dislikes.

➤ Have some of the activities geared towards children. Consider hiring a social director to come in and organize a children's party for the kids while the adults are being entertained somewhere else.

➤ Try not to over plan. You want to offer activities to your guests so they may take part, but they may choose not to take part. That is their choice. Don't overload the weekend with so many activities that everyone is exhausted by the time the wedding rolls around. Maintain a balance in your agenda.

➤ Remember that the wedding and reception are the high point of the weekend. Everything else is optional for most of your guests.

Weekend weddings are meant to encompass all the beauty and love and grace that a one-day wedding event holds, plus give your guests more of a feel for celebrating in a variety of ways. Keep your planning organized and try not to overdo activities. Do your homework, stay organized, and plan ahead. You can then relax and enjoy what should be a memorable weekend for everyone involved!

The Least You Need to Know

➤ If you are bringing guests in to a locale where you do not have family, get some professional help with the planning.

➤ When checking on your wedding date, be sure to check with the local Chamber of Commerce for other events scheduled on that date that may affect hotel room availability, traffic, and so on.

➤ Make sure the hotel where your guests will be staying is "wedding friendly" and cooperative.

➤ Do not over plan. Maintain a balance in your weekend agenda. Consider your guests' interests and needs; give them time to rest and relax.

➤ Remember that the wedding and reception are the highlight of the entire weekend. No other activity should overshadow these two events.

Chapter 19

Mickey and Minnie, Here We Come!

In This Chapter

➤ What is a destination wedding?

➤ How to plan a destination wedding

➤ Some popular sites

➤ Practical tips

In Chapter 18, I talked about weekend weddings. A destination wedding is very similar to a weekend wedding in format and principle, but the kind of location you choose for the wedding is the primary difference between the two. Like a weekend wedding, a destination wedding should offer fun and relaxation for everyone involved. They also require some extra time and organization to pull off successfully.

What Is a Destination Wedding?

A *destination wedding* takes place somewhere you may take a vacation. That is probably the biggest difference between a destination wedding and a weekend wedding. While a vacation in South Bend, Indiana, or Iowa City, Iowa, may not be at the top of your list, you definitely may

 A destination wedding is sometimes referred to as a *travel wedding* (because you travel to the location) or a *honeymoon wedding* (because the destination also serves as the honeymoon spot.)

consider a vacation to Disney World in Florida or to the Hawaiian Islands. Think of it this way: with a destination wedding, the majority of activities you can offer your guests are already in place.

For example, let's say you're a big country music fan. What better spot could you find than Nashville, Tennessee, and Opryland to enhance your destination wedding dreams? Nashville is a stately, southern city filled with beautiful plantations, the home of Andrew Jackson (former U.S. president), and the center of the country music industry. For a weekend wedding in South Bend, Indiana, on the other hand, you have to plan, coordinate, or organize all the activities you offer your guests. Don't get me wrong, destination weddings still require quite a bit of organization and planning to ensure that all systems are go. With a little help from the staff at the site, however, or with other professional help (this is where a good bridal consultant can be a life saver), you can be in for a wonderful and memorable event.

A destination wedding can be as elaborate or simple as you want, depending upon your budget. Many times, families take extended vacations at resort spots and include the wedding festivities. One bride and groom, who were from opposite sides of the country and had met at college, planned their destination wedding so it would be a vacation for both sets of family. They enjoyed a wonderful seven days of fun and excitement before the big event. After the wedding, the couple left for their honeymoon and both families stayed on another two days for more fun and more time to get to know each other.

Keep in mind that with destination weddings, your guests are responsible for their own transportation costs and housing expenses. Very rarely would you have them housed in family homes at a destination wedding unless there were family members in the vicinity.

How to Plan a Destination Wedding

If you have an area in mind or you have some interest you want to fulfill, start arranging for your destination wedding by doing research at the library. Browse travel magazines to get ideas of where you may want to go. Read all you can on a particular spot before you head for the travel agent. You need to be well informed on the area so that you can ask intelligent questions. (Remember lecture #201, "How to Be an Intelligent Wedding Consumer?")

You can contact tourist boards, the Chamber of Commerce, and travel agencies in the area for advice. Almost every large city in the country has a tourist board or tourist information office where you can call to request brochures and resort information.

If you know someone who had a destination wedding, ask for suggestions and recommendations, but be careful you don't compare apples with oranges. Just because you spent time vacationing in the Virgin Islands doesn't mean the resort you stayed at can pull off a wedding. You need specifics about what the resort you want to use can offer in the way of wedding services.

If you belong to the American Automobile Association (AAA), check with them for locations and resorts. They offer a wealth of information, and it's all free with your membership. Many times, they can answer your questions over the phone.

Think about the weather conditions where you are hoping to hold your wedding. Maybe a wedding planned for a remote beach in hurricane season isn't such a good idea. A veil blowing gently in the breeze is one thing, but a hurricane may be overkill. Get some expert advice about the weather at that location at the time of year you are considering.

When choosing a location, think about a spot that may have some meaning to you. One couple, who met at Hilton Head, South Carolina, and had vacationed there several times during their courtship, couldn't think of a more appropriate spot for their wedding. They contacted the hotel where they had stayed previously and knew exactly which balcony overlooking the beautiful beach they wanted for the backdrop for their wedding. Only their immediate family members were present, but the couple could not have been

When selecting the hotel or resort for your destination wedding, always read the fine print in the contracts. Trust me, there is a reason it's so small.

more pleased. After they returned to their hometown from their honeymoon, they hosted a huge reception including dinner and dancing and celebrated with friends and family members who couldn't attend the wedding. During the course of the evening, a video was set up in a

Find out the rules and regulations of marrying at the site you have chosen. Rules change from state to state and from island to island. Don't make the reservations until you are sure you can be married there.

separate room off the main ballroom. It played the wedding service continuously during the evening, and guests could wander in and out at their leisure to enjoy the tape. How fun for guests to see the wedding on tape! It made them feel more involved with the reception because they could witness the actual wedding service.

After you choose a location, you need to select the accommodations you will use. If you have more specific choices to make, such as choosing a particular Hawaiian or Caribbean island, then you'll want to do more research to find just the right resort for your wedding. Take into consideration the extras the resort offers, such as which amenities are free and which ones guests have to pay extra for (golf, tennis, swimming). You don't want your guests spending big bucks on airfare and hotel accommodations only to find that they have to pay every time they use the pool or ask for a clean towel. Find out those details ahead of time.

Just because you have every detail in place and have talked at length with the hotel and the airlines, don't make that first deposit until you are sure you can be married in your chosen spot. Some destinations require a long residency, others require up to a thirty day waiting period after you apply for the license before you can marry there. Take some time now to determine if your dream location actually can become a reality.

Guest Activities

Your guest activities for a destination wedding, unlike the agenda for a weekend wedding, are readily available. Because of the locale you've chosen for your destination wedding, planning activities to keep you and your guests busy will not be a chore.

Again, go with the area. If you're on an island and you have great beaches and fishing at your disposal, make that a focal point. Why not have the rehearsal dinner on the beach? Add volleyball and a picnic supper and your guests can relax, eat, drink, and have fun either enjoying the game or watching the sun set into the ocean.

Let the destination determine what activities you will have guests involved with; the choices are endless. It's up to you and your groom and just takes a little imagination.

Practical Tips

In order to meet your dreams of having your wedding and reception on an island paradise or with a castle as a backdrop, you'll need to make sure you have all your bases covered.

Here are some suggestions to help you utilize your resources and still get to the church on time:

➤ Work with the local Chamber of Commerce or tourist board in the area you have chosen for your wedding.

➤ Hire a bridal consultant from that locale. Many times, the hotels can provide names of local consultants. As I mentioned in Chapter 2, you can also obtain names of bridal consultants in a particular locale or who specialize in destination weddings by contacting the Association of Bridal Consultants in New Milford, Connecticut, at (203) 355 0464. Ask for Gerry or Eileen, and tell them that Teddy sent you.

➤ When you talk with the bridal consultant, whether you choose to work with a private company or a staff member at the resort, make sure that you have all your questions written down before you make the call. Make good use of both your time and the consultant's time. Include all the items you need to discuss: ceremony site, music, floral arrangements, photography, videography, food, liquor, and the fee for staff. You don't want any surprises 2,000 miles away from home. Get those details in writing now.

➤ Make sure you have the legal requirements for marrying in that locale in writing: waiting periods, residency requirements, and what paper work you have to bring with you, such as identification, birth certificates, blood test reports, proof of citizenship, passports, and parental consent (in the case of minors). Be sure you know the age requirement for marrying in that particular locale. This fact varies from place to place; so be sure to check. Work out all these kinks ahead of time!

➤ If at all possible, make a trip to the site before the wedding just to be sure everything is as you want it and there are no hidden agendas with hotel staff. What you are told and how that statement is interpreted by all parties may not be the same thing. For example, you may be assured that the backdrop for your wedding site is a pure white sand beach with crystal clear blue water. The fact that the hotel forgot to mention the oil rigging outfit offshore could be a really big interpretation problem. Sometimes, a face-to-face conversation can save you misunderstandings later on.

➤ Be sure to send a newsletter to those guests who have indicated that they would like to share in your destination wedding. In the newsletter, include information on flights, airlines, hotels, costs, choices of accommodations, what's available on site, dress style for the stay, and anything pertaining specifically to that destination. You can enclose a brochure of the hotel or resort in the newsletter to entice those guests even more.

Don't forget to include in your overall budget the long distance telephone calls that pop up frequently as you plan for this wedding. The telephone is probably the cheapest, fastest, and most convenient way to communicate with the resort staff carrying out your plans. If time is short, you may also look into faxing items back and forth.

➤ Make sure your arrangements are confirmed and you have everything in writing. Look over contracts very carefully. Read the fine print. No surprises, please.

➤ If you are bringing your wedding gown with you, it must be boxed carefully with sheets of tissue paper between the folds. Think carefully before you decide to check it through with the luggage. Losing your wedding gown two days before the wedding would be a big headache. You may put it in a garment bag and hang it on the plane. Linens and silk taffeta are not good fabric choices for travel. Stick with cotton, satin, cotton voile, or a silk crepe for the least amount of upkeep. Check with the hotel or resort about pressing or steaming services.

➤ If you aren't bringing your gown, think about renting one on site, or go with the culture of your locale. Instead of our Americanized wedding gown, go with what the locals would wear. Have fun.

Popular Sites

You can consider any resort area that can accommodate a wedding for your destination wedding. Choose the wedding site as you would chose your honeymoon site. What activities are you interested in? What activities would you like for your guests? Is there a fantasy you want fulfilled, such as spending time exploring a castle, snorkeling off the coast of Bali, or deep-sea fishing in the waters of Bermuda? Whatever your fantasy is, see if you can't find someplace that fulfills it.

It doesn't have to be a big-time resort, either. If there is a state park or nature area that you find particularly inviting and you can envision yourself surrounded by family and friends on top of a mountain, go for it. Make this your special time and offer your guests the opportunity to participate with you as you celebrate your wedding.

Disney World

Disney World in Florida, as well as Disneyland in California, have seen a huge jump in weddings performed on their properties. Both facilities now have full-time staff and departments who handle all the arrangements for destination weddings on their premises. In keeping with Disney's general theme, "Fairy Tale Weddings" is the name of the department that handles arrangements for these weddings. Call 1-800 WDISNEY.

Having been a guest at a destination wedding at Disney World a few years ago, I can say that it did, indeed, have a fairy tale quality about it. The ceremony was held on the lawn in a private area of the hotel. A platform had been erected in the front, and white chairs were set up in rows on either side of an aisle. On the platform were two lovely, large floral arrangements. In the distance, across the lake, we could see the castle. As we entered the site, we were greeted with the music of a string quartet. The fall sun was bright, but not too hot, and the setting was beautiful.

The processional started, and from the side came the minister and the groom with his best man. Down the aisle came the maid of honor and the ring bearer. As we heard the

When traveling by plane, remember that if your luggage is lost, most airlines will give you up to 50% of the value of the contents after a 24-hour waiting period, but you must have receipts. Most of us don't travel with the receipts for the entire contents of our luggage. If you are packing your wedding gown in your luggage, remember to take the receipt. It may not bring your wedding gown back faster, or at all, but at least you'll be partially compensated.

There is a fascinating book on the market called *Places* (Hannelore Hahn and Tatiana Stoumer, 1989) that may help you in finding a unique destination for your wedding. The book's subtitle says it all: "A directory of public places for private events and private places for public functions." Check out this book and let your imagination run wild.

"Wedding March" begin, Cinderella's coach arrived, complete with footman and six white horses. It was a sight to behold. Out stepped the lovely bride, and then she marched down the aisle on the arm of her father.

The ceremony was simple but very sincere. I asked afterwards if their minister had come all the way to Florida to perform the service. They replied that no, he was a local minister who frequently performed weddings at Disney World. We thought he had known the couple for years.

At the conclusion of the service, the couple boarded the coach and were whisked away for the reception. There was something very magical about it.

Hawaii

The islands of our 50th state, Hawaii, are perfect for destination weddings. Whether you want the backdrop of Diamond Head or a deserted beach on Maui, Hawaii probably has what you're looking for.

The perfect climate, nearly all year, is one reason it is such a good selection for a destination wedding. The low season is November through April, when there usually is more rain, but in reality it often only sprinkles. During those months, you can get good prices on lodging. Watch for better airfare prices at that time, too.

You can reach the Hawaii Visitor's Bureau at (212) 947-0717. They can provide you with all kinds of information about the islands.

Las Vegas

If you want something totally opposite from the laid back, relaxed atmosphere of the islands, try Las Vegas. The night life never stops; you can see a wonderful show every night, and a wedding chapel greets you at almost every turn.

One nice thing about Las Vegas is that it is relatively inexpensive to stay there if you choose your hotels wisely. Room rates and food are very inexpensive. (That's because they want you to have more money to spend in the casinos.) If you want a destination wedding and you're on a tight budget, give the friendly folks in Las Vegas a call. The City Tourist Office number is (702) 892-7575.

Cruise Ships

A cruise ship can be an attractive spot for your destination wedding. Whether your tastes take you south to the Caribbean or north to Alaska, a cruise ship can be a real treat for you and your guests.

A destination wedding can be fun, romantic, and intimate for all those involved. It can be a wonderful vacation idea for guests and a good opportunity for family and friends to get to know one another. Whatever destination you choose, just be sure to do your homework and enjoy!

The romantic notion of being married by the ship's captain is false. Unless he is a Notary Public or an ordained minister, he cannot perform the service. What most couples do is to have the ceremony at dock side—off the ship—and then go aboard and have the reception followed by the days at sea for the honeymoon. (Your guests don't go on the honeymoon with you.)

The Least You Need to Know

➤ Destination weddings offer a vacation atmosphere and many of the activities you may want to schedule for your guests.

➤ Make sure that you check about legal requirements for the marriage license in the locale in which you plan to have your wedding.

➤ Wherever you decide to have your destination wedding, work with a bridal consultant either from that area (an independent consultant or one who works with the resort) or a bridal consultant who specializes in destination weddings. They can be invaluable in helping you achieve the type of wedding you desire.

➤ Allow enough time for your guests to plan for this type of wedding; send them informative newsletters to help them prepare.

➤ Try to visit the site before the wedding to make sure it's what you have in mind and to make sure that you have accurately communicated your desires to the local staff.

Chapter 20

Get Serious: Traditional Religious Services

In This Chapter

➤ A look at four different religious services

➤ Some of the traditions and terminology

About 75% of all marriages take place in some form of religious establishment. That may be a church for Protestant, Catholic, and Orthodox services or a synagogue or temple for Jewish couples. While I do not have a degree in theology and don't claim to be an expert, I do have a fundamental understanding of some of the primary parts of the various services. In my research, I also came across some articles written and researched by the Association of Bridal Consultants (ABC). The ABC has graciously given me consent to use some of its material.

Orthodox

The churches of Orthodox rites, including Greek and Russian, hold services similar to a Catholic service. The priest and community control many of the aspects of the wedding ceremony, including what language is to be used. The traditional wedding service is firmly rooted in Byzantine ritual and is quite lengthy.

The Orthodox ceremony is full of symbolism. It is divided into two parts: the Betrothal and the Service of Crowning.

The Betrothal

The Betrothal begins with the blessing of the rings by the priest, who takes them in his hand, makes the sign of the cross, and says, "The servant of God (groom) is betrothed to the handmaid of God (bride), in the name of the Father, and of the Son, and of the Holy Ghost."

The best man exchanges the rings, taking the bride's ring and placing it on the groom's finger and then taking the groom's ring and placing it on the bride's finger. The rings are the ancient symbol of betrothal. The exchange signifies that, in married life, the weakness of one partner will be compensated for by the strength of the other partner. The Orthodox belief is that by themselves, the newly betrothed couple are incomplete; together, they are made perfect.

During the rest of the service, the couple holds candles to symbolize the Lord's light. The bride's bouquet is either held by an attendant or placed on a table.

The Crowning

The Crowning is the climax of the wedding service. Wreaths or crowns are placed on the couple's heads. The bride's headpiece must be removed and held by an attendant if it interferes with the crown. Usually, two crown bearers are included in the wedding processional who walk side by side, because the crowns are joined with ribbon, again to signify unity. The crowns are a sign of the glory and honor with which God crowns the couple during the sacrament. When the crowning takes place, the priest takes the crowns and, holding them above the couple, says, "The servant of God (groom) is crowned unto the handmaiden of God (bride), in the name of the Father, and the Son, and the Holy Ghost. Amen."

The rite of Crowning is followed by the reading of the Epistle and the Gospel. Wine is given to the couple in a common cup denoting the mutual sharing of joy and sorrow. Drinking from the common cup reminds the couple that, from then on, they will share in everything in life.

The priest then leads the couple and the honor attendants around the table in which the Gospel has been placed, symbolizing the Word of God and the redemption by Christ. They circle the table three times to signify the Trinity.

The final part of the service takes place while the priest is leading the couple around the table. The first of three hymns begins. The first hymn celebrates the incarnation of Christ and praises the Mother of God. The second hymn asks the victoriously crowned martyrs to pray for the couple's salvation, and that the couple may live a life worthy to be crowned in heaven. The third hymn glorifies Christ.

Orthodox church members must receive Communion on the Sunday before the marriage ceremony. The church will allow interfaith marriages, but one partner and one witness must be Eastern Orthodox.

It is helpful to have detailed wedding programs printed so that your non-Orthodox guests can understand the symbolism of the service. The service is a very moving and lovely ceremony. Guests will appreciate it all the more if they know and understand what is happening and why.

Protestant

When you talk about Protestant services you are talking about many different denominations: Baptist, Methodist, Presbyterian, Church of Christ, Episcopal, and Lutheran, to name just a few. Add to that the many independent and nontraditional branches, and it becomes quite difficult to provide a "typical" Protestant service.

Since I am Presbyterian by choice and come from a long line of Presbyterians, I will refer to the *Book of Common Worship* as my guide for a standard Presbyterian marriage service. Other Protestant denominations have their own guidelines and may have different requirements for their services. Be sure to check with your minister or officiant. Much will be decided by your minister. Some ministers are very rigid and will not give or take on any point of the service, while others are willing to work with you to make it unique for the two of you.

The standard part of the Protestant service begins with the Words of Welcome where the minister greets the congregation, announcing that they have come to see (bride) and (groom) united in marriage. This is followed by the Call to Worship. The traditional words here are "We are gathered here today to witness the marriage of John and Sally in Holy Matrimony... ."

Following this opening, you may select a reading or two. These readings can be (depending on your minister) Biblical verses, a favorite poem, or some other piece of literature that is appropriate for a religious service. One Bible verse that couples often choose is I Corinthians, verse 13 ("and the greatest of these is love").

At this point, the minister may offer a short sermon to the couple. He may talk about marriage as a commitment or refer to some part of your life where there has been struggle and how you have overcome that struggle. A good minister can make a lovely sermon a very meaningful part of your service.

Next in the service, the minister will ask you to declare your intentions. He will ask a series of questions to which you either answer "I do" or "I will."

Following this, the minister will ask, "Who gives this woman to be married to this man?" Whereupon your dad, choking back tears, says, "Her mother and I." More and more frequently these days, the minister says "who brings this woman to be married to this man" rather than "who gives this woman." It doesn't sound quite so possessive. I've seen a lovely variation on this question in several recent services. Rather than "who gives" or "who brings," the minister asks both families if they will support the union and give it their blessing. The minister may say, "Do you, the parents, accept both (bride) and (groom) as your own? Do you give your loving support to their marriage, and do you acknowledge that from this time forward, their loyalty shall be to one another?" The families then (hopefully!) both answer, "We do."

The next part is the biggie: the marriage vows. Within each denomination, you should have a couple of choices. Sometimes, ministers will let you write your own vows (we'll talk about that in Chapter 22). If you are creative and want to make the service more meaningful, try your hand at that.

After the vows segment, the rings are blessed and exchanged. Usually, the minister will say a few words about the ring being an unbroken circle symbolizing unending and everlasting love.

If you are incorporating a unity candle in your ceremony, this is the point at which you light it. A unity candle is a candle that remains unlit on the altar table. Then, after the vows and ring segment of the ceremony, you and your groom light it to signify the unity of your marriage. Sometimes, the parents also light "family" candles before the service, to represent each family—the bride's family and the groom's family. Some churches do not permit a unity candle because it holds no theological significance, so be sure to check with your officiant.

A unity candle embossed with the wedding invitation. Photo by Wyant Photography, Inc.

At this point in the service, the minister offers a Prayer of Thanksgiving and usually concludes with the Lord's Prayer. Your congregation can either join in saying the Lord's Prayer, or sometimes the Lord's Prayer is sung.

The Minister may ask you (the bride and groom) to kneel for the benediction. Some ministers place their hands on your heads for the blessing, while I've seen others wrap their stoles around your hands as a sign of support.

Following the benediction, the minister, if allowed, will announce you as Mr. and Mrs. John Smith, and the recessional begins.

Roman Catholic

In many respects, the Roman Catholic wedding rite resembles that of the Protestant denomination, with the blessings, prayers, and exchange of vows and rings.

Bet You Didn't Know... The reason the bride is to stand to the left of her groom dates back to the Anglo-Saxon times when the groom, fearing attack from fire-breathing dragons and other menaces, had to keep his right hand free to grab his sword.

The Roman Catholic ceremony, however, is also the Sacrament of Matrimony, one of the seven sacraments Catholics believe are channels of God's grace. The ceremony consists of at least three readings, the nuptial blessing and concluding prayers, and the Sacrament itself.

The Sacrament often is included in a Mass, referred to as a Nuptial Mass. Nuptial Masses usually are celebrated in the morning, but the Sacrament of Matrimony may be celebrated at any time. When an afternoon or evening wedding is scheduled without a Mass, it is customary for the couple and other Catholic bridal party members to participate in a morning Mass, including receiving Communion. It also is customary to receive the Sacrament of Reconciliation.

Marriages are announced by banns, read during Mass or published in a church bulletin. This replaces a traditional Protestant question that's asked at the ceremony: whether anyone knows why the marriage should not take place.

The Catholic Church encourages the couple to help develop and personalize the ceremony, within constraints. Particularly appropriate readings from the Scriptures, prayers, and hymns have been identified and may be used. Other modifications are possible.

After the exchange of vows comes the exchange of rings. The best man gives the bride's ring to the priest, who blesses it and gives it to the groom, who then places it on the bride's finger.

In a double ring ceremony, after the bride receives her ring, the maid of honor gives the groom's ring to the priest; the blessing and presentation are repeated.

The Roman Catholic Church has relaxed many of its former stringent rules regarding marriage to non-Catholics. However, restrictions do apply, some based on church rules and others regulated by the local diocese or parish. It is possible to have two religious ceremonies follow one another or to have an ecumenical service, with another faith's clergyman participating.

The Roman Catholic Church prefers both best man and maid of honor to be Catholic but only requires one to be. The other attendants don't have to be Catholic, but they will be instructed in the required courtesies and reverences.

The Catholic partner is required to promise to continue observing the Catholic faith and to raise children as Catholics, but the non-Catholic partner no longer is required to make that promise.

Some Common Threads Among Christian Weddings

Some common elements among all Christian wedding services include the processional, the recessional, and the placement of the wedding party at the altar. Although individual denominations or churches may have developed somewhat unique versions of these parts of the ceremony, they usually are simply a variation of a standard theme.

The Christian Processional

In the standard Christian processional, the groomsmen enter first, followed by the bridesmaids. The maid of honor is the last adult attendant to enter and is followed by any children in the party, such as a ring bearer or flower girl. The bride is the last member of the wedding party to enter the church and usually is escorted by her father or other close male relative or friend.

Legend
1 = Bride
2 = Groom
3 = Maid of Honor
4 = Best Man
5 = Bridesmaid
6 = Groomsmen/ushers
7 = Flower Girl
8 = Ring Bearer
9 = Father of Bride
10 = Mother of Bride
11 = Father of Groom
12 = Mother of Groom
13 = Officiant
14 = Cantor
15 = Bride's Grandfathers
16 = Bride's Grandmothers
17 = Groom's Grandfathers
18 = Groom's Grandmothers

The Christian processional.

This example shows the groomsmen (or ushers) in pairs leading the processional. They can walk single file or make their entrance at the front of the altar area with the priest. Next, we have the bridesmaids, again single file, followed by the maid or matron of honor, the flower girl and ring bearer, and finally the bride and her father or other escort.

Getting You Down the Aisle

In the Roman Catholic ceremony, the bride's father escorts her up the aisle. When the father gives his daughter's hand to the groom, he joins his wife in the first pew. If a bride's father cannot perform this duty, a brother, uncle, godfather, or close family friend can take his place. In rare cases, a bride could ask the groom's father to take the role. The escort, by tradition, is a man. If the bride has no one for the role, she traditionally walks up the aisle alone.

Positions at the Altar

When the bride and her escort arrive at the front of the church, she lets go of his arm and moves her flowers to her left hand; she gives her right hand to the groom. He puts it through his left arm, with her hand near his elbow. It also is acceptable for the couple to simply stand side by side holding hands.

As for the remainder of the wedding party, you can move them around to accommodate your personal wishes (with the blessing of the priest or minister, of course). Wedding party placement varies depending on your church and its physical setting. The following illustration shows one example of the basic positioning of the wedding party as it arrives at the altar.

Legend
1 = Bride
2 = Groom
3 = Maid of Honor
4 = Best Man
5 = Bridesmaid
6 = Groomsmen/ushers
7 = Flower Girl
8 = Ring Bearer
9 = Father of Bride
10 = Mother of Bride
11 = Father of Groom
12 = Mother of Groom
13 = Officiant
14 = Cantor
15 = Bride's Grandfathers
16 = Bride's Grandmothers
17 = Groom's Grandfathers
18 = Groom's Grandmothers

Traditional positions at the altar for a Christian ceremony.

259

There are no rules for arranging the wedding party; the decision usually is made by the bride who relies heavily on the priest's advice and recommendations from her bridal consultant, if she has one. It should be obvious here that a rehearsal is essential.

Jewish

To understand the Jewish wedding, it helps to have a general understanding of the differences among Jews and Jewish observances. Jewish people divide themselves into Ashkenazi Jews (descended from Eastern European Jews) and Sephardic Jews (descended from Middle Eastern or Spanish Jews). The two sects have very different customs, evident in the celebration of holidays and life cycle events, such as weddings.

Judaism is divided into three basic groups. Jewish weddings differ depending on whether the rabbi and/or congregation is Orthodox, Conservative, or Reformed and depending on whether the customs are Ashkenazi or Sephardic. Even with the varying customs among these groups, all Jewish weddings still have much in common.

The wedding ceremony may be conducted in a synagogue, temple, or other location of the couple's choosing; many Jewish weddings are held at the same site as the reception. Weddings may not be conducted on the Sabbath (sundown Friday to sundown Saturday), on other religious holidays, or during historical mourning periods. The bride and groom should meet with the rabbi shortly after they become engaged to select a date. Because the Hebrew calendar is lunar, holidays are celebrated on different dates each year, so this visit to the rabbi is very important.

According to the most ancient Jewish law, the state of marriage could be attained by the performance, with witnesses, of any of the following acts:

➤ Cohabitation

➤ The delivery of a document (ketuba) by the man

➤ Presentation by the man of an article of value to the woman

Most ceremonies today include the last two of these three, plus the exchange of a specific vow.

The marriage document, called a *ketuba*, is a contract written in Aramaic that outlines the groom's responsibility for and to the bride. It is signed by the groom and two witnesses. Couples sometimes commission artists and scribes to create beautiful ketubas and then have the work of art framed and hung in their homes.

In ancient times, "something of value" often was a coin, but today it usually is a ring. The ring must be of solid gold, with no stones or gems, and it must, at the ceremony, be the groom's property. Today, when many couples select diamond wedding sets, it often is necessary for the couple to borrow a family ring for the ceremony. To do this and meet the ownership condition, the groom must "buy" the ring from the family member and "sell" it back after the wedding.

After the ketuba is signed and the item of value has been presented, the rabbi and the two fathers lead a procession of the groom and male guests into the bride's chamber for the *badekan* (veiling) ceremony. This custom comes from the biblical story of Jacob, who worked for seven years to marry Rachel, only to discover that her father had substituted the older, blind Leah under heavy veiling. A groom still comes to look at his bride before the ceremony and actually places the veil over her.

Once the bride is veiled, the ceremony is ready to begin. How the rabbi and cantor enter is determined by local custom. If the grandparents choose to be part of the processional, they lead off, with the bride's grandparents walking first. The groomsmen follow, one at a time. Following the groomsmen is the best man. Then the groom enters, escorted by both his parents. The bridesmaids enter, single file, then the maid of honor, the flower girl and ring bearer (if you are using children), followed by the bride, who is escorted by both her parents. The illustration on the next page shows a traditional Jewish processional.

Legend
1 = Bride
2 = Groom
3 = Maid of Honor
4 = Best Man
5 = Bridesmaid
6 = Groomsmen/ushers
7 = Flower Girl
8 = Ring Bearer
9 = Father of Bride
10 = Mother of Bride
11 = Father of Groom
12 = Mother of Groom
13 = Officiant
14 = Cantor
15 = Bride's Grandfathers
16 = Bride's Grandmothers
17 = Groom's Grandfathers
18 = Groom's Grandmothers

The Jewish processional.

The illustration on the next page shows the placement of the wedding party after the processional for the Jewish service.

The wedding party usually stands to the left of the *chuppah* (canopy). The chuppah usually is supported by four poles in stanchions, but can also be held by four men during the ceremony, as is frequently done in the Sephardic tradition. Sometimes, a large *tallis* (prayer shawl) is put on the poles and held above the couple to create the chuppah. The chuppah symbolizes the home the couple will establish.

When the bride and her parents reach the chuppah, the parents may lift the bride's veil and give her a kiss. They then replace the veil and walk up under the chuppah on the right side. When her parents are in their place, the bride takes three steps on her own, symbolizing her decision to enter the marriage, and the groom comes to escort her

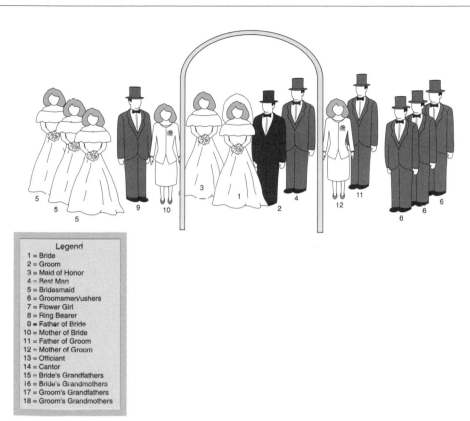

Legend

1 = Bride
2 = Groom
3 = Maid of Honor
4 = Best Man
5 = Bridesmaid
6 = Groomsmen/ushers
7 = Flower Girl
8 = Ring Bearer
9 = Father of Bride
10 = Mother of Bride
11 = Father of Groom
12 = Mother of Groom
13 = Officiant
14 = Cantor
15 = Bride's Grandfathers
16 = Bride's Grandmothers
17 = Groom's Grandfathers
18 = Groom's Grandmothers

Jewish wedding party positions at the end of the processional.

under the chuppah. The groom turns as he joins her, so she is on his right.

During the ceremony, the rabbi reads the ketuba in both Hebrew and English and the couple drinks wine. Sephardic rabbis usually wrap the couple in a tallis, symbolizing their becoming one. The bride (and sometimes the groom) receives a ring. In most ceremonies, the groom repeats a Hebrew vow after the rabbi, with the giving of the ring. The groom declares, "Behold, thou art consecrated to me with this ring, according to the law of Moses and Israel."

At the conclusion of the ceremony, the rabbi will ask the best man to place a wine glass, wrapped in a white cloth or in a special bag the couple provides, under the groom's right foot. The groom will break it, symbolizing the destruction of the temple in Jerusalem, although there are nearly as many interpretations of the meaning of the breaking of the glass as there are rabbis. The bride and groom will kiss immediately after being declared "man and wife" and then run up the aisle into a Yichud.

The *Yichud* is a brief seclusion where the couple can spend a few moments together before joining their guests. If the couple has fasted until the ceremony, this is their opportunity to break that fast. Even couples who have not fasted appreciate a few moments alone in what is usually a hectic and emotionally packed day. Because of this brief seclusion, Jewish weddings usually do not have receiving lines.

Summing Up

This chapter has been an overview of wedding ceremonies of four major religious groups in the United States. It is not intended to be the final word on any of them. Your own minister, rabbi, or priest can be a great help in explaining why something is done the way it is or in giving you additional information about the various parts of a particular service. I urge you to seek his counsel.

Just some final thoughts. No matter what kind of religious tradition you follow, remember that this is your ceremony. Don't be afraid to ask questions. Make sure that you understand what you are saying and why you are saying it. You may be bound by certain rituals and rules, but you can still put a lot of thought and love into this important celebration.

The Least You Need to Know

➤ Even though parts of the wedding service may be quite similar, various religions and denominations can have very distinct rules and requirements.

➤ Meet with your minister, rabbi, or priest early in the planning stages so that you have time to meet any pre-wedding obligations (for example, Pre-Canna classes).

➤ The officiant has the last word when it comes to making decisions about the wedding service.

Part VI
Surviving the Big Event

Well, this is it! The big day is quickly approaching and you are ready. You have met with countless vendors, looked at dozens of bridal bouquets, leafed through numerous invitation catalogs, tried on too many dresses, and have picked out some wonderful favors for your guests to enjoy. This is where all your hard work and dedication is going to pay off. Everything should be in place now. You have a few last-minute details to take care of, and then you just have to get yourself to the church on time.

In this Part, I'll discuss the importance of the wedding rehearsal and how to prepare for your big day by eating right and getting some sleep. Then, I'll walk you through the ceremony, the photography session, and the reception so that you know what to expect on your big day. Read this Part, and prepare for a day to remember.

DADDY!!

CHUCK'S CURIOSITY GETS THE BETTER OF HIM...

Chapter 21

Prepare for the Onslaught

We've discussed nearly all the details you need to know to help you prepare for your wedding. Now, you are zeroing in on the big day. Preparation is the name of the game; it has been all along. Now, even more than ever, I want you to prepare just a little bit more as you move right up to the big day!

Gearing Up for the Big Event

The wedding rehearsal is an important event in the wedding planning process. It is your insurance policy that the members of your wedding cast know their lines, places, cues, what to do, and what not to do come wedding day.

It's *Preparation* with a capital *P.* For example, ushering Grandma to the wrong pew does not make for a lovely day. With a little run-through to work out the bugs and fine-tune the mechanics, you should have all your bases covered.

The wedding rehearsal usually occurs the day or evening before the wedding is to take place. Sometimes, the rehearsal doesn't take place the eve of the wedding. Many times, the Jewish rehearsal takes place the morning of the wedding. Plan the rehearsal for whatever time your individual circumstances dictate. Sometimes, with many members of the wedding party arriving from out of town, you can't logistically work in the rehearsal until early on the wedding day.

Practice Makes Perfect

The whole purpose of the wedding rehearsal is to practice what will take place during the ceremony. As in a play rehearsal, the cast of characters (wedding party) and the director (officiant or bridal consultant) conducts the rehearsal so that all the players know their parts, responsibilities, and duties.

It is very helpful for the musicians to participate in the wedding rehearsal. It not only sets the tone for the wedding, but it gives the wedding party a sense of timing and rhythm for both the processional and recessional and adds dignity to the proceedings.

It is best if the musicians are present for the rehearsal. One of the prime functions of the rehearsal is to practice both the processional (when the wedding party enters) and the recessional (when the wedding party exits). If the musicians are not present, it is more difficult for the wedding party to get a feel for rhythm and timing. I also have found that a rehearsal without music does not provide the true spirit of the dignity you hope to achieve. A wedding should certainly be a dignified event, regardless of whether the ceremony is being held in a church or in your backyard. Wedding parties tend to be louder and more unruly when there is no music at the rehearsal. Sometimes, when you use musicians other than the standard organist or pianist, such as a string quartet or choir, those musicians consider the rehearsal a second performance. In other words, they expect to be paid for attending the rehearsal. While it is not completely necessary for them to be present, it is very helpful. It's a good idea for them to send a representative to determine their placement and how many attendants there are so that they can judge how long the processional will be. Be sure to ask whether your musicians will attend your rehearsal.

There's an old superstition that says a bride is not to participate in the wedding rehearsal. I'm not sure where that came from but it makes no sense. She's the one who's going to be on stage at the wedding, and it makes all the sense in the world for her to walk through her paces at the rehearsal. An actress would never go on stage for a play without first rehearsing. A football or basketball player would not go into a game without practicing with the team beforehand. The same applies for a wedding. Now, you may or may not repeat your wedding vows to each other. You may just be given a cue line and then leave out the actual vows. Both the bride and groom should practice at the rehearsal.

The rehearsal is a good time to try out any bridal accessories, such as an exceptionally long train or veil, that may require some extra attention or special accommodation during the ceremony. One bride I worked with chose to wear a full-length veil that extended four feet behind her on the floor. It was a beautiful sight to see. She did look radiant floating down the aisle on the arm of her father. Dad, naturally, was feeling rather nervous. When they reached the altar area, instead of stepping back away from the veil, he stepped right on it and pulled it completely off the bride's head. He reached down, rolled up the pile of tulle, and tossed it to his wife in the first pew. Words do not begin to describe the look on the mother's face. I now use a "practice" long veil and long train on the bride during the rehearsal, if it's determined that will be a concern. Brides are amazed at how awkward and cumbersome those long veils can be during the wedding and by practicing, it gives them a much better feel for movement and placement.

If you have a long veil or a longer than usual train, you may want to rehearse with it to get a feel for what it will be like on the wedding day. Once a bride puts on the gown and starts dragging around all that extra material, she comes to understand rather quickly how heavy and awkward those appendages can be. With a little preparation and a little imagination, you can avoid an awkward or embarrassing scene.

Whom to Include

Those who should attend the wedding rehearsal include all members of the wedding party, including ushers, flower girl, ring bearer, readers, soloist, musicians, and, of course, the officiant. If you are including train bearers or pages, they should attend. You will also want your parents present, especially if they have a part in the service. Many times, the mothers will light the family candles at the beginning of the service. If they can practice at the rehearsal, they won't be as nervous during the ceremony.

Approach your wedding rehearsal with a relaxed attitude. After coordinating more than 200 weddings, I realize that often this is asking the impossible, but try very hard not to get so upset with the little things that you lose sight of what is taking place. After all, you are dealing with humans, and humans do make mistakes. If there are mistakes made at the rehearsal, try to keep it all in perspective. After all, it is just the rehearsal. Barring any national emergency or natural disaster, you will be married by the time your wedding day comes to an end. Don't sweat the little stuff; you will enjoy the whole process if you can just relax.

Who's the Boss Here?

In Chapter 4, I told you the tale of the clergyman who decided to get back at one bride's mother who had worked against him every step of the way. During the ceremony, in a very public manner, he had the last word and showed her who was in control. Well, the officiant should be in control or in charge of the wedding rehearsal. Some facilities have a wedding director on staff who oversees the rehearsal. If that is the case with your ceremony site, work with that person. Also, if you have hired a bridal consultant, please make sure she knows her role at the rehearsal. Unless she has been asked by the officiant to help out, she should assume a back-seat role; she shouldn't run the show.

Over the years, I have found that the best rehearsals are the ones conducted by the person who will perform the wedding service. What-ever circumstances you face, go in with a positive attitude. Try to work out all the ceremony details long before the rehearsal. It does little good for you or the officiant to be deciding reading selections the eve of your wedding. If at all possible, get those items ironed out long before the rehearsal.

If the officiant does not take charge of your rehearsal, you could be in for some rough waters. The more in charge the officiant is at the rehearsal, the smoother the wedding ceremony goes.

One bride I worked with was a very take-charge kind of person, and she decided to make it her mission to single-handedly direct her rehearsal. Although she gave it her best, she was quite unorganized.

She also insisted that everything be rehearsed to perfection. Halfway through the rehearsal, the officiant, frustrated with the bride's attitude and her constantly saying "But I want it perfect," threw his hands towards the heavens and walked out. This does not generate a warm and fuzzy feeling. It can be frightening to see the man who is supposed to perform your marriage service in less than 24 hours walk out the front doors of the church. If he walked out at the rehearsal, will he show up for the wedding? Who knows? When the officiant walked out, the bride burst into tears, threw down the wedding program, and stormed out. Her mother also burst into tears and ran after the bride. None of the wedding party knew if there would be a wedding the next day. There was, but the tension between the bride and the officiant was thick enough to cut with the proverbial knife.

Remember to have respect for the person who is going to perform your service. Make him your friend, not your enemy. And above all, remember why you are at the rehearsal in the first place. You are here to practice for your marriage service; the day the two of you vow to spend the rest of your lives together. Don't lose track of what's really important.

The Last Big Fling

A discussion of the wedding rehearsal brings to mind one other little item we should talk about—the bachelor or bachelorette party. Promise me one thing, and don't do this for me (hey, I'm not your mother), do it for yourselves. Do not hold this final fling the night before your wedding. It can be a great time to share with your friends, but the bottom line is that you need to be in good shape for the wedding day. If you've been out too late and partied too much, you may not be in any shape to do anything—much less something as important as getting married. All right, enough from Mother Teddy.

Historically, the bachelor party began as a way the townsmen could help a prospective groom get all the philandering out of his system before he took a wife. Today, the bachelor party is an opportunity for the men in the wedding party to get together for a night on the town, a baseball game, or maybe a sailing trip. One groom, who loved to gamble, got his guys together for a trip to Las Vegas for a weekend. Although a more elaborate party than most bachelor parties, they did have a great time, and it gave them a chance to spend some quality time with each other.

continues

continued

If you're a camping nut, why not take your friends to the woods for a camping trip? Fishing and sitting around a campfire telling jokes can be a relaxing—and relatively inexpensive—way to get away from it all for awhile.

Some grooms prefer something less dramatic. Maybe a night in their favorite pub with just a few close friends or ringside seats at a prize fight. Whatever strikes your fancy, try to incorporate those ideas into your bachelor party.

While the men are living it up in a local restaurant, the women can be doing the same thing with a bachelorette party. One of the neatest bachelorette parties I have ever heard about occurred a few years ago. The maid of honor made up a scavenger hunt for the women in the wedding party. The group divided into several carloads and each group was given a list of items to find and bring back to the host site within a certain time limit. Of course, there was no alcohol on the road, but a couple of bottles of champagne did await the winners. The bride later shared with me how much she had enjoyed the evening. Many of the items for which they were searching were things her groom-to-be would like, such as a deck of cards or a book on old cars.

Whatever you decide about pre-wedding parties and your friends, just make sure you play it safe, keep it fun, make sure people know the ground rules, and hold the party several nights before the wedding.

Getting Yourself Ready

Okay, time is marching on. You have made it through the rehearsal in one piece, and you and your groom have been the honored guests at a lovely rehearsal dinner. You say good night to your groom and head home for some much needed rest.

I have tried to emphasize throughout this book how important it is for you to be organized. I don't keep repeating that phrase because I have a limited vocabulary. I say this because of all the ways you can help yourself the best, staying organized and knowing what to do is the key to a successful, stress-free wedding day.

You Are Getting Sleepy

When you come home (or back to the hotel—wherever you are staying the night before your wedding), take a nice, hot, relaxing bath. Now, I'm not a bathtub fan. I much prefer showers, but for this particular event, I think you will find a nice warm bath very relaxing. That's what we're after here. You need to be relaxed so that you can get some much needed sleep. You've probably been going about a 100 miles an hour for the last several months. Now it's time to slow down and savor the day to come.

While you're relaxing in the tub, try sipping some warm milk (not chocolate) or some herbal tea. It's very soothing to the body and soul and research has proven that warm milk releases in the body some chemicals that bring on sleep. As you lay in the tub, focus your attention on a peaceful setting: the green hills of a favorite park, a campfire growing dim, or the brilliance of a sunset. Peace, tranquility, and a sense of calm (using imagery to stimulate that sense); that's what you're after. Put on some soft music to help set the mood or listen to a relaxation tape. Maybe the sounds of water or wind gently blowing can soothe your soul. This is "be good to me" time. Indulge yourself. Try to block out every possible negative vision you can. You want to be at peace—inside and out.

When you finish with your bath, follow your normal night-time routine. Get as much sleep as possible tonight. The wedding day will be exhausting. You need a lot of sleep now so you can feel and look great in the morning. A bride with huge circles under her eyes from lack of sleep is not a pretty sight.

You Are What You Eat

Just as important as enough rest is the right kind of food in your body. As I have mentioned several times in earlier chapters, you must keep yourself on track by eating right and getting enough rest. With all the appointments to keep, fittings to schedule, and vendors to call, nourishing food is important. Try to avoid fast food.

You wake up refreshed from a good night's sleep. Now let's get some good food into you. For starters, if you are not a breakfast eater, try to be one today. Even if it's a bagel and some juice. Just get a little something in your tummy. Believe me, depending on the time of your service, there may not be time to eat later on, or you may be too nervous. If you do enjoy breakfast, then include in your menu some carbohydrates (for energy), some fruit or juice (for vitamin C), and maybe a little protein (milk, cocoa, eggs, or cheese). If you aren't a heavy breakfast eater, don't change now. The important thing is to get your body revved up for the endurance test of a lifetime.

Take to the ceremony site a tray of small sandwiches (without sauces to avoid spills) for the wedding party to nibble on while waiting for the ceremony to start and as pictures are being finished.

If you are relying on family and friends, don't make the decorating so complex that it requires either a long time to arrange or the skill of a brain surgeon to complete. You want your family and friends to be able to enjoy this day, too.

If your wedding is late in the day, it's a really good idea to bring some snacks to the ceremony site for the wedding party to nibble on. You don't have to provide a meal, just some small sandwiches (without mustard, ketchup, or mayo—don't take a chance on staining your wedding finery), and maybe some pretzels and soft drinks. That way, wedding party members who haven't had a chance to eat can get a bite and not be so famished before the reception begins. Also, if you're serving alcohol at the reception, the snacks help to ensure that your wedding party will not start drinking on empty stomachs.

Don't Forget the Decorations!

Remember that sometime early on the day of the wedding you have to think about how to make your reception site look the way you want it to look when the guests start streaming in. If you have made arrangements with the florist and bridal consultant to take care of the details, then you're all set. Relax and skip to the next section about getting yourself to the church. If you have to provide the decorations and do the decorating yourself, you'll need to get the help of some reliable relatives and friends.

It is better to have too much time to decorate than not enough. If you think it will only take you two hours to decorate 30 tables, allow three to four hours and play it safe. This is your wedding day, not a marathon. You want to be as relaxed as you can possibly be.

Get Me to the Church on Time

Over and over again, I remind the brides I work with, and I will remind you, too, give yourself plenty of time to dress for your wedding. This is one time in your life that you probably want to go all out in getting yourself ready, and you don't want to be rushed.

One bride who wanted more than anything to decorate her reception site took on more than she had bargained for. She had already made the centerpieces for the tables, but she couldn't even let her friends and relatives take on the tasks of setting up the room. No, she wanted to personally oversee every detail. So, she worked and worked and the minutes were ticking off her wedding day clock. At 4:30 p.m., and with a 6:30 wedding time, she left the reception site and headed for the ceremony site. She was running late, and the pictures were to start at 5:15. She wanted to take a shower because she had gotten hot and sweaty working on the decorations. She hopped in the shower, turned on the water, and screamed. Hot, rusty water poured out of the faucet. After she calmed down enough to talk and to understand that she hadn't been burned by the water but instead was just covered in rusty water, she grabbed a towel, her robe, her car keys, and ran to her car. Where she disappeared to, no one will ever know, but she arrived back at the church, rust-free, about 20 minutes later. How she ever got her makeup on, her hair dried and styled, and her gown on and still made it down the aisle on time, is anybody's guess. Moral of the story: don't push yourself so much on the wedding day that you are literally out of breath as you start down the aisle. Let others help; delegate some responsibilities. This is one day when you should not rush.

What to Take to the Church

In the Midwest, at least, it seems most brides choose to dress at the ceremony site. They don't dress at home and then ride to the church in their gowns. While this practice will vary depending on your part of the country and your own preferences, you will still need to take some items to the church.

Dressing Off Site

If you dress at home or at the hotel, have someone take these personal items to the church or other facility for you: lipstick, pressed powder for touch-ups, breath mints, and tissues. You also have to make sure that someone—a friend, relative, or your bridal consultant—gets these general wedding items to the ceremony site: guest book (if you are using one at the ceremony) and pen, your ceremony programs, any payments that still have to be made to vendors on the day of the wedding (usually the musicians or limousine company), your unity candle (unless the florist is providing it), and any other decorations that you were to provide. If at all possible, take some of these items to the rehearsal and leave them there or give them to your bridal consultant. If you can get rid of some of these items early on, you'll be able to concentrate on just getting yourself ready and to the church in good fashion.

Dressing at the Site

If you are dressing at the ceremony site, you will have a little more baggage than the bride who dresses at home. For starters, you need your gown, slip, shoes, hose, veil or headpiece, special undergarments, (hey, I want to keep this book G-rated), plus your personal makeup and hair care items.

A particularly nice treat for your wedding day is to have your makeup or hair done at the ceremony site. Come early in your sweats and treat yourself to a professional to do your makeup and your hair. It's a wonderful addition to the day, and photographers tell me the pictures are just that much better. If you plan to have that done, be sure to allow enough time for it.

Something Old, Something New

Whether you choose to dress at home or at the wedding facility, be sure to include in the bag of tricks you are taking with you the items in the verse: "Something old, something new, something borrowed, something blue, and a lucky penny in your shoe."

"Something old" is used to show a sense of continuity. You can use a family heirloom or carry the family Bible or Prayer Book. I wore my grandmother's onyx and diamond ring on my wedding day and carried a hankie from my great-grandmother.

"Something new" equates to hope for an optimistic future. Most brides consider their gown to be their "something new."

"Something borrowed" refers to the old superstition that happiness wears off on others. So if you borrow something from someone who is happy or from a happily married friend, you are to have a happy future.

For "something blue," brides include a blue item of some kind to bolster the favorite old line, "Those who dress in blue have lovers true." Blue has long been considered the color of fidelity, purity, and love. Brides in Israel wear blue ribbons to denote purity and fidelity. Blue also can be associated with the Virgin Mary. Many brides choose to wear a blue garter.

… and "a penny in your shoe." In England it's a sixpence; in Canada, a quarter; and in the United States, a penny. These all help ensure a married life with fortune.

Other customs exist around the world suggesting what a bride should carry on her wedding day. Brides in Greece, for example, place a lump of sugar in one of their wedding gloves to give them the sweetness of life. Brides in Belgium embroider their name in a bridal handkerchief that is framed after the ceremony and passed on to other brides in the family.

The Emergency Kit

Ah, the emergency kit. If you have hired a bridal consultant to coordinate the weekend activities, you can skip this section and move on to the next chapter; she should take care of having these items available for you.

If you are braving this adventure on your own, well, take heed. There are some items you need at the ceremony site, just for "insurance." Of course, you will not need all these things, but it's a good idea to have them, just in case. My kit grows after each wedding. I take items that fill two very large canvas bags, plus an organizer and a tool kit. It's better to be safe than sorry. When you need a big safety pin to hold up the groom's trousers, you don't want to spend time trying to figure out where (in close proximity to the church) you can find such an item.

Bet You Didn't Know... When Lady Diana Spencer and Prince Charles were wed, the princess had a tiny silver horseshoe sewn in the waistline of her gown. The coach they rode in from the ceremony to the reception had a replica of that same horseshoe, in silver of course, attached to the coach. (In this case, however, I guess the good luck didn't rub off.)

Start with the basics: sewing kit, scissors, safety pins (various sizes), tissues, masking tape, and stapler. (You may be surprised at the repairs you can make with masking tape and a stapler.) To that, add a hand towel, wash cloth, soft drinks/juice/water, saltine crackers, static cling spray, breath mints or mouth wash, and sanitary supplies (you never know). There are hundreds of other items you can add, and at every wedding, I discover another item that would come in handy.

Being prepared, both physically and emotionally, and staying organized are ways to keep you on track for your wedding day. It is time consuming, but it pays off when you glide down that aisle relatively stress free and truly a radiant bride.

Go get 'em!

The Least You Need to Know

➤ The rehearsal is a very important part of the wedding activities. Just as an actress wouldn't go on stage without rehearsing her lines, don't show up for your wedding day unprepared.

➤ The person officiating at the wedding should be the person in charge of the rehearsal. Work with your officiant to make the rehearsal go as smoothly as possible.

➤ It's great if musicians can be at the rehearsal. It helps set the tone and mood and adds dignity to the proceedings.

➤ One of the best ways to help get you ready for your big day is to get enough sleep the night before and eat a good breakfast the morning of the wedding.

➤ Allow plenty of time to dress for your wedding; you do not want to be rushed. Pamper yourself.

➤ Be sure to put together a kit of emergency items to take along to the ceremony site for last minute crises.

Chapter 22

I Do, I Really Do

In This Chapter

➤ Some guidelines to writing your own vows

➤ What to include in your wedding service

➤ Sample vows and programs

➤ An overview of the ceremony: what happens after you take that first step down the aisle

Many couples sit in my office and tell me they are going to write their own wedding vows. They know exactly what they want to say to each other and the traditional versions just don't make sense to them. When push comes to shove, however, they find out rather quickly that they either can't do it because their officiant won't allow it, they find it too difficult because they have no experience in writing, or they simply run out of time.

Before you even think about writing your own vows, check with whoever is going to perform your wedding ceremony. If he gives you the go-ahead, get some reference books (I suggest several in this chapter) and then sit down with each other and try to decide what exactly it is you want the whole world to know and understand about your love for each other.

Writing Your Own Vows

When you decide to write your own vows, you and your groom need to sit down someplace (jointly or individually) where you won't be disturbed and think about the things in this world that mean something to you. What all do you want to include? Do you want to totally rewrite the vows segment or only add a few words?

 Never simply assume that you can change any part of your wedding service, including the vows segment. Always clear service changes with the officiant.

Before you can begin this task, you have to know where the two of you are coming from and where you want to go. Is tradition important to you? Do you want to be completely spontaneous and go with the moment? Is it more important to include readings and poetry that have meaning to the two of you? There are many choices out there. That's the easy part. The hard part is putting all the pieces together. One good resource on this topic is a book titled *With These Words… I Thee Wed,* by Barbara Eklof (Bob Adams, Inc., 1989).

It's a great book to sit down with and read vows that cover a whole range of feelings and emotions. This book even provides a questionnaire in the back for each of you to fill out. Once filled out, you can see where the two of you have similarities and common threads. Working through this questionnaire should give you some form of "theme" for your vows.

After you have the go-ahead from your officiant and you have decided what is important, your next task should be to look at some sample vows for ideas.

I, Mary, Take You John

If you are a traditional couple and you want to keep that flavor, you may only want to change a word here or there and keep most of the traditional words.

One of the more traditional vows segments goes like this:

I, (name), take you (name), as my wedded husband.

You can probably find several variations on this line. A vows segment from *The Protestant Wedding Sourcebook*, for example, reads as follows:

Before God and these witnesses, I, (groom), take you, (bride), to be my wife, and I promise to be true to you, and to be faithful to you as long as we both shall live.

Another selection from the same book reads as follows:

I (groom), take you, (bride), to be my wedded wife; and I do promise and covenant to be your loving and faithful husband; for better, for worse, for richer, for poorer; in sickness and in health; so long as we both shall live.

These examples, while still quite traditional, add a word here and there to give the vow more meaning. Sometimes, just changing the word to more modern terms can make the vow seem more personal. For example, insert "you" instead of "thee."

Get some ideas from these samples and change the words around to put your feelings and thoughts about each other into words with which you are comfortable.

Mary, Join Me as We Venture into the Cosmos

If you are not a traditional couple and you want something very different and unique, you have some more work to do.

Your best bet may be to pull out parts of several vows segments, mix and match them to fit your needs, and then see what you come up with. It takes time and concentration, but the end result may be something the two of you can cherish the rest of your lives.

One couple had chosen an outdoor setting for the ceremony and had asked an officer of the court to preside. They wanted to limit the religious aspects of the service, but still have something meaningful to the two of them and to their families. There were some traditional elements they wanted to keep. They studied several books, and after much cutting and pasting, they came up with these vows:

I, (name), acknowledge my love for you in front of our family and friends. I respect you as a person and in doing so, invite you to share in my life as I hope to share in yours. I promise always to recognize you as an individual. I promise to be true to you in good times and in bad, in sickness and in health. I will try through kindness and understanding to work with you for the life we have envisioned. I will love you and honor you all the days of my life.

In this sample, the couple wanted it clear to all involved that they would continue to be individuals as well as a couple. They told their guests that they would have respect for each other, would treat each other with kindness and understanding, would love and honor each other (some of the old traditional stuff, but it works), and then promised to be true to each other in good and bad times.

This couple felt very good about these words. The vow meant more to them because they had such a large part in putting it together.

Finding Some Inspiration

The following books can help you get started if you want to write your own vows:

The Protestant Wedding Sourcebook, by Sidney F. Batts, Westminster/John Knox Press, 1993.

Weddings, A Complete Guide to All Religions and Interfaith Marriage Services, by Abraham J. Klausner, Alpha Publishing Company, 1986.

Wedding Readings, by Eleanor Munro, published by Penguin Group, 1989.

Words for Your Wedding, by David Glusker and Peter Misner, Harper & Row, 1983.

Christian Wedding Planner, by Ruth Merzzy and Kent Hughes, Tyndale Publishers, Inc., 1991.

Customizing Your Service

Even if you can't do anything with your vows, there are other items that you can add to your service to make it more personal (if you have the blessing of the officiant). Some couples are just too overwhelmed to even consider rearranging the actual ceremony, but others do little things here and there to make the ceremony truly their own.

Some Unique Ideas to Consider

There are several areas within the ceremony you can expand on to give your wedding a unique flair. Music is one of the easiest ways to add some personality to the service. Again, check with the musicians at the church or site to make sure you are not breaking any rules, and then let your imagination soar.

One couple sang to each other during the service. It was beautiful because they were both professional musicians. (As I stated in an earlier chapter, you may not want to try this one.)

I've actually had several couples use singing as a way to make their wedding ceremony unique to them. One father sang to his daughter after they reached the altar. He chose "Climb Every Mountain" from *The Sound of Music*. It was very moving, and when he reached the part, "… till you find your dream," there wasn't a dry eye in the church. I told you earlier about the bride who burst into "When I Fall in Love" at her wedding. Her groom didn't know it was coming, and the look on his face was priceless. (It's times like these when a good videographer is worth his weight in gold!)

Be careful that you don't add anything to your ceremony that greatly increases the pressures of the day. You already may be on emotional overload, so don't make it harder on yourself. Don't consider singing at your own wedding, for example, unless you know you can deal with the added pressures of performing.

If you aren't into singing or songs performed by someone else, think about using music in other ways to make your service truly yours. See if you can add chimes or a bell choir (a group of musicians who play bells). It would be very fitting for a wedding.

Readings are other avenues to use to make the service more individual. Be sure to check with the officiant first. You may choose either a religious piece or both a religious piece and a traditional, classic piece. You may want to write something for the service. One bride hired an actor to read Elizabeth Barrett Browning's famous piece, "How Do I Love Thee." Before that reading, I had never been particularly fond of that piece. After hearing it read as it should be, however, I definitely changed my mind. Selections from *The Prophet*, by Kahlil Gibran, are also popular contemporary readings, or you may like a particular e.e. cummings piece and want to work it into your service.

While a professional actor may be a nice touch, readings are a great way to include close friends who are not otherwise part of the wedding party. One bride asked a close friend whose mother had died tragically two months earlier to do one reading. Then, in the "Prayers

of the Faithful" at the Nuptial Mass, the congregation prayed for the reader's mother. A nice, thoughtful touch showing that the bride—even on her day—was a caring, loving person.

One bride I worked with had her wedding gown made. She then took some of the leftover material and made small handkerchiefs for both mothers. She had their initials embroidered on the hankies and wrapped a single rose in each one. On her way down the aisle, she stopped first to present one to her mother-in-law and then stopped to give one to her mother. It was very touching, and I'm sure those hankies are framed and hanging on someone's wall.

One of the most memorable wedding ceremonies I have ever witnessed was a wedding I coordinated before I had even considered getting in the business. (You'll meet Cindy and Lee in Chapter 27 when they share their survival tips.) They worked very hard on the various parts of the service and thought through the rationale for why they wanted things the way they did. They had done their homework and each part of the ceremony had meaning. The highlight of the ceremony was a candle lighting service. Not only did the couple light a candle, but they shared their light with the ushers who lit candles and then walked down the aisles lighting the candles of every guest on the end of each pew. That guest then turned and lit his neighbor's candle, and so on. The light spread across that church with the feeling of a warm blanket covering you on a cold night.

The minister had just concluded a lovely sermon in which he talked about the inner light we all have and how we must pass that light on and make the world a better place. When all the candles were lit in the church, 500 guests sat in the glowing candle light while the couple turned towards the congregation. With a look of love and hope in their eyes, they raised their candles up and the congregation followed suit. That entire church was lit up by candle light. There was the feeling of togetherness and hope for the future, not only for the couple, but for each member of the congregation. It was a very moving experience. To this day, when people talk about that wedding, they always comment on the candle lighting service.

Where to Draw the Line

Okay, you want a truly unique service. You want a service that causes your guests to say as they file out: "Oh, that was wonderful. The ceremony meant so much to them (you and your groom)." You want to make it your ceremony, not some carbon copy script that half the brides and grooms in the United States use, but you don't want to go overboard.

It's as easy as K.I.S.S—keep it simple, sweetie. Just because you love music does not necessarily mean you should engage the Philharmonic Orchestra, the Mormon Tabernacle Choir, a string quartet, two trumpeters, and an organist. No, let's do one or two of the above and call it quits. If you have the budget to hire the orchestra and the choir, please call me. I want to talk to you. (Just kidding.)

Adding one or two unique features to your service is probably enough. You don't want guests so overwhelmed by the individuality of the service that they lose track of what is really taking place.

So, K.I.S.S. And enjoy!

Sample Wedding Programs

A wedding program details how the service will proceed and who is involved. Programs can be a single sheet of paper (perhaps rolled and tied with a ribbon or engraved on fine paper and monogrammed with the couple's initials) or a small booklet. A wedding program enables guests to follow along during the service and see who's in the wedding party.

Following are two sample wedding programs to give you some ideas. The first is a very simple program, while the second is more elaborate.

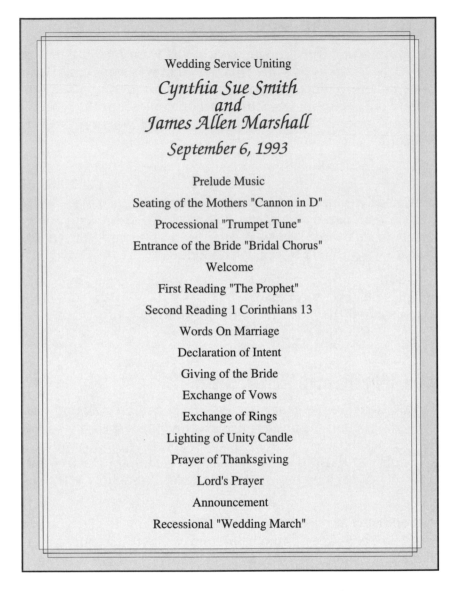

Wedding Service Uniting

Cynthia Sue Smith
and
James Allen Marshall

September 6, 1993

Prelude Music

Seating of the Mothers "Cannon in D"

Processional "Trumpet Tune"

Entrance of the Bride "Bridal Chorus"

Welcome

First Reading "The Prophet"

Second Reading 1 Corinthians 13

Words On Marriage

Declaration of Intent

Giving of the Bride

Exchange of Vows

Exchange of Rings

Lighting of Unity Candle

Prayer of Thanksgiving

Lord's Prayer

Announcement

Recessional "Wedding March"

A simple wedding program printed on a single sheet of paper.

Prelude "Endless Love"	Gospel Father Lawrence Rhiel
"Here I Am Lord"	Matthew 19:3-6
"On Eagle's Wings"	Homily
Seating of Mothers Theme from "Ice Castles"	Solo - "If You Ask Me To" James Johnson
Lighting of candles	Exchange of Consent
Reading "The Lady of Shalot" - John Miller	Blessing and Exchange of Rings
Processional "Air on G": - Bach	Prayer for the Couple
Entrance of Bride "Bridal Chorus"	Solo - Unity Candle
Greeting and Opening Prayer Father Lawrence Rhiel	"Love of a Lifetime" James Johnson
First Reading	Prayers of the faithful Father Lawrence Rhiel
Sirach 26:1-4, 16-21 Susan Miller	Response "Lord Hear Our Prayer"
Responsorial Psalm	Nuptial Blessing
Second Reading	Solo - "The Lord's Prayer" James Johnson
1 Corinthians 12:31-13:8a Mary Ann Miles	Sign of Peace
Readings John Miller	Final Blessing
"Sonnet XLIII"	Response - Amen
"Love"	Solo - "Feels Like Heaven" James Johnson
Solo - "The Wedding Song" James Johnson	Recessional "Wedding March"

Wedding Service Uniting
Cynthia Sue Smith
and
James Allen Marshall
September 6, 1993

A more elaborate wedding program booklet.

As an extra touch, you can add a brief note about the wedding participants. For example:

Maid of Honor, Lynn Jones
(Lynn has been the bride's best friend since 1974)

Reading, "The Lady of Shalot"—John Miller
(John is the groom's younger brother)

This Is It: The Ceremony!

All systems are go. You've been through the rehearsal. You got a good night's sleep. You even ate a little breakfast this morning. Now, you're in the back of the church holding on for dear life to your dad. Your guests are all seated. Your groom's mother and your mom have been seated. The candles are lit. The music is playing. Your heart is beating faster and faster; you may even have little beads of sweat breaking out on your upper lip. The processional music starts for the bridesmaids, and then you hear the trumpet fanfare and you take that first step. You know, they always say, that first step is a big one.

Take a deep breath. Seriously. Controlling your breathing has a calming effect on your body and your mind. Relax and walk S L O W LY. After all, this is one walk you want to make the most of. You want to get mileage out of this trip down the aisle. You want to be poised, proud, happy, maybe even a little teary-eyed. This is your moment. If you haven't seen your groom before the service, this will be the first chance you have to gaze at each other (although, it will be a quick gaze).

Bet You Didn't Know... "The Wedding Song" (you know, the one that begins "As it was in the beginning...") written and sung by Neil Paul Stookey of Peter, Paul, and Mary fame is a popular wedding number. Did you know that he has never profited from royalties? Actually, neither has anyone else. He set up a foundation that receives all proceeds from royalties. As of March, 1994, over $2 million has gone to charity. That's a true humanitarian.

As you walk down the aisle, make eye contact with your guests. Let them know, visually, that you are glad they're here. One of my favorite pictures from our wedding is the one of Daddy and me walking down the aisle and, in keeping with my character, I'm just chatting away to guests along the aisle. But that's me, and the photographer captured the moment perfectly.

When you reach the altar, depending on what type of service you have, you may either leave the arm of your dad or stay with him until the officiant asks the famous "who gives this woman..." question. When you reach the altar area in a Catholic service, your groom comes over to you, you give dad a kiss, and then you turn to walk up to the altar with your groom.

Now you're in the hands of the officiant. And, trust me, he has probably done this about a 1,000 times and likely hasn't lost a couple yet. Just take your time, wait for the officiant's lead, and try to remember every moment of this most wonderful experience. Personally, I remember nothing except walking down the aisle, talking to guests as I passed, saying "I do" several times, and then kissing so loudly at the end of the service that I thought I would die of embarrassment. It did give a humorous pause to an otherwise very serious ceremony.

As you are standing during the ceremony, do not lock your knees. Keep them flexed. Locked knees lead to only one thing, and that's fainting. You don't want that during your wedding service.

During one service, in which my favorite Catholic priest was presiding, the priest asked the best man for the ring. From my vantage point in the back of the church, I could see the best man digging in his pocket for this ring. Next I heard a "plink" and the sound of something rolling across the wooden floor near the altar. As I looked towards the altar, I could see the priest chasing this now wildly rolling ring all over the altar area. Finally, he stomped on it to stop its forward motion, picked it up, and walked back to the wedding party. He stood there for a moment, looked the groom right in the eye and said, "And this is your best man?" The wedding party burst into laughter. The congregation laughed. It was wonderful because it was natural. It wasn't made up or planned; it just happened. Instead of getting all upset and distressed, go with the flow of things. Let the officiant guide you through, and make sure your best man doesn't have slippery fingers.

The ceremony is complete now, and you are about to leave the altar area. You have just pledged your life to this wonderful man, now your husband. Having planned ahead of time what would happen next, the officiant pronounces you husband and wife (not man and wife anymore), and you hear the chimes, or the peal of bells and music and you're off down the aisle.

If you decide to use a traditional receiving line, you have to determine in advance where it will be placed and who will participate. It was once considered proper etiquette for all the bridesmaids to stand in the receiving line. While not wanting to incite those who still believe in the etiquette police, there really is no purpose to including all the bridesmaids. That's part of the old etiquette standard that needs some help being revised. Guests are more interested in seeing you, your groom, and your respective parents than in shaking hands with ten of

Bet You Didn't Know... The receiving line comes to us from the ancient Greeks who believed that the bride on her wedding day was blessed. Those who touched her had the blessing rub off on them.

your closest friends that they may never lay eyes on again. The men in the wedding party seldom stand in the receiving line, except, of course, for the fathers, who may or may not take part. They may choose to mingle with the guests.

After you have decided where to place the line and who will stand in it, build in some extra time for that whole process to happen. If you're on a tight schedule, for whatever reason, you want to make sure you have the time to accomplish a formal receiving line. If you expect 200 guests for your wedding and you are doing a traditional receiving line, expect for that process to take about 40 minutes. Sometimes, it may take less time or more time, depending on the guests, and (don't ask me why) the weather outside. If it's hot outside or rainy, the line will move slower; if it's sunny and cool or even cold, it will be quicker.

The following illustration shows one way to have your parents and you and your groom line up for the receiving line. It is optional for the fathers to stand in the line. Guests enter the receiving line from the left and move to the right.

mother of the bride   mother of the groom   bride   groom

Positions of participants in a traditional receiving line.

If you have a divorce situation in your family and you don't want to put parents in a receiving line, consider just you and your groom releasing the rows and greeting your guests there. Instead of the ushers returning after the recessional and escorting the mothers out and then letting the rows leave systematically, the wedding party exits and the couple comes back in and releases the rows. You would start with the bride's side. Your parents stand, come greet you in the center of the aisle, and then exit. You then move to the groom's parents and do the same thing. You zigzag your way to the back of the church. I have found this system works beautifully in divorced families or where we have a large attendance. The couple still has the opportunity to greet their guests, but it moves much more quickly than a traditional receiving line. The following example illustrates this method of releasing guests.

Long before you start back down the aisle, you need to decide whether or not you are going to have a receiving line. A receiving line is a traditional way for guests to greet you, your parents, and possibly some of the wedding party after the wedding. You form a line outside the ceremony area—someplace with easy access and a good traffic flow (people, not cars). Guests move through the line, introducing themselves, shaking hands, and giving out hugs and kisses.

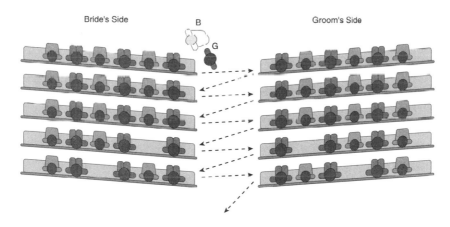

Greeting guests while releasing rows at the end of the ceremony.

After you have released the rows or finished with the receiving line, one of two things happen. You are either needed to do more photography if it wasn't all taken beforehand, or you can exit the ceremony and head for the reception and party time!

Taking the time to carefully plot out the order of events that will occur at the ceremony site will help your day run as smoothly as possible. (And you can reduce your stress level!) This is where expert advice from professional folks who have been through this before will help. Even if you only buy a couple of hours of time to meet with a wedding coordinator, I think you will find it very beneficial to your planning.

The Least You Need to Know

➤ Get advice from your officiant before you start working on writing your own vows. Make sure it is okay for you to vary from the traditional words.

➤ You don't have to go all out to make your wedding ceremony unique. You can add little touches here and there to make it reflect both your personalities. Some great books are available that can give you some ideas.

➤ Don't go overboard. Remember to K.I.S.S. (keep it simple, sweetie).

➤ Decide early whether you want to include a receiving line in your plans. Consider your time factor, the number of guests, and the physical area you have to work with. An alternative to a receiving line is for the couple to greet guests as they release the rows one by one after the recessional.

Say Cheese!

As we mentioned in Chapters 6 and 11, photography is a vital part of your wedding day activities. When everything is said and done, when the last dance has been danced and the final crumb of wedding cake has been eaten, you will want some way to hang onto all the wonderful memories you've just created. Photography and videography can help accomplish this. You want to make good use of your time spent with the photographer or videographer. You need to have the details ironed out before he even arrives at the church (time, what pictures you want, if there are special shots you want him to capture). Aside from that, let the photographer guide you through the special moments of the day that should be captured on film. After all, he's the one with the "eye" for photographic moments. Allow him some freedom to use his creativity.

When to Take Those Pictures

One of the biggest dilemmas couples face today is how to work in time for the wedding pictures. When I was married, it was considered bad luck and improper to see each other before the walk down the aisle. I remember being at the church for our wedding. I was in the sanctuary checking the flower arrangements when someone yelled, "The groom is here!" I made a mad dash back to the dressing room nearly falling over a wastebasket and for what—to hide from the man I was about to marry? Doesn't seem to make a lot of sense now, does it?

As far as we know, the tradition of keeping the bride and groom apart before the wedding probably developed in the days of arranged marriages. That way, the groom would not see the bride and back out of the wedding if he didn't like what he saw. The question you and your groom have to answer is "Do we want to see each other before the ceremony?" This is a personal choice, but before you make up your mind, let's talk about available alternatives. Basically, you can choose from three time periods for your wedding photography.

All Before the Wedding

This is probably my first choice of when photos should be taken. Most photographers will tell you that they not only get better pictures when they do everything beforehand, but it also relieves some of the pre-wedding tension. If you do everything before the service, you are more relaxed than if you take the pictures after the service, when you're wondering what's happening at the reception and if everything is okay. If all the pictures are taken before, you are free to leave the ceremony site along with your guests. Couples tell me they enjoy the wedding and reception so much more because they aren't worried about pictures. Grooms tell me that there is still something very mystical, magical, and romantic about the moment when the organ goes into "Bridal Chorus" and the bride starts her walk down the aisle. Even if they have seen their bride before the ceremony, it is still a very moving moment.

One thing I do for my clients who want to take all the pictures beforehand is to find some private time for the couple to see each other in their wedding finery. The bride gets dressed in her gown and veil while the groom is putting on his tuxedo. I find a private room somewhere at the ceremony site, take the bride to the room and then bring in the groom. Then I close the door and give them some private time. Some couples use this time to give each other their gifts or cards. I even had one groom who sang to his bride. I have learned over the years that this private time may be the only quality time the couple will have the entire day until they get in the car to exit the reception. Some couples find this hard to believe, but experience wins out here. Once that ceremony starts, you're on a roll and things don't calm down much until late into the reception. You may want to gaze longingly at your groom as you walk down the aisle, but there is so much else going on that this usually is not possible. Also, depending on the site, once you start down the aisle and the congregation stands (as they usually do), the groom's view of you—and you of him—is obstructed by the guests (unless of course, you are both 8 feet tall). Once you reach the altar, you're off and running, usually at a gallop, with the ceremony and then the reception. That's why I say that some private, quality time early in the day before pictures start may be the only quality time you can find.

If you choose to have all your wedding pictures taken before the service, allow enough time to accomplish this task. Your photographer should give you a timeline for the picture schedule. For example, if you are taking all the pictures beforehand, the photographer may start taking pictures with you and then add your groom. Your parents may be next in line. He will build up the photography session so that he finishes with the entire wedding party. Thus, you don't have

Allow enough time to accomplish whatever photography style you have chosen. It's always better to allot too much time for this than too little.

lots of people standing around with nothing to do but wait to have their pictures taken.

Try to build in some extra time for just relaxing after the pictures are completed. Posing for pictures is work. Don't let anyone tell you differently. If you can build some extra time into the day for just relaxing and maybe even slipping off your gown and resting for a while, it can make all the difference in the world later on.

After the Ceremony

You may have to take pictures following the ceremony if you choose not to see your groom until after the wedding, or you may be scheduled into a church where there just isn't time to take pictures beforehand. If you are having a Catholic wedding at 6:30 p.m. in a church in which Mass is scheduled for 5:00, for example, the only way you can have pictures taken before the ceremony is to go to the church very early in the afternoon and take them at that time.

In most cases, the photographer should be willing to come in and do some candid shots, perhaps in the dressing room or at your home while you are adjusting your veil, or maybe a picture of you and your mom. The bulk of your photos will be taken after the ceremony, however.

Trying to finish pictures without the entire wedding party is difficult. Make sure your wedding party knows when and where the pictures will be taken and who is expected to be photographed. Never assume that they know what your plans are.

You need full cooperation from your wedding party. Let me repeat that. You need your wedding party, your parents, and anyone you want included in the photos to be cooperative with the photographer. Pictures taken following the wedding will take some time, but they don't need to take hours. Make sure everyone understands that pictures will be taken immediately following the ceremony and receiving line (if you are having one). One bride did not make that clear and three of the ushers headed directly for the reception. They had to be called back to the church so the pictures could be finished.

For pictures after the ceremony, the photographer probably will reverse the strategy and begin with the large group shots, working down to the shots of just the bride and groom. Sometimes, he may photograph the parents first so that they can leave and greet guests at the reception.

Before and After

Probably one of the most common ways to work in all the photos you want taken is to take some before and some after the ceremony. If you are determined not to see your groom before the wedding, this is probably the method you will choose for getting all the shots you want.

When you have some photographs taken before and others taken afterward, the photographer usually starts with the bride and then adds her parents, maybe the bridesmaids, and then perhaps the groomsmen. In other words, the photographer takes as many pictures as possible without you seeing your groom before the ceremony.

If you are truly not comfortable, for whatever reason, with seeing each other before the ceremony, do not let anyone—photographer, your mother, his mother, bridal consultant—talk you into going against your wishes. This is something that is definitely up to you.

The photographer can do the same with the groom. He can photograph the groom, his parents, and groomsmen, and then get a picture of the groom and the bridesmaids. Just try to get as much as possible out of the way before the ceremony so photographs won't take so much time following the ceremony.

Following the ceremony and your receiving line (if you are using one), you can do the larger pictures: the couple with the entire wedding party, the couple with the parents, and so on. It shouldn't take too long if you work with the photographer. He's not a magician; so get your wedding party there on time, let them know what to expect, and smile.

At the Ceremony Site

If your wedding is taking place in a church with an altar area, don't assume that all your pictures have to be taken at the altar. Your photographer is your best judge of what will photograph nicely and what won't. I have learned over the years to trust their judgment. They have an "eye" for seeing things that someone without a photography background is likely to overlook. So while you may insist that you have a picture taken with the pipe organ in the background, if the photographer says it won't work, it is probably because through his camera it looks as if you have horns coming out of your head. This doesn't mean there aren't other settings within the church or ceremony site that you can use for backdrops.

One church I have worked with has a beautiful cherry staircase leading to the upstairs sanctuary. At Christmas time, it is always decorated with ribbons, greens, and gold balls. For weddings, it is usually decorated to coordinate with the flowers in the sanctuary. Many brides have had their pictures taken on that staircase.

Maybe your church has a small chapel that is picturesque. Check ahead of time to see whether the church allows you in other areas. If they give you the go-ahead, look around and explore. Look at the outside of your facility. Some of the most majestic wedding photos I've seen are of wedding parties or the couple alone outside with the church as the background.

If the photographer is not familiar with the setting, ask him to meet you there before the wedding day so he can see what he will be working with. He may find a backdrop that will photograph well that you hadn't thought about.

Finding Other Hidden Treasures

Of course, you will want pictures taken at the ceremony site and at the reception, but you may want to consider using some other sites to add some different backdrops to your pictures. There are hundreds of choices out there; use a little imagination.

One bride, who dressed at home and whose parents boasted a beautiful garden and yard, had some of her formal pictures taken there. It was a lovely May day, not too sunny (outside pictures are best when taken on overcast days so that the subjects of the pictures aren't all squinting), and the photographer was able to get some great pictures.

Maybe you have a garden or a park in your area that you've admired for years, or maybe there is someplace special to you and your groom and you want a photo to remember it by. One couple married in a lovely outdoor ceremony near a lake where they had spent many of their dates fishing. When they had finished the formal pictures, the groom turned to the photographer and said, "I want a picture of us by the lake." So, we hopped in a golf cart (that was our mode of transportation) and drove to this secluded lake. The fall foliage was at its peak and the lake was crystal clear. There were even some Canadian geese floating by. The photographer posed the couple in front of the lake and the colorful trees; a goose even cooperated and swam by right on cue. That picture will mean more to that couple than most of the others because the setting had special meaning for them.

Your wedding pictures are meant to last a lifetime. When everything is over, they are what you have left to remember this special time. Work with the photographer to help capture the very essence of your day.

Adding Videography

In Chapter 11, I talked about adding videography to help capture your wedding memories. Videotaping your wedding and reception is a great way to make sure you don't miss any of the day's events. A good videographer can capture on a single frame what a still photographer cannot.

When you decide to add video to your wedding day, make sure the videographer and photographer are willing to work with each other. Sometimes, this is a difficult task. They are each concerned with their own work (and should be), but they need to cooperate with each other to help give you the best possible coverage of your wedding. If they are professionals, there should be no problem. They are there to do two entirely different things: one to take photographs, one to get on film the events as they unfold. What you don't want to see when you get your pictures back is a shot of the videographer holding his camera. Actually, you don't want to see the videographer or the photographer on film.

Most video companies will send a representative, if not the camera crew, to the ceremony site during the rehearsal to check out placement and entrances so they can set up the equipment to get the best vantage point possible. They will also want to talk with the officiant to find out what is acceptable and what is not. While you want them to have a good vantage point, you may not want them to be too visible to the guests. After all, this is a wedding ceremony, not a TV production. You should be able to have a good tape of your ceremony with two cameras.

If your videotape won't be edited, then you probably will have shots of the photographer on the tape. Since it has not been edited, "what you see is what you get."

One video company a bride hired came to tape the ceremony at the church with not one, not two, but five cameras. I kept waiting for Dan Rather to appear at any moment. There were wires and tape all over the floor. When they plugged their microphone into the church system, the minister suggested that it was not a good idea. The church had some problems with the system and he didn't want anything to go wrong during the ceremony. The videographer assured the minister that everything would be fine. Famous last words. Everything was not fine. In the middle of the ceremony, a hard rock station was blasted

throughout the church sanctuary. Needless to say, the couple was very embarrassed and upset that this happened during their ceremony. The bottom line here is try not to turn your ceremony or reception into someone's electronics extravaganza.

The Least You Need to Know

➤ Pictures can be taken at different stages and different time periods during the wedding day. Make a decision early about whether you want to have all the photos taken before the ceremony, after the ceremony, or whether you want some taken before and the last few afterward.

➤ Look around the ceremony facility and see if you can find some unique backdrops to use for your wedding photographs.

➤ Consider using sites other than your ceremony facility, such as a park, garden, or someplace special to one or both of you.

➤ Work with the photographer to make sure you have plenty of time to complete all your pictures. Let your wedding party know when photographs will be taken, and ask them to be on time and to work with the photographer.

➤ If you decide to add videography to your wedding day, make sure it is as unobtrusive as possible. This is a wedding, not a television production, so try to keep the electronics to a minimum.

Let the Party Begin!

In This Chapter

➤ Planning your reception agenda: when to do what

➤ Handling gifts at the reception

➤ Implementing security

➤ Making your grand exit

You're done with the formalities at the church, and you are feeling somewhat more relaxed. The religious and legal portions of the day are over. Now, prepare to be the guest of honor at one of the greatest parties you have ever attended. Whether you are having a small, intimate celebration with only family and a few close friends or the party of the century with dinner and dancing till dawn, you and your groom want to enjoy it. Let others do the worrying for now. You want to concentrate on your new husband and your friends and family who have come from all over to share in this day.

Activities to Include

What happens when you arrive at the reception? Should there be some kind of order to the events? Can you just mingle and do things as the spirit moves you? The answers are both "yes" and "no."

Remember that this is your reception. The agenda needs to be of your choosing, not because Cousin Sarah says that a reception is supposed to include this and that. Discuss your options and what you want to see happen at the reception. For example, do you want a formal affair with assigned seating for a served meal, or do you want your guests to be free to move around, help themselves to food and drink, and mingle with the other guests? Do you want to throw a bouquet and garter? Do you want a rigid dance order that specifies who dances with whom and when? Setting an agenda helps determine how the activities will flow.

Agenda

Call it whatever you like, but even at an informal, family-only reception, there should be some kind of an agenda. You need an idea of what events are to take place and an approximate time of when each should happen. In order for your agenda to be carried out, you need someone to help move the events along. This is another place where a bridal consultant with experience can be invaluable to your plans.

 Here is another great opportunity to make a relative or close friend feel very special. Instead of relying on an MC, a DJ, or bandleader, why not have someone you know (and who knows the guests and can pronounce their names!) handle the introductions. Obviously, it should be someone who can stand up in front of a crowd and speak without tripping over his tongue!

Many couples want to be introduced as they arrive at the reception. This can be accomplished by working with your band or DJ. Ask them to do the honors if you aren't using a master of ceremonies (MC) for the evening. Most are more than happy to assist. Consider whether you want your entire wedding party to be announced or just you and your groom. Also, be sure that each individual or couple knows where to move after the introduction. Decide whether you want them to walk to the head table or directly to the buffet line. The type of food you are serving for the reception will dictate some of these decisions.

Usually, ushers/groomsmen are introduced first with the bridesmaids they walked with at the ceremony. Then the children attendants are introduced (if they are old enough to participate in this; otherwise, they can be acknowledged at the table where they are seated with their families). The best man and maid of honor are introduced next, followed by the new couple (that's you).

You've been introduced and you are famished; get something to eat. Your guests can wait for a little while and you should be able to enjoy this meal. Put everything else on the back burner. If you are having a formal seated dinner, this will not be a problem. Guests will also be seated and waiting to be served.

Bet You Didn't Know... The term "toasting" dates back to the sixteenth century. Those attending a function placed a spice-laden crouton in the bottom of a wine glass. It was either for flavor or nourishment (who knows). Anyway, the last person to drink from the glass and find the "toast" not only claimed it but was also given good wishes.

When you are finished eating, you may want to schedule in a toast or two. Traditionally, the best man offers the first toast of the evening. He stands, gets the guests' attention, and makes a toast to the two of you. The toast should be simple and sincere, and he may choose to share a funny (and tasteful) story. Your groom thanks him and offers a toast to you, his new bride. After that, it's an open floor (anyone can offer a toast or it can stop there).

When a toast is proposed, all should rise—except the person or persons who are being toasted. In the examples just given, both the bride and groom would remain seated for the best man's toast. For the groom's toast, only the bride would be seated.

Following the toast and depending on what you have decided to do, you can go right into cutting the cake. This is another place you will want formal photographs, so make sure that your photographer knows the order of events.

How to Cut the Wedding Cake

Cutting a wedding cake is an art. Don't let anyone tell you otherwise. If the catering staff is willing to cut the cake for you, by all means, let them. If you don't have any expert assistance available, however, and this task becomes the responsibility of your volunteer cake server who may never have attempted this task before, the following diagram may provide some assistance. Be sure to share this information with your server so that she can be prepared for the big day.

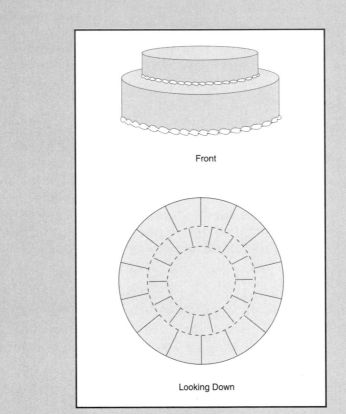

Front

Looking Down

Diagram for cutting the cake.

Always remove the layer you want to cut. Never cut a layer while it is on top of another layer. About two inches from the outside of the cake, make a circular cut all the way around the cake. Then from the outside in, to the cut, slice pieces off. Repeat this process, moving in two inches at a time, all the way to the center of the cake.

Your photographer will work with you on where you should stand at the cake table. Follow his guidelines and suggestions so that he can get the best possible photograph. According to tradition, the groom places his hand over yours and together you cut the first slice. The angle from which the photographer wants to shoot and the way your cake has been constructed usually determine where you make the cut for the first slice. Sometimes, the photographer may ask you to pretend to make the first cut from a higher layer so that the angle is better for the photograph. After he has snapped the picture, you would then normally cut the first slice from the back of the bottom layer of the cake.

Have a plate and napkin ready at the table to place the cake on and to wipe sticky fingers. Then you take turns feeding each other a small piece of cake. Notice the word *small*. I find it very interesting when a couple gets into a food fight while they are feeding each other the cake. Must be all that wedding tension finally coming out.

Sometimes, after the cutting ceremony, the cake is taken into the kitchen, sliced and served. At one second wedding, however, the bride and groom cut the entire cake while their children served the guests. It was a nice way to involve the children and recognize that so much of a family's life centers around food and serving others.

If your reception includes dancing, the dancing can begin following the cake ceremony. Your groom is the first person you dance with at the reception, and some couples choose a favorite song for that first dance. You can either dance the entire first dance with your new husband, or the bride's father can cut in and finish that first dance with his daughter. Some brides request the first dance with their groom and the entire second dance with their father. A popular song for the dance with dad is "Daddy's Little Girl." (Check with your local music store for sheet music if the band or DJ doesn't have it.)

Bet You Didn't Know...
As with many of the wedding traditions we still observe today, the cake cutting dates back to ancient times. In ancient Rome, the couple would share a hard biscuit, taking only a bite from it. The wedding officiant would then take the remaining biscuit and crumble it over the heads of the couple. It was thought to bring bounty to the couple, good luck, and many children. Guests at these ancient weddings would rush to the site where the cake had crumbled and try to obtain any leftover crumbs for their own good luck. Over the centuries, this cake crumbling has evolved into modern wedding guests having a piece of cake at the reception or taking a piece home with them.

Don't make the dancing segment of the wedding so complicated that the cast needs cue cards to tell who's dancing with whom and to what song. I normally recommend two or three special dances.

Once you have the first dance or two out of the way, it's time to let loose and get the party moving. This is where the homework you did before you chose your DJ or band should pay off. If your dance floor is filled with dancers most of the night, you get an "A" for all your advance work.

Later in the reception, if you choose, you can throw the bouquet and garter. Here again, you will need help to make the announcement. Ask for all single women to join the bride on the dance floor. Work with your photographer, too. Let him determine the best placement. It is customary for the bride to turn her back to the single women and, after a countdown, toss the bouquet. Tradition has it that the woman who catches the bouquet will be the next to marry.

Now it's the groom's turn. Instead of using a chair to sit on while the groom removes your garter, why not ask the best man to kneel on one knee so you can sit on his leg? It makes for a great picture and is certainly warmer than a cold chair. Sometimes, the band or DJ provides a drum roll here and then plays "The Stripper" for the actual garter removal.

When the groom has the garter in hand, you move off the dance floor and with his back to his single male friends, he tosses the garter. Again, the next to marry is the man who catches the garter.

Remember, you don't have to incorporate any of these customs into your reception. After all, this is *your* reception, and you should plan your agenda around the things you want to include.

There may be more things you want incorporated into your wedding reception. Some sororities and fraternities have rituals they perform during the evening. Maybe there is someone you want to honor with a special dance. One father purchased a magnum of champagne at the time of his daughter's birth with the intention of opening it on her wedding day. He did this and it was quite a nostalgic moment for the family as he talked about the little girl who had grown into a lovely young woman.

Handling Gifts at the Reception

According to proper wedding etiquette, all wedding gifts should be sent to the bride's home or her parent's home before the wedding. In our busy, hectic society, however, guests sometimes fail to abide by this rule. Often, you have numerous wedding gifts to deal with at the reception. When you talk with the reception site manager, ask to have a table specially set up in the main room for wedding gifts.

Your gift table needs to be in a place that is hard to access, such as a distant corner away from any exits. It's much harder to walk clear across the dance floor with gifts than to grab one and go out an exit. Make it hard to get to and away from, and you'll take home the gifts intended for you.

Assign someone to greet guests and take any gifts they may bring to the reception. He doesn't need to stand "guard" over the table all the time, just be there at the beginning of the reception to help guests. If you anticipate receiving cards containing monetary gifts, have either a basket or box placed on the table to collect those. If you use a basket, make sure you empty it frequently during the evening. Cards can walk away even more easily than wrapped presents. The best solution here is to have a sealed box that can only be opened by breaking the seal.

Do not have this table set up in an outer lobby. There are too many sticky fingers out there, and you want to make it as difficult as possible for a would-be thief to exit with your wedding gifts.

Always write a thank-you note for the gifts you receive, even if it's as simple as "Thank you for the lovely wedding gift." Your guests will appreciate the acknowledgment that you did receive their gift.

You should not open gifts at your wedding reception. The only time where that might be appropriate is a small family-only reception where you can do the honors without creating too much hassle. Always have someone record who gave you what so that you can send thank-you notes.

Security

You may think security is a strange subject to discuss in a wedding planning book, but nothing is farther from the truth. Weddings can bring out the good, the bad, and the ugly in your guests. Throw in a little too much to drink, and you can have some fireworks that you didn't expect or want.

Most of the larger facilities used for receptions have security guards who are on the premise and "patrol" the area just in case they are needed. They are not there to embarrass you or intimidate your guests, but when you need them, you'll be glad they're around. A rowdy group of groomsmen, who had consumed way too much alcohol, decided that dancing on top of the tables at the reception would cap off their evening very nicely. The catering manager asked them to get down and tried not to make a scene. It was the end of what had been a very long day. The parents were upset. The couple had already left for their honeymoon. The catering manager tried one last time and when he couldn't get them to move, he called security. Not a pleasant sight, but a needed one. The men were escorted off the property and driven to the hotel where they were staying.

If you are serving alcohol at your reception and your reception facility doesn't provide security, you may want to look into hiring a security guard for the evening.

Designating the Designated Driver

Any discussion of alcohol brings up the topic of watching out for those who have indulged too much. When I first started in this business, I would see people drinking to excess at almost every wedding reception; that usually is no longer the case. It doesn't matter the age of the guests or the age of the couple, I just don't see the overindulgence I once saw.

What I do see is a more attentive society who is taking it upon themselves (and rightly so) to make sure guests are sober enough to drive when leaving a reception. I have had couples take car keys from their guests and only turn them over when the driver was taken home by someone who had not been drinking. I have had parents book cab companies to come gather guests after a reception and deliver them safely to their homes or hotel. On several occasions, couples have rented buses or trolley cars to transport guests from the reception back to the hotel. There are all kinds of ways for you to make sure guests from your wedding reception do not leave the reception and drive under the influence of alcohol.

The best way to protect yourself from any chance of liability is to make sure that you are working with a licensed liquor agency in your state and that they are checking the IDs of guests who appear to be under age. It is everyone's responsibility to make sure that each guest who leaves is capable of driving a car. You don't need the memory of a terrible auto accident involving one of your wedding guests. Take some time now and develop a plan for seeing that you have a safe and happy reception.

Child Care

"Child care?" you ask. "What is she talking about?" Well, for openers, if I live to be 100 I will never understand why parents cart their toddlers and babies to weddings and receptions, especially evening weddings. Parents don't enjoy the time spent at the wedding or reception when the baby is along. There is nothing enjoyable about trying to keep a crying baby still during the wedding vows or trying to con Junior into not playing leap frog on the dance floor with the other two dozen children.

If your guests insist on bringing their children, try to provide some activities that kids will enjoy. You can apply the following ideas to both your ceremony and reception.

Children like to be kept busy; children are basically very busy little people. And I love kids; truly, I do. (Ask my kids. Well, you can ask them now that I've finished writing this book.) Plan activities for the kids. If the church or reception facility has a separate room, ask to use that room as the "entertainment lounge." Give it a fancy title so the kids think they're getting a great deal.

It helps to know in advance the ages of any children who may be attending the wedding and reception so that you can plan appropriate supervision and activities. Consider including an additional enclosure card with the invitations you send to those with small children. This card can have blanks for the names and ages of the children, and guests can return them in the same envelope as the reception response card.

Maybe rent some cartoons and bring in a VCR and TV for "movie night." Provide some kid snacks and nonsugared drinks (apple or orange juice). Have coloring books out, some crayons, some easy-to-read books for the older children, puzzles, trucks or cars, maybe some blocks. A good resource here is to check with a local university (early childhood department) or a high school home economics class (family development) to see if you can hire students to come in and work with the children. Notice I said "work with" not "watch." There is a vast difference between the two.

House Sitters

During the final consultation with my clients, I suggest that if they don't have a good security system on their property, they consider hiring a house sitter to stay at their home during the ceremony and reception. At the very least, you need to make sure the neighbors know what is happening on the wedding weekend, and ask them to watch out for anything or anyone unusual in the area.

Burglars know when weddings are happening. They watch for them. These potential party poopers scan the newspapers for wedding and engagement announcements and marriage license announcements. They know that there will be a lot of movement, a lot of gifts arriving at the home, and that they can count on the family being gone for hours the day of the wedding. Don't give them the opportunity to steal you blind. With a little preparation now, you won't be sorry later.

It is also a good idea to add a rider for your wedding gifts to your insurance policy. This is a short-term policy that you can usually add through your homeowner's or renter's insurance policy. It doesn't cost much, and it can save you thousands of dollars if you happen to be unlucky enough to be robbed.

Making Your Grand Exit

The time come has come, my dears, to make your getaway. It was once thought that the couple should leave the reception at some point so that all the guests could stand around and throw rice at them. Rice is now out (it's too easy for someone to slip and fall on it), that's for sure, but rice has been replaced by birdseed or, better yet, rose petals. The showering simply means good luck and, according to legend, also promotes fertility. But I'm getting ahead of myself here.

 Petals, either fresh or dried, are a wonderful alternative to the birdseed. They don't get caught in your clothes and hair, and they smell wonderful. They are natural, so you don't have to worry about the environment. Check with your florist.

One bride lost a $100 deposit when a guest, not knowing the rules, passed out birdseed to the guests to toss. The church claimed the deposit as a clean-up fee.

You and your groom need to decide when you want to leave your wedding reception. Most of the couples I work with want to stay

310

for the whole reception. After all, it is a party for you, given in your honor. Most of these couples don't want to miss anything: the fun, the music, the dancing, and talking with friends they've not seen for months. So, if that's what you'd like to do, go for it.

But let's say you do want to leave earlier than most of your guests. Maybe you have a plane to catch or you just want to find some time for yourselves. If you are changing clothes at the reception, then you need to do that before you leave. It will be easier on you not to travel in a long gown, complete with train. Besides, you can leave your gown with your mom or a good friend to be taken to the cleaners. (Yes, it will need to be cleaned after your wedding.)

After you have both changed clothes and gathered the items you need to take with you (hopefully your luggage for the honeymoon will already be in the car), it's time to say good-bye to your folks. Now, most times, moms and dads at this stage of the game are glad things have gone well. They're happy, they're sad, they're tired, and

It is best to check with a reputable dry cleaner before your wedding to see about having your gown not only cleaned but preserved. This is a process where after the gown is cleaned, it is packed in an air-tight box and sealed. This process will protect your gown for many years from the aging process or bugs.

they love you. Give them a hug; thank them for this wonderful day and for all of their support. Do the same with your groom's parents. And then, make your exit. If you have petals or birdseed you want guests to toss as your make your mad dash to the waiting car, have one of your bridesmaids gather guests by the exit and pass out the birdseed or petals.

The photographer will want to capture this moment on film. Give him time to get set up and then run, do not walk, to the car and wave good-bye. Now, you're off. You're alone for the first time since earlier today or maybe even the previous day. Have a great honeymoon.

The Least You Need to Know

➤ Talk to each other about what activities you want to include in your reception (introduction of the wedding party, the cake cutting, first dance, tossing the bouquet and garter, and so on). It's important to plan a reception agenda so that the reception has a continual flow and so that the photographer can be set up for each activity.

➤ Check with the reception manager about having security available during the festivities. It's good to have some expert assistance if guests become rowdy or out of control.

➤ Although etiquette dictates that wedding gifts be sent to the bride's or her parent's home before the wedding, some probably will be brought to the reception. Have the reception manager place a table for gifts in the main room of the reception and ask a friend to direct guests bearing presents to this table.

➤ Check into hiring a house sitter for your home for the periods during the wedding weekend when you will be gone for extended periods. Also check into purchasing a short-term rider to your homeowner's or renter's insurance policy to protect the value of your wedding gifts in case you are burglarized.

Part VII
Tales from the Altar

How do brides and grooms ever survive this thing called a wedding? How do they manage to enjoy the day? What would they change if they could? The couples in Chapter 27 have some stories to tell; they may have some advice that can help you. Read on for some solid suggestions on how you can survive the big event!

Part VII also reveals some vendors' insights and tips to help get you through the whole process more easily. They, too, have survived many a wedding.

We'll also take a look at some popular wedding trends around the country. You find out what is currently popular in photography packages, wedding cakes, reception menus, centerpieces, and wedding transportation. You can also get great ideas for your own wedding by seeing what other couples are trying.

Chapter 25

Tips from the Pros: What's Hot, What's Not

In This Chapter

➤ Bridal consultants offer advice

➤ Trends around the country

One of the benefits of belonging to an international trade association is the opportunity to meet people from all over the world who share a common desire: to provide the best possible services and products for our wedding clients. Over the years, I have had the pleasure of hearing other professionals speak and the opportunity to share ideas about our profession. I have learned so much from them, and I want to share some of this valuable information with you.

This chapter includes tips and advice from professionals to you, the prospective bride and groom. These wonderful consultants have also included trends they are witnessing in their particular area of the country. Enjoy this free advice as you read on.

Bridal Consultants

Bridal consultants have only one thing in mind: helping you enjoy your wedding. Here are some suggestions, new ideas, and advice from some of the best.

Merry Beth Julnes

Merry Beth Julnes from Kirkland, Washington, owns and operates Aisle of View. She is an independent bridal consultant and has been in business since 1989. Her goal is to make each wedding a unique, exciting, and memorable experience for her client.

"When guests leave the wedding I want them to be able to say, 'Oh, that was so like Sally and John.' It can't be something generic that will work with every wedding. If we tried the same idea at the next wedding, it might not work."

Merry Beth shared one of her success stories with me that can help you formalize some ideas for your own wedding.

In the biographical information for the bridal consultants in this chapter, I have listed any professional ranking a consultant may have achieved within a trade organization. In the Association of Bridal Consultants, there are three levels of distinction based on course of study, number of years in business, references from peers and clients, and activities within the Association. The three levels are Professional, Accredited, and Master. To date, there are only four Master Bridal Consultants in the world.

She was working with a couple who's first names both began with the letter *R*. We'll call them Rita and Ryan. One day while Rita and Merry Beth were doing some errands for the wedding, Rita mentioned in passing that her friends were teasing her about the upcoming wedding, saying, "Oh, it's Rita and Ryan, Rita and Ryan"—making friendly fun of their identical initials. Merry Beth instantly had a mental picture of the "Rolls Royce" logo with the double R in it and realized that here was an opportunity to make this wedding unique and very classy, too. So, that's what they did. The double R logo, similar to the Rolls Royce logo, became Rita and Ryan's logo, which they had monogrammed on everything: invitations, RSVP cards, thank-you notes, programs, napkins, table centerpieces, a balloon display, a sculptured cake—all monogrammed with the double R. As the grand finale, Merry Beth scheduled a Rolls Royce to pick up the couple after the ceremony and chauffeur them to the reception. What had started out as teasing turned into a most successful and classy wedding.

Martha Cook

Martha Cook of Weddings By Design in El Cajon, California, has been in the business of wedding consulting for eight years. She also talked about the need for brides and grooms to find something unique in their wedding and expand on it. The uniqueness may be in their musical selections, choice of flowers, or an ethnic background from either side of the family from which the couple can draw food or traditions. "Whatever you do, all the pieces need to fit together to create a beautiful picture for the wedding you want."

"Traditional weddings are still the most desired by brides today even if the bride is rather untraditional," says Martha. "Using color and style can create a theme for any wedding." One example she used was a bride who loved bows and who created a theme of bows from the invitations to the cake. Beautiful, lush bows with long cascading ribbons decorated the church and were used on the bridesmaids' arm bouquets. Another bride chose deep red roses to accent everything, including the 1940s style black dresses worn by the attendants. Another idea is to use all white with gold accents to create a very elegant and formal setting."

Scarlett Lewis

I first met Scarlett Lewis at a conference in Indianapolis in 1988. She and her former partner had just been filmed by CBS for a segment of "48 Hours" dealing with weddings. She's a lovely lady and knows of what she speaks. Scarlett hails from Austin, Texas, where she owns Scarlett Lewis & Associates.

When I asked Scarlett what she would like to offer to brides-to-be, she paused and said, "Try to use a bridal consultant who has been in the business long enough to know the vendors' strengths and weaknesses. It takes years to build relationships and mutual respect in order to achieve maximum productivity that can result in benefits for the bride." She did suggest that if you are not using a bridal consultant to at least type up a complete itinerary for the wedding day and give it to all the participants at the rehearsal. "It's important to have the wedding day time schedule, seating chart, photography schedule, and all other vital information in writing so that everyone is fully aware of their responsibilities."

Christine Young

The Wedding Directory is the consulting business owned by Christine M. Young of Rockland, Massachusetts.

She offers these tips for the bride-to-be:

➤ Putting guests' names and addresses on index cards and then alphabetizing the cards is a big help. It enables the bride to eliminate duplicates from parents' and fiancé's lists and will also serve as a list for mailing thank-yous for shower and wedding gifts.

➤ When calling a reception facility to check on availability and you are told they are booked for the date you are inquiring about, don't hang up—ask if they have received a deposit on the date. This information is generally not offered but is given when asked. With a follow-up phone call, you may find it has suddenly become available because the original bride never actually signed a contract and put money down.

Lois Pearce

Lois Pearce lives in Hamden, Connecticut, and owns Beautiful Occasions, an event planning firm. She's been in the business since 1987 and is an Accredited Bridal Consultant. She offers these suggestions:

➤ Stop talking to everyone about your wedding. Each additional opinion clouds your vision of your dream wedding. Once you ask for advice from your well-meaning friends and family you will continue to receive it, solicited or not.

➤ Consider an "afterglow," a morning brunch where out-of-town guests and family can gather to continue the wedding festivities. Brides and grooms say good-bye from there rather than at the end of the reception.

➤ To keep costs down, choose a morning or afternoon reception. For mornings, have a brunch reception. For an afternoon reception, consider serving hors d'oeuvres and cake rather than a full meal. People tend to drink less early in the day. Limit the cocktail hour.

➤ Allow your florist and photographer to use their creativity. They are artists, and you will stifle their work by being restrictive. Search for the professional with whom you have the best personality match and who suits your budget. Then allow the person to do his job.

Kay Krober

Kay Krober is from Indianapolis, Indiana, and has been the proprietor of Kay Krober Bridal Consultant for three years. Kay is quite creative and extremely organized. She offers a couple of suggestions here for a different type of wedding.

Instead of the traditional flower girl dropping petals as she walks down the aisle, "a unique approach can be to have the flower girl give roses to the guests in the aisle seats. We use decorated baskets for sweetheart roses that have been wired by the florist to resemble long-stemmed roses. As the flower girl walks down the aisle, she randomly selects persons seated on the aisle to receive one of the roses. It is not necessary to have a rose for every pew. Older flower girls seem to enjoy giving the roses, a symbol of love. If several children are to be in the wedding, some might drop petals and some hand out roses."

Kay also suggests that if you are using an aisle runner, you should have it in place before the guests arrive. Then seat all guests from the side aisles for the following two reasons:

1. Early guests are more likely to move over to the center aisle—the better seats for those arriving early. Later guests may be seated on the outer seats, which prevents earlier guests from having to move over or be stepped over if they want to hold their aisle seats. Rope off the back of the center aisle with a garland of greenery and flowers made by the florist to coordinate with the aisle decorations, ribbons and tulle, or a simple ribbon with bows at pews on either side.

2. One of the most goof-prone moments at the wedding is the pulling of the aisle runner by two ushers immediately before the processional. They are asked to do a difficult task for which they have no experience and are seldom instructed properly. The runner rolls out crooked, wrinkled, or twisted. Often it becomes loosened at the altar. The lovely atmosphere is disrupted as the men try to make adjustments. If the runner is pulled and secured before the guests arrive, the ushers will be relieved and the ceremony will be more graceful.

Cyndi Basker

Cyndi Basker, who was quoted in Chapter 18 for her experience with weekend weddings, owns Celebrated Events in South Bend, Indiana.

Besides all her expertise with weekend weddings, she provides this tip for you:

"Many churches now prohibit rice throwing or birdseed tossing. Instead, get small bottles of bubble blowing liquid, have an usher or someone pass these out to guests as they exit the church. Then when the bride and groom emerge from the church, guests can blow bubbles at them.

"Also, as a couple dances their first dance, have bridal party members blow bubbles on them for that Lawrence Welk touch! It is very sweet and looks romantic, dancing in the bubbles."

Cheri Rice

Cheri Rice hails from Anoka, Minnesota. She is a Master Bridal Consultant through the Association of Bridal Consultants and owns The Personal Touch Bridal Agency. She's been in the business of helping brides since 1979.

Cheri also likes to use ethnic touches when appropriate and shared the story of a wedding couple with Scottish and Irish heritage. The couple hired a bagpiper to greet guests as they arrived and as they exited the church. She says it was a very pleasant experience and that the family was thrilled to have some of their family heritage incorporated into the wedding.

Cheri also shared one idea with me that she uses in place of the traditional guest book. Instead of the guest book at the church entrance or at the reception, you can place sheets of paper (all colors) along with crayons, colored pencils, and felt tip markers on a table at the entrance of the reception (obviously, this won't work at the church). A hostess, similar to a guest book hostess, explains the idea to guests and hands out the supplies. The guests are asked to write a message or draw a picture, whatever moves them at the moment, for the couple. There is a basket placed by the exit for guests to leave their "artwork" when finished. When the papers are all collected, the couple can have it made into a book. The paper should have a defined writing space so as to leave room for the book to be bound. Some guests caught on right away. Others had to think about what they wanted to say or draw for the couple. What a unique way to share in the couple's special day and new life together.

Norma Edelman

Norma Edelman owns The Wedding Casa in San Diego, California. She has been in the business of helping brides plan their weddings since 1981 and knows how to tell it like it is.

Norma coordinated 74 weddings in 1994. For the majority of her weddings (most of which are held outdoors), both the ceremony and the reception are held at one location. "You loose three things when you move from the ceremony site to a separate reception site: time, money, and guests. I keep them all at one location and that makes it more affordable."

Mary Jane Miles

Mary Jane Miles is from Evansville, Indiana, and is the owner of The Perfect Wedding. And truly, she does help create some "perfect" weddings. She has this suggestion for creating some family tradition:

If you don't already have an item for your wedding that has been a family tradition, start one yourself. Have a white or ivory pillow made for the kneeler and embroider the names of the couple and their wedding date on the underside. Each family member who uses it can add their names and dates.

She suggested the following idea for a unique and inexpensive favor: "After the dinner, have a friend pass out scratch-off lottery tickets to each *adult* guest. Everyone has fun finding out if they are a winner, and someone may even be generous enough to donate a lucky ticket back to the bride and groom."

Randie Wilder-Pellegrini

Randie Wilder-Pellegrini owns Cordially Invited, an event planning firm in Beverly Hills, California. She opened her business in 1977, following a career in marketing and public relations.

Randie advises couples to "take time before the wedding to savor every minute and enjoy the planning of your most special day. That's why there are bridal consultants—to take away all the stress of the preparation so the couple can just enjoy." Randi also advises her clients to get a massage the day before the wedding to help them relax for this once-in-a-lifetime celebration.

Dorothy Penner

Dorothy Penner has been in the wedding industry since the early 1970s. She was a buyer for a bridal salon for years and now does weddings and event coordinating all over the country. She lives in Louisville, Kentucky. She's quite a lady, has lots of experience, and loves this business.

She offers this suggestion: "If the bride's gown has a detachable train, have the material from the train made into a christening gown for the first baby." What a wonderful family heirloom to be passed down.

Frank Andonoplas

Frank Andonoplas owns Bridal Consulting and Wedding Planning by Frank in Chicago, Illinois. Frank is one of the fine men we have working in this industry. He loves what he does and from what I've observed, he is also very good at it. Frank has attained the distinction of Professional Bridal Consultant.

Most times, couples are nervous at the altar. This can sometimes cause their hands to swell and cause problems with the ring ceremony. I tell couples at the rehearsal to just put the ring on as far as it will go and not to force it. When they walk back up the aisle, they can usually slide the rings into place easily.

Another suggestion I offer is for the bride to write her mother and mother-in-law a note before the wedding. I place these notes in their pews with a pretty lace hanky.

Trends Around the Country

Some of the trends mentioned in this section may give you some ideas that you can incorporate into your plans, or they can let you know if something you want to include is currently "in." The trends are listed by region and have been provided by some of the best consultants from around the country.

Pacific Northwest

Merry Beth Julnes from Kirkland, Washington, says that in the Pacific Northwest the trend seems to be toward elegant and traditional services in formal church weddings. Some photographers in her area offer photographic packages that include many candid shots; however, brides in the region seem to be leaning more toward the traditional posed formal pictures in the church and at the reception and away from candid shots.

East Coast

Christine Young from Rockland, Massachusetts, says the trend on the East Coast seems to be toward limiting the alcohol offered at weddings to wine, beer, and champagne. A full bar is sometimes still offered if a budget is not a concern, but more couples are choosing not to offer a full bar even when it is within their budget. The risk of overindulgence is an increasing worry for many couples. Here are other increasing wedding trends on the East Coast:

➤ Donating leftover food to food banks.

➤ Printing invitations on recycled paper.

➤ Using food stations, especially when the reception is held in a large estate house or historic home, because it enables the guests to utilize all the rooms.

➤ Providing amenity baskets and flowers in the rest rooms.

JoAnn Gregoli, a Professional Bridal Consultant from Denville, New Jersey, and owner of Elegant Occasions, Inc., notes these trends in her area:

➤ *Favors.* Couples are no longer spending money on items that are not needed; instead they are making donations to charitable organizations.

For the environmentally correct couple, tree seedlings and tree seed packets are the latest rage.

➤ *Cakes.* Since many people are having a hard time deciding on a cake flavor, more couples are opting for a multilayer, multiflavored cake; thus, offering their guests a choice of wedding cake flavors. Fresh flowers now adorn the tops and sides of cakes, eliminating the plastic bride and groom.

➤ *Coffee bars.* With coffee bars springing up all around the country, specialty coffees are now being offered as part of the wedding package. Cappuccino and Espresso are offered regularly.

➤ *Costs.* Wedding costs are so high in the Northeast that all parties are now sharing the expense—it is no longer the responsibility of the bride's family.

➤ *Transportation.* Vintage cars and trolleys are the newest rage in northern New Jersey.

Lois Pearce from Hamden, Connecticut, says the East Coast trends she is seeing include the following:

A *blusher veil* covers the bride's face for the processional and sometimes remains down until the end of the ceremony when the groom lifts it to kiss her. In some ceremonies, when the bride and her father reach the altar area, the father may lift the veil before the ceremony begins. At one time, the blusher, or face veil, was always used but has been used less often in the last 15 years.

➤ The trend is away from full-service bars. Couples are more conscious of the liability factor and that guests are not drinking as much hard liquor as in the past. More wines and assorted beers are being served. Brides are moving more towards elegance. Less fluff is being used on dresses and headpieces, with more silk fabrics and traditional crowns, headbands, and ornamental bows for headpieces. Blushers, fingertip, and chapel-length veils are removable with just the headpiece for the bride to wear during the reception.

➤ Bridal gowns are now more versatile: a more formal look for the wedding, with either a removable jacket or removable longer skirt for a semiformal look for the reception.

➤ Grooms are also choosing two separate looks for the wedding and reception. A full tuxedo for the wedding and a colorful vest and tie for the reception.

➤ Bridal parties are still wearing a common color, but not always the same style of dress.

Northern California

L'Affaire Du Temps is an event planning firm in Milpitas, California, owned and operated by Patricia Bruneau. Pat offers some of the following general trends she sees in Northern California:

➤ Couples are hiring professional bridal consultants more frequently.

➤ More couples are paying for the wedding themselves.

➤ Photographers are including casual engagement photo sessions into the photography package and displaying the pictures at the reception.

➤ Destination ceremonies and honeymoons (for example, Hawaii) are becoming more popular with a reception for friends six months later.

➤ Videographers are being used quite regularly.

➤ Limousines, Rolls Royce automobiles, and horse-drawn carriages are still popular forms of wedding transportation.

➤ Cummerbunds and bow ties are being made from the same fabric as the bridesmaids dresses.

➤ Brides still want a blusher for the ceremony.

Here are some trends in wedding ceremonies that Pat is noticing:

➤ Outdoor ceremonies are being performed all year around.

➤ Couples are writing their own vows and incorporating children in the case of second marriages.

➤ More couples are incorporating family heirlooms, such as a childhood Bible carried by the bride, a handmade ring bearer pillow, or a cake top that parents or grandparents used.

➤ Couples are facing each other or their guests during the ceremony instead of facing the officiant.

➤ Grooms are escorting their mothers down the aisle.

Pat is noticing the following trends in receptions held in the Northern California region:

➤ Mansions, country clubs, and hotels are still the most popular locations.

➤ Less traditional wedding favors are being used. Instead, truffles, wildflower and tree seed packets, monogrammed wine glasses, and small perfume bottles tied with ribbon are becoming popular.

➤ Head tables are being used less frequently.

➤ Receiving lines are obsolete.

➤ Open bars are disappearing, and guests are drinking less alcohol.

➤ The couple's engagement photograph is matted and framed and then displayed on an easel at the reception. Then guests can sign the matting instead of a guest book.

➤ A video or slide montage of the couple is being shown during dinner.

➤ More brides and grooms are taking dance lessons to be prepared for their first dance at the reception.

➤ No more matchbooks or monogrammed napkins.

➤ Fresh flowers on the wedding cake are replacing a plastic cake top.

➤ Each tier of the wedding cake is a different flavor (carrot is very popular).

➤ Children invited to a wedding have a special room to spend time in that is complete with movies to watch, coloring books, and games.

➤ Disposable cameras are placed on each table for guests to use to help capture the moments at the reception.

➤ Brides and grooms frequently are toasting their parents and guests.

➤ Formal introductions of the bridal party at the reception are still popular, for example, the couple is being introduced as Mr. and Mrs. Ken & Tina Smith.

Southern California

Also located on the West Coast, but in Southern California, is Claire Webber. Claire says that "unlike the '80s, the '90s are fairly stream-lined. People tend to see weddings as the most important party they will give. They still want value for their dollar, but they also want the best."

"Romance is back. That and a natural look. Couples want the old world romantic look and they want attention to detail."

Norma Edelman of San Diego notes a few trends she is seeing in Southern California. First of all, she doesn't see full bars anymore. Mostly she is seeing the limited bar concept: beer, wine, and champagne. She also sees couples using more DJs than bands. Norma commented that in Southern California there is already in place a mixture of ethnic backgrounds, especially Hispanic. She says couples try to incorporate aspects of these cultures into their weddings.

Favors are not very popular in Southern California. If couples use favors, it probably is something as simple as Hershey kisses scattered on the reception tables.

Reception food is almost always a buffet rather than a sit-down dinner. She never uses aisle runners. However, she does see lots of interesting transportation ideas for the couple to make their grand exit. They use small, ocean-going boats called "Harbor Hoppers" to take the couple from the reception to the hotel or to an awaiting car. It's a great idea to incorporate the ocean (since it's right there) into the wedding.

Midwest

Cheri Rice from Anoka, Minnesota, notes that birdseed and rice are out. They are not allowed anymore in Minnesota. The environmentalists are saying that birds can actually eat too much birdseed and kill themselves. In place of birdseed, she sees some confetti, but even more popular is for guests to blow bubbles as the couple exits.

Mary Jane Miles of Evansville, Indiana (near the Kentucky border), says, "In the last five years, I've seen more seated dinners than buffet or hors d'oeuvres receptions. Hunter green and navy blue have replaced the "black and white" wedding as far as colors go. Because of those rich, deep colors, the brides have been choosing stronger colors for their flowers. We just aren't seeing pastels." She also noted that she sees a lot of ivory or candlelight color for the bride's gowns instead of white.

South

Scarlett Lewis from Austin, Texas, says trends in Texas (which is usually considered the South) are towards traditional, sophisticated, and classic weddings—not trendy. Her clients' weddings average 300–500 guests and, because of these large numbers, usually involve a heavy hors d'oeuvres buffet instead of a seated dinner.

The Least You Need to Know

➤ Wedding styles and traditions are changing depending on the region of the country in which you live. In the Midwest, the trend is away from a reception buffet and towards a served dinner. The opposite is true in Southern California where the trend seems to be toward serving buffet style.

➤ On the East Coast, some environmentally friendly changes seem to be in place, such as using recycled paper for invitations, donating leftover reception food to charity, and giving donations to charity in their guests' names in lieu of favors at the reception.

➤ In the South, the trend seems to be toward large, sophisticated weddings in a traditional, not trendy, style.

Chapter 26

THE SHOES ARE
A BIT MUCH, DEAR...

Free Advice from Some Experienced Vendors

In This Chapter

➤ Advice offered by bridal apparel retailers, florists, photographers, a travel agent, a party store owner, videographers, caterers, a tent rental store, and musicians

➤ Additional questions to ask your photographer and videographer before you sign the dotted line

---

I don't know where else you can go these days and not have to pay for the advice that follows. These generous vendors have graciously provided some great ideas, tips, and suggestions to help make your wedding planning and your wedding day as trouble-free as possible. Most of these folks have been in their respective businesses for years. What they have to offer is invaluable because of their years of experience. In addition, they all love what they do and truly want your wedding to be a special day.

Gowns—Bridal Retail

As I discussed earlier in the book, your wedding gown and bridesmaids' dresses can be an expensive purchase. Read on to find out what advice these bridal salon owners and the Director of Retail Services of the Association of Bridal Consultants have to offer about purchasing your gown.

Betty Heine, The Bridal Cottage

Betty Heine, owner of The Bridal Cottage in Terre Haute, Indiana, suggests: "Remember, this is YOUR wedding, so be yourself. Allow enough time to try on several styles of bridal gowns. You will know when you find THE ONE. Wait until you have chosen a wedding gown before you begin selecting a particular style of headpiece and veil. Select a couple of bridesmaid's dresses for your attendants' approval. Stick to your choices. Don't let one person's opinion sway you. Allow enough time to order. We are at the manufacturer's mercy as far as delivery is concerned."

Mary Kelley, Director of Retail Services, ABC

Mary Kelley, the Association of Bridal Consultants' (ABC) Director of Retail Services, formerly owned a bridal retail salon in the Midwest and offers the following suggestions for you:

"It's important that the bride (and her attendants) be aware prior to shopping for their gowns that the sizing is not the same as ready-to-wear. Bridal sizes run smaller. That means if she usually wears a size 10, she probably will wear a 12 or 14 in bridal apparel. These garments are made to fit so closely to the body (unlike most ready-to-wear styles) that one size doesn't fit all. If on a manufacturer's size chart a bride has a size 10 bust, a size 12 waist, and size 8 hips, the store probably will recommend that she order a size 12 (the largest measurement). A reputable store owner can sleep very well at night knowing she gave the best possible recommendation if she recommends a size 12 and tells the bride up front that it will fit correctly in the waist, but the bust and hips will have to be altered. Have the bride get involved in choosing the right size so that she feels comfortable with the choice. Brides and bridesmaids should also understand that these gowns are intended to be altered or custom-fitted to each individual person. They are not custom-made by the manufacturer to a woman's measurements. Inside seams are purposely left raw so that custom fitting can be

330

done easily. If the bride and bridesmaids are aware of these facts before they go shopping for gowns, they will be much happier with the final outcome.

"It's a very good idea for the bride to go in and try on her gown and check it over as soon as it comes into the store. The store only has a certain number of days to return any gown with which there are problems. If the bride doesn't come in until two months after she is notified that her gown has arrived and there's a problem with the gown, she may well be out of luck as far as returning it to the manufacturer for repairs or replacement.

"Bridesmaids' gowns take about 8–10 weeks for delivery. There is less chance of a bridesmaids' order shipping extremely early because they are less likely to have 6 or 8 different sizes and colors in stock. Bridesmaids should also come in to try on their gowns as soon as notified. Five of the six gowns may be perfect while one may need replacement, but it may not be noticeable until the dress is tried on. Also, if one gown has to be returned to the manufacturer, the entire order may be sent back to ensure that all gowns are from the same dye lot. It's amazing how 'off' one gown can be if it comes from a different dye lot.

"Almost all manufacturers charge extra fees for certain changes: larger sizes (over size 18), rush cuts, rush shipping, some phone orders, some colors. These charges are usually passed along to the consumer as extra charges. They are not charges the shops just invent to make extra money. These are actual charges billed to the shop that they must then pass along to customers."

Ellen Prange, The Bridal Suite

Ellen Prange from The Bridal Suite in Huntington, Indiana, says, "The biggest help a bride can be to a bridal shop is to not wait so long before ordering her gowns. Bridal wear runs small. Don't be offended if the shop takes measurements and orders a size larger than you wear in ready-to-wear apparel. We must order from each manufacturer's measurement charts and they are all different. Also, don't expect every shop to carry all the dresses you see in the bride's magazines. Sometimes if we don't carry it, we can order it, but not always." And finally she urges brides, "Always ask what alterations will cost. Our shop does not charge for alterations, but we are in the minority. Most shops do charge."

Seamstress

If you prefer to have your gown or your bridesmaids' dresses designed and made for the wedding or if your gown needs alterations (some salons offer a discount if you go elsewhere for the alterations), then you'll need to find an accomplished seamstress.

Sue Thompson, AAA Sewing Suite

Sue Thompson owns AAA Sewing Suite in Terre Haute, Indiana, and is an accomplished seamstress. She offers these tips to future brides regarding their sewing needs:

 Bustling your gown refers to the pulling up of your train at the back of the gown so that you can move around more freely at the reception. This is usually accomplished by sewing tiny hooks and eyes or ribbons at appropriate spots on the back of the gown and train.

"If you choose to take your gown to a seamstress for alterations, be sure to bring the shoes and undergarments that you will be wearing with your gown for the wedding. If you're having your gown made from scratch, visit the seamstress before you buy material and patterns. Many times, they have patterns or can mix pattern pieces for you to create a unique gown.

"Always be sure to ask about the best way to bustle your gown.

"Be sure to ask whether the shop can restore older gowns or make the bridesmaids' dresses and maybe matching cummerbunds and ties for the men."

Florists

Flowers add so much to both the ceremony and reception sites: beauty, fragrance, and an aura of romance. It takes a great deal of planning and work by a professional florist with an eye for design to put the full magic of flowers to work. Read on to discover what some experienced florists advise.

Joyce Mills Edelsen, Joyce, A Floral Specialist

Joyce Mills Edelsen owns "Joyce, A Floral Specialist" in White Plains, Maryland. She is an award-winning floral designer and has been in the floral industry for 25 years.

Joyce offers this advice to the wedding couple:

"Interview the florist. You want someone who will listen to your dreams. This includes a reflection of your wishes, your physical size, the wedding style, the season, time of day, color, and most of all your budget.

"Obtain a photo or sketch of the gown and bridemaids' dresses. Bring a fabric swatch with you to the interview for color ideas. This information will be very important to the florist so they can offer you the best suggestions on bouquet styles.

"Select your florist 6–12 months in advance so they can reserve the date, time, and location on their calendars. Fine tune the order in the months ahead, and always review your order 1–2 months prior to the wedding.

"The bride and the financially responsible party should go to the first floral consultation (too many people will hinder your decision making). The consultation should convince and assure the bride that she has made the correct decision and the floral order is in good hands.

"The traditional split on expenses is like this: the bride's family is responsible for the largest portion of order. The groom's portion is usually the rehearsal flowers, the bridal bouquet, the men's bouton-nieres (the bride gives the groom his), and the mothers' and grandmothers' corsages."

Alison Hunter-Novak, Flora Scape

Alison Hunter-Novak, American Institute of Floral Designers, owns Flora Scape in Springfield, Illinois. I met Alison this past summer at a seminar in St. Louis. I was impressed with the questions she asked of the presenter. Here's what Alison has to say to brides-to-be:

"In selecting your florist, the most important thing is to book the date at least six months before the wedding. Final selections and exact floral descriptions should be made three months prior to the wedding. Though an initial consultation before that time can help with budget, color, and style choices, final selections made three months prior to the actual wedding date are not only adequate, but can cut out much time in consulting. By then the couple has made most of their plans and selections, and fewer changes are made between that time and the wedding day. This way, more realistic price estimates can be made. The professional florist should choose quality and flowers based on what is in season. Color and style should be the bride's choice. Never under-estimate the powers of a professional florist."

David Kurio, David Kurio Floral Design

David Kurio owns David Kurio Floral Design in Austin, Texas. He's been in business for ten years and from our conversation, obviously loves his business.

David offers this concept to the bride:

"When a bride calls and books us, we ask her to sit down with some wedding publications and look through those to get a feel for flowers. We ask the bride to find pictures of flower bouquets and displays she both likes and dislikes and to put those into a folder. When she comes in for the appointment with those folders, we can look through them and will have a better idea of her likes and dislikes. It saves all of us time. By using this method, we can see something similar in a publication and pull the same idea from our portfolio. Then we can incorporate the colors and design style with her wedding flowers. We always ask her to bring a sample of the fabric of both the wedding gown and the bridesmaids' dresses, and a photograph of the dresses if at all possible.

"I recommend that brides use a bridal consultant. They can be a real life-saver, both in terms of saving money and headaches."

Reba Butts Schopmeyer, Reba's Flower Shoppe

Reba's Flower Shoppe, in West Terre Haute, Indiana, is right in my own backyard and is owned by Reba Schopmeyer. Reba takes her bridal work seriously and always gives 150% to her clients. She offers this advice:

"When talking to brides who are uncertain about using fresh or silk flowers, I explain that the most important thing they will have ten to twenty years from now are their wedding pictures. Nothing enhances the pictures more than the beautiful color and form of fresh flowers.

"Once we have collected all the preliminary details on the wedding, the bridesmaids' flowers are selected first. The image of the wedding is most often determined by the color and character of the bridesmaids' dresses and the flowers they will carry. If she chooses baskets of daisies, the wedding will be quite different than if her flowers were orchids. The color of the bouquet is the most important characteristic of the bridesmaids' bouquets, followed closely by the style of the bouquet."

Jack Sitarski, Poplar Flower Shop

Jack and Jim Sitarski own Poplar Flower Shop in Terre Haute, Indiana. I have worked with these gentlemen over the years and found them to be professionals and excellent designers. Jack works more with weddings and offers these tips:

"Choose your wedding colors before talking to your florist about flowers. Coordination of dress colors and flowers will be much easier if the bride provides small swatches of dress material.

"Set your budget before meeting with your florist. A professional florist wants to give you the best value for your money.

"Please, please limit the number of people you bring with you to the consultation. It's been my experience that the more people the bride brings with her, the more difficult it is for her to make decisions concerning *her* wedding."

Claire Webber

Claire Webber from the San Francisco Bay area owns Claire Webber Florals and Events by Design. Claire is a florist and an event designer. She can take an ordinary hilltop and turn it into Camelot, or she can take a large hall and turn it into the most elegant setting for a celebrity wedding. She not only works with flowers to help create these scenes, but she also incorporates fabric treatments, greens, plants, props, linens, chair covers, and special sound and lighting. She has been in business since 1988 and serves a national clientele.

For some advice to a couple, Claire says:

"Hire a designer who will help you create the big picture that suits you best and is within your budget. Working with a designer who has an ongoing relationship with the various vendors you will need will help you shuffle your budget and get your best value for your dollars.

"It is important for the couple to use a bridal consultant during the planning stages. If that is not in your budget, at least hire a wedding coordinator for the day. There are so many details that are not part of a design package, such as giving direction to the ushers and making sure the bridesmaids are all dressed on time."

Photographers

Smiling pretty for the photographer can be helped greatly by understanding what the photographer is trying to accomplish and knowing a little about wedding photography. In this section, several experienced and knowledgeable wedding photographers offer their suggestions.

G. Gregory Geiger, CPP, Gregeiger Company Unlimited, Inc.

Gregory Geiger, CPP (Certified Professional Photographer), of Gregeiger Company Unlimited, Inc. in Orange, Connecticut, has photographed weddings all over the country. I have seen his work several times and have always been quite impressed. He offers some questions that you should ask the prospective photographer in the initial stages of planning:

➤ Do you have any particular philosophies about your approach to photographing wedding events?

➤ Do you have any set goals as you approach each wedding?

➤ How long do you expect to be with us on the day of the wedding? Beginning at what time? Until when?

➤ How can we best help you perform your duties while photographing our wedding?

➤ What kind of educational background and/or experience have you had in developing your photographic technique? When was it last updated?

➤ How will you present the preview pictures for our final album selection? What kind of time frame are you looking at for preparing the preview pictures for selection? Are you providing us with proofs or slides? May we keep them? For how long? Are they for sale?

➤ How can people who live out of town order, pay for, and expect delivery of reprints and/or albums?

➤ How much money would you expect us to spend before you think we would be completely happy with our wedding coverage?

Geiger also suggests "calling an industry organization or association to provide you with names of reputable wedding photographers in your area. And although it may offer a list of members, it should not be taken as a recommendation. If your photographer does belong to such a group, however, call the association to learn its policy concerning back-up vendors if yours is not cooperative or suddenly goes out of business. Once you've chosen a photographer, ask if he or she is familiar with the site of your wedding. If not, you should visit it together. If you're dealing with a studio that employs a staff, as opposed to an individual, ask for the home telephone number of the photographer you have requested. Don't hesitate to call if you have any questions or want to verify the time and date."

Wayne Manuel, Wayne Manuel Studio

Wayne Manuel Studio is also located in Terre Haute, Indiana, and Wayne's been in the business for years. In fact, he photographed my wedding and has over 1,000 weddings under his belt.

He tells me that, "Today's bride and groom want a large album covering the entire event, with formal portraits as well as candid coverage. The time frame for that can last from early afternoon well into the evening hours.

"Almost without exception, today's brides and grooms do not mind seeing each other before the ceremony and have the majority of their photographs taken just prior to the service."

He offers this sample photography guideline for a 4:00 p.m. wedding, with all portraits taken before the service:

1:15 Bride photographed alone

1:30 Groom photographed alone

1:45 Both families, including children, parents, grandchildren, and grandparents

2:45 Entire wedding party, including the officiant

3:30 Finished! Sanctuary cleared and ushers are ready to greet and seat guests.

Manuel also says, "It is imperative that all people be on time, dressed, and ready to be photographed at their designated time. This is a must!"

"Lastly, the mental attitude of the wedding party is most important. If everyone is happy and excited about the day, everything else is possible. These are the couples who get the great albums."

Don and Madeline Wilson, Studio 2 Photographics

Don and Madeline Wilson, owners of Studio 2 Photographics in Terre Haute, Indiana, are also creative photographers. They love the challenge of going the extra mile for the client. Below, Madeline offers some advice to prospective brides:

"Hire a photographer who will make the day *your* day and not his or her day. The photographer is there to make your day worry-free as far as the photographs go. You should be able to trust this person and let him or her guide you through the photographic moments.

The photographer should be easy to work with and personable. In addition, your photos probably will be better if the photographer's assistant is also a photographer and not just a glorified dress handler.

"Back-up equipment, back-up equipment, back-up equipment!! We work with four cameras and three flash units. Never trust a photographer who doesn't use back-up equipment. Cameras can malfunction without the photographer even knowing it. We have everything on two separate cameras. Everything! That equates to a worry-free day for you.

"Ask whether the photographer you are considering hiring uses two cameras. If he or she says, 'No, but it's never been a problem,' it may be that this photographer is due for one. Try to find a photographer who works with back-up equipment on a routine basis."

Jim and Lois Wyant, Wyant Photography

Jim and Lois Wyant, from Wyant Photography in Indianapolis, Indiana, are another pair of great photographers. Watching them shoot a wedding is truly a pleasure. You can view examples of their wedding photography in the four-color photo section in this book. The Wyants offer this advice for brides- and grooms-to-be:

"The United States does not require a license, examination, apprenticeship, or degree to practice photography. So how can you judge those calling themselves Professional Photographers? Here are some guidelines to help you determine true professionalism.

➤ *Professional.* By definition, a professional is one who exemplifies high standards within a profession and brings great skill and experience to that role.

➤ *Credentials.* P.P.A. (Professional Photographers of America), founded in 1880, is the world's oldest and largest association for professional photographers. The organization provides educational services and sets standards of professional performance for its more than 14,000 members and 250 international affiliated organizations. The P.P.A. degree program is the foremost appraisal of the professional photographer. The 'Master of Photography,' an earned degree, is presented only to those photographers whose superior competence and technique have been recognized in exhibit competition. The photographic Craftsman Degree (Cr.Photog.) is awarded for teaching, lecturing, and service to professional photography associations. (Note of caution: Many photographers claim to be 'Masters,' 'Artists,' and so on, but be sure to check for diplomas and proper credentials.)

➤ *Ethics.* Always consider a photographer's honesty, attitude, and character. For example, make sure that images viewed in brochures, albums, and so on are indeed the work of the photographer you are considering.

➤ *Organizations.* Membership to most professional organizations requires little more than dues-paying. Look for someone with active involvement and participation in competition, which indicates an interest in learning, sharing, and creative growth.

➤ *Competition.* Take note of any awards received by the photographer. This is an excellent measure of talent, technical knowledge, and artistic ability. Be sure recent honors are documented and are awarded through professional organizational competitions, such as those of Professional Photographers of America (P.P.A.), the Professional Photographer's Organization (P.P.O.), and/or the regional or state affiliates of these organizations.

➤ *Marketing.* A Yellow Page listing or clever advertisement does not automatically signify 'professional.' Because photography is a visual profession, viewing a photographer's work is the best way for you to judge the quality, professionalism, and value.

➤ *Consistent Quality.* Look around the consultation room at the images displayed along with the images in albums. Do they all display the kind of quality you're looking for or do some of the images fall short? Ask yourself, 'Which level of quality can I expect to receive?' Pay close attention to the photographer's expertise in the areas of lighting, posing, and composition.

➤ *Education.* Ask where the photographer has studied to gain his skills, and if he is continuing his education.

➤ *Emotional Impact.* Technical skills are important, but the ability to reach beyond the 'rules' of photography is the mark of a true professional. Look for images displaying expression, enthusiasm, and feelings."

Travel Agents

Whether it's "Aloha" or the Mickey Mouse theme song for your honeymoon, the expert help of a great travel agency is a must for perfect planning. Experienced travel agent, Steve Schrohe, offers some sound advice for honeymooners.

Steve Schrohe, International Tours

Steve Schrohe, President of International Tours in Terre Haute, Indiana, suggests that brides-to-be seriously consider all-inclusive resorts or cruises for their honeymoon. "Nothing is more special than a honeymoon. When newlyweds go to an all-inclusive resort or on a cruise, most meals, drinks, and entertainment are included in the original purchase. This alleviates sticker-shock related to meals and entertainment and allows the couple to live it up throughout their trip, as most items are prepaid." Schrohe notes, "Often these packages (particularly the cruises) are sold well below the published brochure price and represent a tremendous overall value.

Don't be afraid to let your travel agent know your budget. A good agent will be happy to match your dreams with your wallet and can let you know which honeymoon spots are popular and affordable."

Party Supply Store

Whether you want to get only your invitations or all your wedding party supplies in one stop, a good party store is a must. Below is some practical advice from one store.

Sandra Martin Baete, M-R Wedding and Party

Sandra Martin Baete, from M-R Wedding and Party in Clarksville, Indiana (just across the river from Louisville, Kentucky), offers couples some advice on decorating with a difficult color scheme.

"Many times, a bride will choose a beautiful color such as coral or periwinkle for her wedding. These colors are widely available in brides-maids' dresses, mothers' dresses, and flowers. However, they are not always easy to find in other areas, such as decorations. This is where a little creativity and flexibility can go a long way.

"Double-stuffing balloons (putting one inside another), twisting two colors of tulle together, and custom mixing of such items as float-ing candles can help assure a pulled together look. You may also be able to special order an item in your color. Wedding professionals are here to help. If you just ask if something is available, you may be pleasantly surprised.

"Also, do not get overly concerned about matching everything exactly, as long as all the shades complement each other and don't clash, it will look great.

"If you've picked a color that you just can't seem to match, such as iridescent navy, don't panic. All you really need is one item in your color—perhaps a wide fabric ribbon down the center of the table with everything else done in white. (By the way, a black balloon inside a transparent royal blue balloon makes a beautiful iridescent navy.) Remember, the key to success here is flexibility and creativity."

Videographers

Wedding videography is a wonderful way to help capture the memories of your day as they unfold. In earlier chapters, I talked about what to look for when you choose a videographer. In this section, you get some valuable advice from two professional wedding videographers. One professional trade organization dedicated to videographers is the Association of Professional Videographers (APV) located in Duncanville, Pennsylvania. If you have questions, contact either Rosanne or Burt Conrad at 814-695-4325.

Lance and Burt Holland, Holland Video Productions

Lance and Burt Holland are co-owners of Holland Video Productions in Atlanta, Georgia. They've been producing wedding videos for the past five years and average about 50 wedding videos per year. (That's a lot of tape.)

Lance and Burt offer some points for you to consider when decid-ing on a videographer:

"VHS video tapes are meant to last for between 10 and 15 years. This can be much less if they are played frequently. Therefore, you will need some way of making duplicates in the future. This could be from a master tape, a submaster on a high-quality format, the original raw footage, copies of the raw footage, or at least a copy of the master which is stored safely. Ask your videographer what options you have for watching the video many years down the road.

"Find out if the videographer will attend the rehearsal. No matter how many weddings the video company has shot, this is essential for assuring there are no surprises during the wedding.

"The best questions to ask your videographer are, 'What is the biggest mistake you made filming someone's wedding, and how did you fix it? Was the couple satisfied?' Also, you should ask the videographer these questions:

➤ Who will be editing the tape? How much time is spent editing?

➤ Who will be shooting the wedding?

➤ What is your policy toward making changes *after* the tape has been edited?

"Demo tapes are good tools for narrowing down your choice of videographers, but make sure you see at least some of what an entire tape looks like.

"Always ask for references. Number of years in business and number of weddings produced is important, but make sure all of those past clients have been satisfied."

Jim Wright, Video Magic Productions

Jim Wright, owner of Video Magic Productions, in Clinton, Indiana, has been doing wedding videography for 14 years. He is a true artist in every sense of the word and every one of his videos is unique to that couple. Here are his suggestions:

"The single biggest problem facing most wedding videographers today is the misconception that we can capture credible footage in just about every conceivable lighting situation: from the father and bride entering the church through an open door with a blazing sun at their backs, to the murky shadows of a one hundred and fifty year old mausoleum lit by the twinkling of too few candles.

"Light is nature's oldest special-effect: a genie capable of painting life's robust and myriad images at 30 frames per second across the canvas that is video tape... but only if the brush is grasped correctly.

"Often what the bride envisions for this, the most romantic day of her life, and what the videographer delivers a few weeks later are poles apart. Visiting several videographers early in the planning stages of your big day can allow a finished product that finds the best of both worlds—yours and the videographer's.

"Unlike the still photographer who documents the wedding through a series of staged shots, the videographer is charged with capturing the emotions of the day: unrehearsed, unexpected, and in constant motion.

"Armed with a little pre-planning and basic knowledge, the bride and her consultant can find a nice balance between what is expected and what is delivered."

Caterers

I've talked at great length throughout this book about food for your reception. Food is an important aspect to any wedding reception. In this section, catering managers provide you with some more "food" for thought.

Amy Acklin, Donna Rader, and Ted Spragg; Marriott Corporation, Education Services

Amy Acklin, Donna Rader, and Ted Spragg are the catering managers for Marriott Corporation at one of my favorite local reception sites: St. Mary-of-the-Woods College, located outside the city limits of Terre Haute, Indiana. The St. Mary's facility itself is quite elegant, and working with Marriott makes my life and the couple's lives worry free. These three professionals offer the following suggestions:

"Have an idea of what your budget is and plan the location, meal type, and size accordingly. It is hard to make a large, elegant place appropriate for a small punch and cake reception. But it is just as difficult to get the full benefit of a full meal reception if it is overcrowded and the facility is in poor condition.

"When choosing a menu, do not be satisfied with a set menu if it is not what you want. Any good caterer will work with you on setting a menu and its presentation to match your expectations. Keep in mind that this is your event and it should be the way you want it to be.

"When you begin planning your reception, look at the starting and ending times. When the reception begins at 4:00 p.m. and ends at 8:00 p.m., your guests most likely will make a meal out of your menu whether you have hors d'oeuvres or a full meal. The costs will be fairly similar. A full menu after 9:00 p.m. most likely won't be eaten as a meal, especially if it is a buffet. Hors d'oeuvres may be the better way to go at that time. The caterer should charge less after 9:00 p.m. than during a meal period.

"If you choose to serve alcohol, your best bet is to hire a bar caterer who has sufficient liability insurance. One liability ordeal can wipe you out financially if something happens and you don't have proper coverage. It is also good to provide alternative beverages all evening. Examples would be coffee, iced tea, and soda. Shutting down the bar 30 minutes before the entertainment stops is always a good plan to follow."

Jerry Green, The New Savoy

Jerry Green, president of The New Savoy in Bronx, New York, has been in the business of catering weddings, parties, and nightclubs for 30 years. With that much experience, his advice is important.

"Be very honest with the banquet manager regarding your budget. A good banquet manager is capable of saving you money if you are truthful with him.

"Always have a definite wedding date or alternate date in mind. Many banquet managers will not take you seriously unless you have a specific date. Be as outspoken and forthright as you can. If you say very little to the banquet manager he may not feel you are a serious customer. Never tell an experienced banquet manager what you think he wants to hear. He has too much experience and will see right through you. Always be pleasant and polite. You will receive twice what you give."

Rolo Miles, Indiana State University Food Services

Another Marriott branch is on the campus of Indiana State University, Terre Haute, Indiana. Their catering manager, Rolo Miles, offers the following suggestions:

➤ Seek out the best quality catering that you can afford. Ask around; deal with reputable caterers. Don't have your family cater your wedding.

➤ Don't just assume that your caterer will take care of decorating. Look at some pictures of their presentations.

➤ If possible, try to attend an event put on by the caterer that you think is the best.

➤ Get *everything* in writing. Don't assume *anything*!

➤ Make sure you put on the invitation what type of reception you are having, such as buffet, seated dinner, or hors d'oeuvres.

➤ Remember, listen to the caterer. They are professionals and have the experience to assure you a wonderful reception.

Jacquelynne T. O'Rourke, Edelweiss Caterers

Jacquelynne T. O'Rourke has owned Edelweiss Caterers in Danbury, Connecticut, for many years and is referred to as an "off-site" caterer in our chapters on catering. Off-site caterers do not work in one facility; they work in diverse locations.

I met Jacquie at a conference two years ago, where she was one of the speakers on catering. I think you will find value in her advice to couples:

"Whether the bride selects a gorgeous mansion, an incomparable garden reception, a modern art gallery, or a historic museum, the caterer should be qualified to assist her in all phases of planning the wedding reception.

"Ask about the little extras, such as immaculate service staff with white-glove presentation, petite strawberries in the guests' champagne glasses, butler-style hors d'oeuvres, carving stations with chefs in white jackets, and flaming Crêpes Suzettes prepared at each guest table.

"Your caterer should have the ability to help you select and order all your required rental items. Depending on your physical setting, those should include linens, china, silverware, crystal, tables and chairs, tents, and so on. Ask questions concerning damage waivers, time of delivery, and pickup of everything.

"Request several references and call each previous bride, especially if her reception took place in the same facility that you are considering. Schedule a complimentary 'tasting' of some of the entrées that you are contemplating.

"Finally, this day should be free from worries and stress, and the proper caterer will make you feel like a guest at your own wedding!"

Tent Rental

Whether you need to rent tents, tables and chairs, maybe fountains, portable bars, or even white lattice arches, a good rental store is where you need to begin to shop. Tent rental, in particular, will be addressed in the information below. (Remember Chapter 17 and my strong recommendation that you have a good back-up plan if you are planning an outdoor wedding? A tent makes an excellent back up.)

Carole LeMond

Carole LeMond, owner of Tent Rental Unlimited in Evansville, Indiana, offers these suggestions to couples planning those wonderful outdoor weddings:

"The most important tip I can offer is to remind you to make sure that when you rent tents for your wedding you have enough square footage of tent to cover *all* guests. Then relax and don't worry about the weather. A tent can be cooled or heated."

"Tents for a wedding normally are installed on a Friday with the removal on the following Monday. This enables the bride to further utilize the tent for the rehearsal dinner or a brunch following the wedding."

Music

Over the years, I've heard music blend with the ceremony and reception and I've heard such outrageous songs that the hair on the back of my neck stood straight up. In this section, two professional musicians offer some things to consider when you are deciding on music for your ceremony and reception.

Bill Cain, Keyboard Musician

Bill Cain, of Terre Haute, Indiana, is a talented professional musician. When I know that Bill is our organist or pianist for the ceremony, I know we are in good hands. Bill offers the following practical advice for couples:

"When determining your vocal selections, ask yourself if the song that sounded so perfect at the local hotel lounge on Saturday night is really the song you want your grandmother to hear at your church wedding.

"Also, when you are using a music selection that is available only on tape or CD, ask yourself if it's really fair to the musician to ask him to transcribe that music onto sheet music so that it can be played at your wedding."

Kenny i Orchestras

Kenny Ilg is president of Kenny i Orchestras in Somers Point, New Jersey. His bands perform all over the East Coast and get rave reviews wherever they go. They are truly magical music makers. Kenny offers the following advice for selecting musicians for your reception:

"Volume is a key item when selecting the 'make or break' factor of the reception—the music! Not only does the band have to be conscious of volume but sensitive to all those involved in the wedding: the consultant, photographer, caterer, videographer, and, of course, the guests.

"Auditioning the band is crucial. Recommendations are extremely important and may come from people who have enjoyed the entertainers at previous events. A referral from a reception site or caterer also can be respected.

"Note the band's poise, professionalism, volume, selections, overall appearance, and timing. Remember that their personality is a mirror image of the elegance and excitement level of the party.

"Ask the band leader several key questions: Is their contract clear regarding getting exactly who you've hired, especially guaranteeing that the leader or MC will be present? How early does the band report to the site? Do they have liability insurance? Can they provide music for the cocktail hour if it is in a room separate from the dinner dance? The music helps to make the dream wedding a reality. Select it with care!"

The Least You Need to Know

➤ Make sure you order your wedding apparel as far in advance as you can. Ask about alteration costs. Make sure that you go back to the shop to try on the dress as soon as you are notified that it has arrived.

➤ Select your florist and book your wedding date with the florist as far in as advance as possible. Actual floral decisions don't have to be made until about three months before the wedding, after you have finalized your wedding colors, style, and budget.

➤ Find a competent travel agent to help you plan your honeymoon. Tell the agent your budget and let him help you stay within it. Consider inclusive deals, such as all-inclusive resort getaways or cruises.

➤ Party supply stores can help you find wedding decorations and accessories in hard-to-find or coordinating colors.

➤ Be careful in your music selections. Make sure that the songs you want to use don't have to be transcribed to sheet music from a tape or CD. If you are using a band or other musical group, try to see the musicians perform before you hire them.

Chapter 27

True Confessions: Couples Tell How They Survived

In This Chapter

➤ Brides and grooms share their wedding stories

➤ What worked for them

➤ What they would change

A long time ago, I learned to listen to others who have experienced something that I am about to. After all, those with the experience have been through the ordeal.

In this chapter, eight brides and grooms share their wedding days with you. You should find some wonderful ideas in this chapter. They share hints and tips that worked for them and made their weddings easier to live through. They also tell you the things they would like to have changed.

Read on and learn from these brides and grooms. They have all survived to tell about it.

Eight Wedding Stories

CYNTHIA KAY STEWART AND LEE F. GUTHRIE

Date: August 10, 1985

Hometown: Fremont, California

Guests: 500

Attendants: 8 bridesmaids, 8 groomsmen, 6 ushers, flower girl, ring bearer

Colors: Mauve and pink

Reception: Buffet dinner; DJ for dancing

Invitations: Thermograph

Programs: Printed

Comments: Wrote their own service

This wedding is an especially sentimental one for me. When Cindy and Lee asked me to help them coordinate their wedding because I was such an organized person, it caught me completely off guard. I had never even heard of a bridal consultant, but I gave it a try just to help them out. Little did I know what helping them plan their wedding would lead to. I wasn't even thinking about a career change at the time, but that's another story.

Cindy and Lee did their homework. They knew they wanted a truly meaningful ceremony—one in which they could incorporate their own ideas. They spent time researching customs and working with their officiant to have this wedding service be truly their own. And all their work paid off!

With 500 guests attending, they opted for a buffet dinner reception for the ease of their guests. The church and the reception were located within walking distance of each other and shared a common parking facility.

Cindy decided on silk flowers and used the various shades of pink to accent the mauve dresses. For the church decorations, she had baskets of flowers on either side of the altar table, pew ribbons, and candelabra. She kept it simple.

This is the wedding ceremony I talked about in Chapter 22 in which the couple incorporated the lovely and meaningful candle lighting service. It was the highlight of the service; to this day, I can still see the look on both their faces as they gazed out into the congregation.

Tips from Cindy

"Stay on top of the bridal shop for your bridesmaids' dress order. I took it for granted that everything had been ordered properly until I received all the dresses one week before the wedding in the *wrong* color.

"Make sure your musicians, or anyone in the wedding party for that matter, doesn't have too much "fun" at the rehearsal dinner. You want everyone to be in good form for the big day."

SHERON J. DAILEY AND THOMAS B. TUCKER

Date: May 13, 1990

Hometown: Blackhawk, Indiana

Guests: 175

Attendants: Matron of honor, best man

Colors: Spring

Reception: Three-choice entrée, seated dinner; orchestra for dancing

Invitations: Original design (painted in different colors with matching place cards for the reception)

Comments: Outdoor ceremony

This is probably one of my most outstanding wedding memories. Sherry and Tom are not your traditional couple, but they have a very romantic story. They met on an airplane. Yeah, right. No, actually, they were assigned the same seat. After the flight attendant had straightened out the seating mix-up, they ended up sitting next to each other. By the time they reached their destination, they had exchanged telephone numbers. Tom was in international business and lived in Boston. Sherry is a university professor and was living in Indiana. They are from two entirely different backgrounds, but you know what they say about opposites attracting... .

In the planning of their wedding, they worked hard to make it truly reflect their personalities. The ceremony was scheduled for outdoors on their lake property; however, they put a different twist to it. Guests were invited for 5:30 p.m. for cocktails and hors d'oeuvres. A string quartet began playing music inside the tent (which was there as a back-up for inclement weather). At 7:00 p.m., the guests moved to the lakeside where the ceremony was to be held. When guests entered the area for the ceremony, each guest, both men and women, were given flowers—either to pin to a lapel or to hold as a bouquet. It was a nice touch. There was no real processional. Sherry and Tom entered to "Water Music" by Handel. Their attendants simply stood with the minister.

The actual service had been written for them by some dear friends. It was filled with humor, warmth, and meaning. Friends and family spoke during the service telling us stories and adventures and sharing more with us about who Sherry and Tom really were. It was a very personal and touching service.

They had guests travel from as far away as Italy, where Tom had done business for years. In fact, the wedding cake was not a typical wedding cake. It had been made in the shape of Italy and was covered with kiwi, strawberries, and cream cheese (representing Italy's colors). Very original and again, something that reflected their uniqueness.

Tom and Sherry wanted a formal dinner for their guests, and a choice of three entrees was offered. On the response card, guests had indicated which entree they preferred, and then on each place card was a sticker telling the server what the guest had ordered.

Tips from Sherry and Tom

"First of all, and above all, we believe that the bride and groom must decide *together* why they are 'having a wedding' instead of simply 'getting married.' Getting married is quick and simple, but having a wedding takes planning and understanding who you are.

"As we planned for our wedding, we thought a great deal about our individual pasts and our future together. We realized, above all, that although we were both mature chronologically (Sherry was fifty; Tom was fifty-eight), and that while both of us enjoyed substantial careers that brought us numerous and significant rewards, emotionally, we were teenagers! We held hands in public, rushed across crowded rooms to greet each other, and said, 'I love you' at the end of each telephone call.

"We wanted to bring together our friends and families so that they could meet each other. We told people months in advance so they could plan. We sent out our invitations six weeks in advance so folks could make travel arrangements.

"I urge you to prepare throughout every phase of the planning for the 'worst case scenario.' If you are planning an outdoor wedding, assume that it will rain and build your plans around an indoor wedding which you can—spontaneously and simply—move outside when you are pleasantly surprised with gorgeous weather. If you plan for live music, assume that the first violinist in your string quartet will break her arm, and be prepared for someone to hum her part as you march down the aisle."

One thought from Sherry for brides: "Be rested. I wanted to take a nap on my wedding day so that I would be rested and would look it. I got my wish.

"Above all, we urge brides and grooms to cherish—and not to fear—their uniqueness. Traditions grow over time and, in fact, become traditions because more often than not they 'work'; but on your wedding day you have an inalienable right to do what will make you the happiest. And everyone else has the responsibility to make it work for you."

ROBIN HESS AND CURTIS L. COFFEE

Date: June 13, 1992

Hometown: Indianapolis, Indiana

Guests: 120

Attendants: 4 bridesmaids, 4 groomsmen, 2 ushers, flower girl, ring bearer

Colors: Mauve and pinks

Reception: Hors d'oeuvres; DJ for dancing

Invitations: Engraved

Programs: Printed

Comments: Single location for both ceremony and reception

When I first met Robin, I was impressed with her organization. She had been a bridesmaid many times. She knew exactly what she wanted the day to be like and how to go about accomplishing that task.

Robin found the perfect gown. It was out of her price range, though, so she had a gown made. It was blush—not white or ivory—but a pale blush pink.

The church where the wedding was to take place had a lovely hall attached. Robin decided to have the reception there and not move guests around. At the initial planning, she thought they would only have about 75 guests because the groom was from Texas and she had not lived in the city in which the wedding was being held for several years.

She wanted the "Great Hall," as it was called, to be transformed into a gorgeous reception site. She rented crystal, china, silver (not stainless steel), and linens. The tables were covered with pink floor-length skirting and an overlay of white lace fell about halfway down the table. Pink linen napkins were fan folded at each place and the florist topped off the table with a lovely arrangement of lilies and pink roses. Robin used votive candles all around the room and in the windows to give a soft glow to things. The entrance room to the hall was where we put the guest book and a table display of Robin and Curt's baby pictures plus their engagement picture. As guests passed that table they were greeted with a "menu" board. Robin had the menu done in calligraphy, mounted, and framed, and stood it on a pretty gold easel. When everything was finished, it was quite lovely.

Guests were served hors d'oeuvres and Italian Cream wedding cake (Robin's favorite). Robin and Curt danced their first dance to a song they had choreographed for that very moment.

Tips from Robin

"I would definitely do all photographs *before* the wedding ceremony, except for candids, of course. Also make sure that someone sees to it that the photographer and videographer are not in each other's way.

"As a veteran bridesmaid who always dressed at the church, and always hated the confusion, I dressed at home and rode to the church in a limo. I'm very glad I did that. My silk gown made the trip fine and it was fun to see the neighbors sitting on their front porches watching to catch a glimpse of me as I left for the ceremony. Having someone at the house to provide an extra pair of hands would be a good idea.

"I have mixed feelings about receiving lines. We used one simply because Curt's parents were from out of state and probably no one would have met them otherwise. I like the idea of having the couple release the rows. That seems faster.

"Take as much time off before the wedding as possible. I took three days, but a week would have been better.

"Be prepared for a let-down after the festivities are over.

"I would recommend using a seating plan and place cards even for a buffet dinner. I also would recommend not choosing anyone for your wedding party who you think might be difficult to work with."

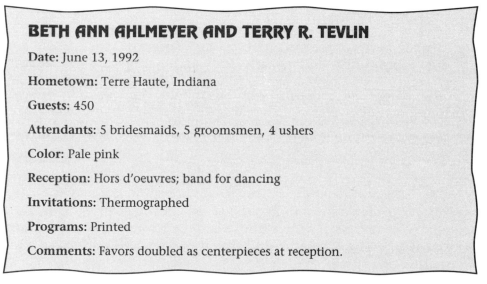

BETH ANN AHLMEYER AND TERRY R. TEVLIN

Date: June 13, 1992

Hometown: Terre Haute, Indiana

Guests: 450

Attendants: 5 bridesmaids, 5 groomsmen, 4 ushers

Color: Pale pink

Reception: Hors d'oeuvres; band for dancing

Invitations: Thermographed

Programs: Printed

Comments: Favors doubled as centerpieces at reception.

Beth is very organized and knew exactly what she wanted. She and Terry had dated for five years before they married and had time to see other weddings and take notes.

They had all the pictures taken before the service, which helped immensely. With 450 guests to greet, time marched right along after the ceremony.

The church was very simply decorated with aisle candles, flowers on every other pew and flowers baskets on the altar. The bridesmaids carried arm bouquets of white silk roses, pearls and ribbons. The brides-maids wore full-length pale pink suits which easily could be worn again.

At the reception, in keeping with their simple format, the only table decorations were the favors for guests. They were clusters of pink shiny fabric tied up with ribbons. In the center was a collection of jelly beans. It was fun and the guests enjoyed figuring out what was inside.

Beth was the only bride I've worked with who walked down the aisle all by herself. Her father is deceased and she wanted no one to take his place.

Tips from Beth and Terry

"For memories of the reception (because time goes so quickly) place disposable cameras on the tables for your guests' perspective of your reception. Have someone announce where to leave the cameras when all the film is used. Several of ours left with our guests.

"Beth's father is deceased; she had his wedding ring tied to her bouquet.

"Take all your posed pictures before the wedding.

"Check to make certain the band knows and can play the song you have chosen for your first dance. We picked "Unforgettable," which we had heard at an earlier wedding. However, without asking us, the band decided they couldn't play it well enough and played a tune neither of us liked.

"The photographs we have of our wedding are wonderful. I only wish now that we had taken more. Because we knew our photographer didn't like to do candid photography, we had a friend use his 35mm camera to get some casual shots."

JULIE ANN DORSETT AND SCOTT ROBERT DECKER

Date: August 1, 1992

Hometown: Sugarland, Texas

Guests: 325

Attendants: 5 bridesmaids, 5 groomsmen, 2 ushers, 2 flower girls, 1 ring bearer

Colors: Ivory and hot pink

Reception: Seated dinner; band for dancing

Invitations: Thermographed

Programs: Printed and tied with ribbons

Comments: Bride's parents hosted a brunch the following day for out-of-town guests, wedding party, and close friends

Julie was living out of state during the planning stages of her wedding. We did a lot of our work over the phone and through her mom, who lives locally.

The church was decorated with large green plants, palms and other greenery, and large candles. The altar table was covered in an embroidered tablecloth falling to the floor, a unity candle, and votive candles.

We used aisle candles on the pews with greens and flowers. Julie kept all the flowers to white. She wanted simplicity. The bridesmaids carried arm bouquets of roses, snapdragons, and baby's breath.

Julie and Scott left the ceremony in her grandfather's 1956 Desoto convertible Indianapolis Pace Car! A classic! It was great to see the look on the their faces when they exited the church and saw that car awaiting them. They made their mad dash amid tosses of rose petals.

The reception tables were decorated with rose bowls filled with fresh flowers and a tall candle. After the meal was served, the guests danced to a band.

A brunch for out-of-town guests, close friends, and family members was held at her parent's home the next morning. It was a great way to unwind and spend some quality time with people who had come from all over to be part of their wedding day.

Tips from Julie and Scott

"The most important thing that we did was to plan and give ourselves plenty of time to get things done. One thing is for certain; everything will not go as planned. You will get invitations back with wrong addresses or misspellings. Order products and services in plenty of time to have them corrected if necessary. Also, one of our more helpful ideas was to use visualization. Go into a quiet room and play out every detail of the wedding through your head and try to think of every possible thing that could go wrong. Also remember that you did all the planning; if something goes wrong, chances are your guests won't even know the difference.

"We used family and friends to help with tasks. We didn't take on all that responsibility for the weekend. Instead we did what we needed to for ourselves, including a massage for Julie. The results were a stress level at zero.

"One of our most difficult decisions was whether to take pictures before or afterward. We wanted a traditional wedding and that, we thought, included us not seeing each other. We did decide to take all the photos before. It was great! You still get that "wedding rush" during the processional and ceremony and still have a few minutes to spend quietly with the groom before everything begins. You are more fresh and do not have to worry about reapplying make-up. This allowed us to leave the church in the midst of petals and be in the caravan to the reception.

"I would advise getting a checklist for the photographer if he doesn't already use one. Our photographer didn't get some shots we expected and we were disappointed. If you want it taken, write it down.

"One of the most relaxing things we did was not to leave for our honeymoon until two days after the wedding. This allowed us time to spend with our friends and family who were there only for the weekend. It took off the pressure of having to make an early morning flight after a night of partying.

"We served a brunch the next morning to out of town guests, family, and close friends. It was great to see everyone in a relaxed atmosphere before they had to depart. It also was a great way to unwind some from the wedding day energy level.

"And finally, obtain the services of a top-notch wedding consultant to help guide you through this most important event!"

SUZANNE MARIETTA AND MARK ALAN UNGER

Date: March 5, 1994

Hometown: Terre Haute, Indiana

Guests: 200

Attendants: 6 bridesmaids, 6 groomsmen, 2 ushers, 1 flower girl

Colors: Black and white with gold accents

Reception: Hors d'oeuvres; band for dancing

Invitations: Thermographed

Programs: None

I was hired by Suzy's future mother-in-law as a gift to Suzy. Suzy's mother lives in Florida and because of the distance, couldn't help much with the planning. Suzy and Mark knew what they wanted. They wanted a nice service and a relaxed, fun reception.

They used lots of greenery and white twinkle lights at the church. We put white lights on some topiary trees along the side of the altar. In the center, the altar table was covered with a lovely cloth. The unity candle was the focal point there. Suzy and Mark also used aisle candles with greenery and bows. Her bridesmaids wore mid-calf length black cocktail dresses which they can definitely wear again. They had matching black sequined shoes. They all wore their long hair up and it gave a finished look to the wedding party. Their flowers were casablanca lilies with gold ribbons and greenery. It was very elegant.

At the reception, Suzy borrowed rose bowls and placed a large white candle in the center. The caterer used white table cloths and black napkins. He placed a black napkin under every rose bowl. The florist put some greenery and babies breath around the rose bowls. Suzy finished off with some gold confetti and the effect was a simple, inexpensive, yet very attractive centerpiece.

Mark and Suzy did not want guests to wait on them to arrive before they could eat. As guests entered, they could help themselves to food and beverage. The band played background music. It created a great party atmosphere. Guests were enjoying themselves long before the couple arrived.

Tips from Suzy

"Guests do not notice if you do not use an aisle runner. The ushers really don't like to deal with it and I think they probably find it embarrassing. I did not find having a program essential. Try to make the reception simple. Do not go over board on petty things: aluminum ash trays, mints, nuts, matches. Make sure you have a correct count for ordering your invitations. I had way too many. Buy things as you go along. For example, buy stamps weekly, as well as thank-you notes and gifts for attendants. That way it's not such a big expense all at once. Borrow some items from your friends and families. Make it fun! Do not get stressed out. Be beautiful, and remember, this is your day!! Enjoy it. It also doesn't hurt to get some professional help, in the way of a bridal consultant, for your big day."

CAROLYN MICHELLE CULP AND KENNETH WILLIAM WYGLE

Date: April 9, 1994

Hometown: Sagamore, Ohio

Guests: 325

Attendants: 6 bridesmaids, 6 groomsmen (groomsmen also ushered), flower girl

Colors: Ivory and navy

Reception: Hors d'oeuvres; DJ for dancing

Invitations: Thermographed

Programs: Engraved

Comments: Monogrammed boxes containing truffles were given as favors

---

Carrie was also an out-of-town bride, so we talked on the phone and worked through her mother. Both Carrie and Ken were very organized and knew the style and type of wedding they wanted. They wanted the ceremony to be meaningful, and they wanted their guests to enjoy themselves at the reception. That is one reason they chose to have an hors d'oeuvres reception instead of a buffet or seated dinner. Actually, this reception had food stations with heavy hors d'oeuvres rather than the lighter finger food fare.

Carrie loves flowers, and she was married in April, remember? What flower is blooming in April? And Terre Haute just happens to boast a tulip factory. We used hundreds and hundreds of multicolored tulips. It was breathtaking. Carrie was also very fond of tulle and ivy. The florist came in and designed the staircase leading to the sanctuary with garlands of tulle, ivy, and french ivory braid ribbon with a gold edge. *Every* pew in the entire church had a pew bow made of the same french ribbon. They chose two large arrangements of mixed spring flowers to adorn the altar area. She chose not to use candles.

Instead of the traditional organ, she used a string quartet for the music. For Carrie's entrance, a trumpeter was added to the string group.

The bridesmaids wore street length navy dresses with a viole wrap-around skirt. They were attractive dresses and the women could wear them again. Each bridesmaid carried 18 assorted colored tulips tied with the same french ribbon. Carrie carried 24 ivory tulips.

When they arrived at the reception, guests were greeted with ivory table cloths and centerpieces of large vases with 24 tulips in each and 5 votive candles around the base. Every table displayed tulips of a different color, and it was a very, very beautiful sight.

Food stations were used for this reception and it worked very well. Assorted hors d'oeuvres were offered, plus heavier foods such as pasta dishes, a carving station for small beef sandwiches, and a seafood station, which included shrimp and lobster.

Tips from Carrie and Ken

"We were so very relaxed because we knew our bridal consultant was in charge of the details. We think having her help made a huge difference and allowed us to concentrate on one another rather than on the functions of the day. If a bridal consultant is not in your budget, at least ask a friend or family member (NOT mom or a bridesmaid) to handle some of the details and be informed in case help is needed.

"We also loved being apart all day and seeing one another for the first time at the BIG moment. (Carrie said, 'It made my heart beat faster seeing Ken when I walked in ready to marry him.')

"On Friday before the Saturday wedding, we saved time for us to have lunch alone. It was fun to run away from the hectic planning to laugh and take an hour to celebrate in private. After all that goes on surrounding the big day, time is so important to remind us that we love being together. We did have one rule at lunch: NO talking about the wedding, aside from the excitement and joy. No stress allowed for our time alone.

"Regarding wedding showers and wedding gifts: Try to have at least one couples' shower to celebrate with family and friends. The wedding is for both the bride and groom. This shower is a fun way to get the guys involved, too. We took our time in opening our wedding gifts and cards. We wanted to savor the well-wishes from family and friends. We made it a special time to do this.

"If the wedding is in the late afternoon or evening, find something special to do with your wedding party. Ken played golf with his guys and I took my bridesmaids out for a luncheon. We both had fun spending time with those who were close to us.

"Make sure you make your preferences clear with the band or DJ about song selection. Meet with the music people to confirm everything. Music has a profound impact on the atmosphere you want to create.

"We felt overwhelmed at one point during the reception due to all the guests who we wanted to see and who wanted to congratulate us. While we wanted to have time to thank everyone for coming, we didn't want to get cornered. Looking back, a receiving line at the church would have eliminated the overwhelming attention of our friends and family and allowed us to give everyone the chance they wanted and us an opportunity to say thanks to them for coming.

"Make the honeymoon two weeks!!! Our one week was glorious but we were sad to end it so quickly. Two weeks would have been delightful after all the time, energy and work of planning the wedding, not to mention the emotional wear and tear. Besides, it's not every day you vow to spend the rest of your life with someone. Celebrate!

"One very important point to remember: No matter what *might* go wrong or what might happen throughout the planning and the strong desire for a perfect day, by midnight on the selected date, you will be married. Nothing else is as important as that. As far as we were concerned, if we were husband and wife by the end of the day—it was the perfect day!"

ERIN SUE ROWE AND BRADLEY BROWDER

Date: September 10, 1994

Hometown: Indianapolis, Indiana

Guests: 200

Attendants: 6 bridesmaids, 6 groomsmen, 4 ushers

Colors: Champagne, ivory, and white

Reception: Hors d'oeuvres; dancing

Invitations: Thermographed

Programs: Printed and tied with ribbons

Erin and Brad are two of my most recent clients. Both live out of town and wanted some help pulling all the loose ends together on the home front.

Erin chose champagne-colored dresses for her attendants. Her gown was white and ivory, a very lovely creation which suited Erin's personality. She brought color into the picture with the flowers. The bridesmaids all carried arm bouquets of different colors and kinds of flowers. There were stargazer lilies, roses, baby's breath, sweet peas, just an array of lovely flowers to complement the dresses.

Erin wanted something different for music and chose a string quartet to play the prelude music, processionals, and recessional. She placed a sound activated tape recorder in the music loft to record the music.

This couple also wanted a relaxed atmosphere and decided to serve a heavy hors d'oeuvres reception. The centerpieces were interesting and inexpensive. Erin rented hurricane globes and placed a tall ivory taper in the center of each. Around the base she gathered ivory tulle in a "cloud effect" and sprinkled it with gold confetti and glitter. It was very simple, but very elegant. The candlelight caught the gleam of the glitter and made everything sparkle.

Tips from Erin and Brad

"We really had a wonderful time and there aren't too many things we would change. However, there are a couple of points we feel are important.

"Hire your wedding consultant at the beginning of the planning stages *before* problems arise!

"We strongly recommend taking all the formal wedding photos before the ceremony. It really relaxed all of us and gave us the opportunity to enjoy the entire reception.

"Most importantly, think positive. We reached a point during the planning where we felt there was no possible way that *all* the details were going to fit together. But, magically, everything seems to fall into place! Don't be too hard on yourself, and have fun!"

A Final Word

Over the years, I have learned so much from the delightful women and men I have had the pleasure to work with. They have taught me a lot about weddings and what is important. In this chapter, they have had the opportunity to share some of their experiences with you. Each of these weddings, while having some similar qualities, was uniquely different. It amazes me, even today, after almost 10 years in this business, how different each one of us is and how we can use that uniqueness to our benefit in planning a memorable wedding day.

Enjoy your planning and your time together. I hope all your dreams come true, and may you always live "happily ever after."

The Least You Need to Know

➤ Make your wedding a reflection of both your personalities, your dreams, and your desires.

➤ Take one idea—something unique to you (your love of music), or something you've read about (maybe in this book), or thought about (in your dreams)—and try to incorporate it into your wedding plans.

➤ Reread the tips and advice offered by the brides and grooms in this chapter. It's free. It comes from folks who have experienced what you are about to, and it is sincere.

Index

Q-R

quality time
    brides/grooms alone
        together, 362
    with parents, 11-12

rabbis, *see* officiants
Rader, Donna, 343-344
readers, 84
readings, customizing
    ceremonies, 283-284
receipts, organizational
    systems for keeping, 4
receiving lines, 290-291, 355,
    362
reception assistants, 84
reception cards, 142-143
Reception Site Worksheet, 124
receptions
    agendas, 302-306
    buffet receptions, 111
    cake and punch receptions,
        109
    centerpieces, 116-117
    child care, 309
    cutting costs, 185-186, 318
        locations, 321
    decorations, 354, 356-357,
        359, 361, 363-364
    disposable cameras,
        174-175
    eating before brides/grooms
        arrive, 360
    favors, 172-174, 321
    formal dinner receptions,
        111
    getting away, 310-311
    gifts, 307
    guaranteed numbers of
        guests, 54, 115-116
    hors d'oeuvres receptions,
        110, 361
    music, 68-69, 145-146
    party supplies, 340-341, 360
    reserving sites, 318
        capacities, 50-51
        planning around big
            events, 40
        reception managers, 51
        services and restrictions,
            51
        types of sites, 49-50
    sample menus, 112-113
    seating plans, 355

security
    alcohol-related inci-
        dents, 307-308
    helping guests leave
        after drinking, 308-309
services, 108
sizes of sites, determining
    needs, 108
record-keeping, organizational
    systems for, 4
references, 15
registering for wedding gifts,
    146-147
Rehearsal Dinner Worksheet,
    77-78
rehearsal dinners, 71-76
    responsible behavior, 351
rehearsals, 267-272
religious ceremonies
    Christian
        altar positions, 259-260
        Orthodox, 251-253
        processionals, 257-258
        Protestant, 253-255
        Roman Catholic,
            256-257
    Jewish, 260-264
reminder lists, organizational
    systems, 4
renting tents, 346
repeat buying power of bridal
    consultants, 16
reservations
    florists, 65-67
    honeymoons, 88-93
    hotels for weekend
        weddings, 235-236
    musicians, 67-69
    photographers, 61-63
    reception sites, 49-51, 318
        planning around big
            events, 40
    rehearsal dinners, 72-73
    videographers, 63-64
response cards, 14
restoring wedding gowns, 184
returned invitations, 358
rice
    attendants, 84
    throwing, 310-311
Rice, Cheri, 320
ring bearers, 82-83
ring pillow, cutting costs, 187
rings
    fitting over swollen hands,
        322
    history, 5

rite of passage, stress caused
    by, 193
roasted camel, 52
Roman Catholic ceremonies,
    256-257
rose petals
    petal attendants, 84
    throwing, 310-311
royal wedding (Charles and
    Diana)
    Just Married sign, 163
    lucky items, 277
    wedding gown, 157
Russian Orthodox ceremonies,
    251-253

S

San Antonio, Texas honey-
    moons, 92
San Diego, California honey-
    moons, 92
Schopmeyer, Reba, 334
Schrohe, Steve, 340
Scottish theme, 320
scrolls, 143
seamstresses, 332
seasonal weddings, 215-220
security
    alcohol
        alcohol-related inci-
            dents, 307-308
        helping guests leave,
            308-309
    child care, 309
    gifts at receptions, 307
    house sitters, 310
semiformal weddings, 22
Seven Weeks Before the
    Wedding checklist, 99
shoes
    brides, 157
    men, 158-159
    outdoor/garden weddings,
        222
showers, 177-178, 362
shows (bridal), 5-6
silk flowers, 133
Sitarski, Jack and Jim, 335
sites
    ceremony
        determining wedding-
            party sizes, 79-80
        selecting, 42-44
    destination weddings,
        246-249

T

U-V

W-X-Y-Z

Who Cares What You Think?

WE DO!

We're not complete idiots. We take our readers' opinions very personally. After all, you're the reason we publish these books! Without you, we'd be pretty bored.

So please! Drop us a note or fax us a fax! We'd love to hear what you think about this book or others. A real person—not a computer—reads every letter we get, and makes sure your comments get relayed to the appropriate people.

Not sure what to say? Here's some stuff we'd like to know:

➡ Who are you (age, occupation, hobbies, etc.)?

➡ Which book did you buy and where did you get it?

➡ Why did you pick this book instead of another one?

➡ What do you like best about this book?

➡ What could we have done better?

➡ What's your overall opinion of the book?

➡ What other topics would you like to purchase a book on?

Mail, e-mail, or fax your brilliant opinions to:

Tom Godfrey
Product Manager
Alpha Books
201 West 103rd Street
Indianapolis, IN 46290
FAX: (317) 581-4669

CompuServe: 74140, 1306
Internet: 74140.1304@compuserve.com

**alpha
books**